BUILDING BRAND IDENTITY

A Strategy for Success in a Hostile Marketplace

Lynn B. Upshaw

John Wiley & Sons, Inc.

New York ■ Chichester ■ Brisbane ■ Toronto ■ Singapore

Author's Note: The text and exhibits of this book contain references to the positioning and personality of various brands and are based on published reports and the author's observations of the marketplace. Except where noted, these observations do not necessarily represent the opinions of the companies which market these brands or of their communications agencies.

This text is printed on acid-free paper.

Library of Congress Cataloging-in-Publication Data:

Upshaw, Lynn B.
  Building brand identity: a strategy for success in a hostile marketplace /
  by Lynn B. Upshaw
  p.   cm.
  ISBN 0-471-04220-X

Printed in the United States of America

10 9 8 7 6 5 4 3 2 1

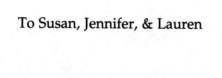
To Susan, Jennifer, & Lauren

Contents

Acknowledgments

First, my sincerest thanks to Pilar Webster of InfoWeb for her outstanding research work. And, to my assistant, Jayne Winter-Nico, for her continuing help. I'm also grateful for the ideas and input I'm exposed to every day from some of the brightest marketing minds I know, especially John Faville, Dianne Snedaker, Bruce Campbell, Barry Layne, Michael Llewellyn-Williams, and Jerry Hamilton. And special thanks to my brother, Jim Upshaw, for his valuable advice.

Virginia Vann of Southwestern Bell provided me with all the information and good counsel I could hope for, and we're all very grateful to Mac Geschwind for his enthusiastic support of our work.

Thanks also to my agent, Mike Snell, and my editors at Wiley, John Mahaney and Ruth Mills.

Finally, my gratitude to my infinitely patient family: my daughters Lauren and Jen, and my wife, Susan, who offered me her encouragement and copyediting skills when I needed each most.

Preface

Brands have no right to exist.

They are not guaranteed by the Constitution. There's no economic law that expects them to fuel supply or demand. They carry no inbred immune system. It's possible to sell a product or service without creating an elaborate brand; in fact, it happens all the time. It would take some major adjustments, but global economies would eventually survive if brands were to fall out of sight and never be heard from again. While brands have admittedly become the foundation of our commercial markets, they are—as hard as it might be to accept—dispensable.

All of which is particularly sobering when you consider that there are growing forces in the marketplace that are systematically damaging and even destroying some brands, and keeping many others from reaching their full potential. As *Advertising Age* editors wrote in October of 1994: "Assaulted by private labels, fighting for shelf space and combing for new ways to reach media-saturated consumers, marketers find the job of creating and sustaining brand names tougher than ever." That challenge is as real for service brands, durables, and business-to-business brands as it is for those sold in the supermarket.

The same challenge leads to the central message of this book: When a brand is under attack from threatening forces within a hostile marketplace, its best defense (and the source of its best offense) is a formidable brand identity.

How is a strong identity built? Marketing is too filled with natural disasters and serendipity to permit formula answers. But successful marketers are beginning to figure out ways to improve their odds: by dissecting a brand and being painfully candid about what's usable for identity building, and what should be repaired or discarded altogether. By digging deep into a brand's prospect base to understand who a brand should be selling to and what motivates them to buy, not just for groups or segments, but for individuals. By assuming that it's the buyer who positions a brand, not the seller, and that the hardest working positionings are unshakably credible coming from the right brand, and urgently relevant to the right customers. By creating a personality that's strategically true and irresistibly human. By blending their positioning and personality into one of the most distinctive brands in the customer's life. By borrowing good ideas from brands that have already created strong identities. And by readying a brand for the slightly terrifying, incredibly fertile new world of interactive marketing.

A brand's identity has always been the most influential and most easily leveraged part of its accumulated equity. To accomplish aggressive objectives in a business environment that's holding marketing people more accountable than ever, it's worth the time and effort to define what a brand's identity is, and how it can be strengthened to combat those factors that might otherwise slow it down or even destroy it. *Building Brand Identity* is a reminder of what brands have always needed to succeed, and a call to build a stronger presence in the marketplace. Above all, it's a proposal to think in new ways about tools marketers have had available since their first day on the job, and about new tools that are just now coming to their attention.

Building Brand Identity is also about realities: the realities of the individual customer who is in need of products and services, yet subject to more distractions, and harboring more skepticism than ever before; the realities of the brand team, which are not always aligned to help them accomplish their brand goals; and the realities of the brand itself, which is a living player in the theater of the marketplace.

Throughout this book, we will be referring to "brand stewards," an increasingly popular term in marketing circles. Brand stewards are those, such as brand managers, marketing managers, or category managers, who are directly responsible for the welfare of a brand. Brand stewards also include those who work on brand assignments at marketing communications agencies and who have (or should have) a major influence on a brand's marketing programs. Even beyond core team members, brand stewards may also include any others who have some say about how a brand is sold in the marketplace. That can widen the membership rolls quite a bit to include marketing researchers, business analysts, R&D folk, those who run the retail operations, the sales or broker force, the quality-control managers, the customer service people, and many others who in some way contribute to the brand identity.

The other term you will be reading frequently on these pages is "brand team." When Procter & Gamble and other companies popularized the brand management system, the idea was to place primary responsibility for a brand on a single individual's shoulders. The brand, in that system, was to be run as an entrepreneur might run his or her own business. Today, brands and their identities are often managed by a cadre of team members who ideally complement one another. A modern brand team uses the energy and synergy of many contributors, rather than primarily relying on the leadership of a lone manager.

Brands are the flags of marketing. They stake out a certain territory and inform the world that what lies within sight of the flag belongs to those who fly it. At least that's the way it's supposed to work; now branding is riskier and less predictable. Events in the past decade have proven that there are no certainties in the world at large. That's not true in the world of marketing. We can be certain that it will be much tougher for brands in the future to design the right flag, let alone to fly it.

Near the corner of 56th Street and Fifth Avenue in Manhattan, surrounded by upscale jewelry stores and boutiques, there is a small museum and gift shop dedicated to the global icon known as Coca-Cola. At Coca-Cola Fifth Avenue, the past and present Coke brand is celebrated with real and recently manufactured memorabilia of the "Always Coca-Cola" culture, spotlighting more innocent days as we like to remember them. Walking by the Coke displays, listening to the sounds of tourists that blend with the brand's campaign theme song piped in from above, a visitor is struck by the global importance of this single brand whose identity has made it the most valuable label in the world. In the 1980s, Pepsi had dented the Coke identity with its "The Choice of a New Generation." Coca-Cola Fifth Avenue is

Atlanta's response: We will own the way we were and the way we want to be. It was like an opponent telling Steve Young that they were going to take away the San Francisco 49ers' running game and force them to pass. Fine, we'll take it.

Not many brands can be a Coca-Cola, but every brand is created with an identity of some kind: a name, a graphic symbol, a meaning, an expectation, a covenant with its users, a promise for its prospects, a place in someone's life, a space in everyone's marketplace. That identity is a gift, awarded at birth, free of help or hindrance, there to be nurtured or squandered.

It's the job of the brand steward to take that gift and make the most of it, and the goal of this book to help make that happen.

PART ONE

Building Brand Identity

1

The Brand Identity Strategy

It is shopping day in the year 2020. Thirty million Americans order goods and services via in-home interactive telecomputer programs, but you are one of the majority who still prefer to pick up what they need at multilevel shopping experience centers. The truth be told, you are slightly terrified by the more than 65,000 products and services to choose from, nearly 20 percent of which can be customized on the spot to fit your specific needs.

To help you sort through the overwhelming array of choices, you start with a visit to the bank of virtual reality headsets near the center's entrance so you can plan your shopping before venturing out onto the moving trams that run down each aisle. As you visually "walk," you are accosted by so many brands that the impact of each is washed away in a sea of colors and superlatives slashed across package facings. The brands remind you of orphaned pups at the humane society, scrambling for some attention that might lead to an embrace and a trip home.

You are oblivious to the factors that have determined what's for sale: which brands the store can make the best margins on, what the most recent sales reports have proven are the most popular options, and what your previous 10 purchases have determined are your personal favorites. Private labels—a class of top-notch products now commonly called "best brands"—dominate the majority of categories. One-third of all brands are rotated off the shelves every 90 days, replaced immediately by new items that turn more quickly based on daily scanner projections. Only the number 1 and 2 brands in each category are allowed to remain on the shelf on a semipermanent basis. Newly introduced brands are given three to five weeks to make their move, or they are promptly discontinued.

Because the grocery and drug chains have better scanning data than manufacturers, marketers are often the last to know when their brands have failed. This rapid turnover has led to unprecedented increases in new product introductions, now numbering 30,000 per year, 27,000 of which are actually variations on a base product. In fact, 85 percent of all brands have created "extended families," flankers and line extensions with only minor product differences between them.

You decide to stop at the center's "Lifestyle wing" where shoppers are offered hundreds of services, including home mortgage refinancing, office cleaning services, and wedding/funeral arrangements. (Each service can be "experienced" before committing to a purchase, of course.) Today, you will use the vacation services that are sold by a broker—also an employee of the retailer's holding company—who is licensed to represent virtually all airline, cruise ship, hotel, and rental car corporations in the United States.

Unlike in the product wing of the center, the myriad of service brand names are never mentioned by the in-store broker; only your destinations and your specific travel needs are discussed. Your vacation is completely customized, using frequent-user programs so complex that only the broker's information manager understands them. There are many travel packages that fit your vacation's specifications, so you must sort through 17 nearly identical offers.

Before, during, and after your shopping experience, you and your loved ones are subjected to a continuous stream of advertising, sales promotion, and price merchandising, exposing them to a commercial image of some kind every 9.6 seconds during waking hours. Selling messages crop up on everything from major league baseballs to stop signs in municipalities that are particularly hard-pressed for funds.

In the experience center alone, you've been told that there are well over 500 separate advertising vehicles along the way, such as 25 interactive kiosks, fifty 21-inch video monitors ingeniously placed among the *food and drug facings, 75 ads embedded into removable mosaic tiles on the floor, and a soothing voice that continuously whispers the specials of the day into your headset. You are reminded of your son's high school term paper, which he called, "Overload: Is It Time to Ban Advertising?" He got an A-minus.*

As you pass the "News of the Day" projection screen, you read that the Time Warner/Yankelovich/Rolling Stone research organization has discovered that only 16 percent of the American public can recall a single product or service brand name on an unaided basis. Of those, most can only remember the one called "Best Brand."

Brand Building in a Diffused and Confused Marketplace

Today that scenario may sound a bit far-fetched, but in a few years it may be hard fact.

The holy order of brands has been one of the few things that we could count on to remain stable in our unstable economy. That is no longer the case. Who marketers sell their brands to, what they sell, and how they sell them, are all mutating at an exponential rate like some commercial Andromeda strain. There are days when many wonder if marketing as we know it will survive the decade. Not to worry, it won't.

Disruptive forces have created a hostile environment for traditional brands that threaten their very survival. Nevertheless, what you just read is not inevitable if marketers act now to analyze and revitalize the core of what they are really selling, namely, their brands' identities.

To begin, let's take a look at what brands face on a good day:

■ *America's consumer-driven economy has been fundamentally restructured, permanently altering our definition of value. Lower-priced product and service brands have been legitimized as mainline options, even for those who can afford more expensive alternatives.*

Millions of Americans lost their jobs during our most recent recession, including many who were used to a comfortable life.

Unlike in the past, those jobs will never return. Defense workers at all levels will never again draw a paycheck in that field; middle management slots in scores of industries have been dropped permanently from the organization charts; clerical employees by the tens of thousands have been preempted by executives who type their own documents and answer their own phones at their desktop workstations. Many have been forced to retrain themselves for entirely new careers or face the unemployment line.

These are life-changing experiences that have made people rethink the household budget, and wonder whether products and services that cost more are really all that necessary. Along the way, many lower-priced products and services have been upgraded in quality and now approach parity with their premium competition. And, it's not just those with less to spend who are interested in these bargains. We are all partaking of lower-priced brands, and pocketing the change without looking back.

These new views of value have redefined what brands are, and what they must bring to the marketplace.

■ *More marketers than ever are in the business of customized excess.* According to just about everyone, the end of the mass-marketing era passed over us in the dead of night like some lunar eclipse. Its demise was first predicted by Alvin Toffler in his 1970 book, *Future Shock.* Ten years later, he confirmed in *The Third Wave* that, "The mass market has split into ever-multiplying, ever-changing sets of mini-markets that demand a continually expanding range of options, models, types, sizes, colors, and customizations."[1]

We are now living in a world of "mass customization,"[2] an economy propelled by renewed individualism and kaleidoscopic tastes, prompting sellers to produce customized goods and services at every opportunity. Consumers consider it their right to demand their own version of whatever is offered for sale. TWA sells customers virtually any type of vacation plan they desire through their customized Getaway programs. American Greeting Cards generates more than $35 million a year with their CreataCard machines that enable shoppers to design their own cards from scratch. Hertz #1 Club Gold receives your reservation and has a car of your choice waiting for you in a weather-protected stall. Marriott's Honored Guest program provides the room style you want (given space available) without any extra effort on your part.

At the same time, consumers don't necessarily feel that they need all that is being offered to them. In a 1992–93 year-long study by Willard Bishop Consulting, respondents said that the marketplace was filled with too many "me-too" products.[3] As more consumers express that sentiment and retailers reduce the number of SKUs (stock keeping units, aka size/flavor shelf slots) allocated for each brand, companies such as Procter & Gamble, Unilever, Kraft/General Foods, and many others have shed marginal brands. Depending on the category, the number 1 and 2 brands are likely secure, but the rest are up for grabs.

■ *Product/service parity is blurring the distinctions between brands.* There are precious few meaningful differences between PC hardware models, beers, long-distance carriers, airlines, juice beverages, stereo systems, insurance plans, and detergents—except in the way that they are packaged and presented to the consuming public. Technology is making it easier for competition to duplicate every innovation, and nearly impossible to hold onto a product or service advantage for any length of time.

Apple Computer learned that the hard way in the early 1990s when its strategy of relying on technological prowess fell victim to price wars, the expansion of the Microsoft Windows software and the successful cloning of IBM PCs. Eventually, in the fall of 1994, the company was forced to open its operating architecture to cloning, and to seek alliances to survive as a hardware supplier.

As parity becomes the norm, consumers are more likely to discount the entire concept of premium brands. This trend is exacerbated by the blurring of brand impressions brought on by a wave of brand alliances and co-branding in a wide spectrum of product and service categories.

■ *Retail discounting and the life-and-death power of the retail trade are forcing brand stewards to re-think how they market their traditional packaged brands and service brands.* Over the past decade, distribution leverage shifted from the manufacturer to the retailer in the United States, just as it had years ago in Europe and Canada. Retail chains used to be simply the conduit for the sale of packaged brands; now they are iron-willed gatekeepers, armed to the teeth with state-of-the-art information technology, as determined to sell their own higher-margin private label brands as they are in stocking the nationals.

As analyst Gabe Lowy of Oppenheimer & Co. has pointed out, "The changes (in the retail environment) are bigger than Procter & Gamble, bigger than Philip Morris, bigger than Unilever. Manufacturers no longer control what happens in stores. When Wal-Mart can tell you how many units of any given (product) have been sold in the last 60 seconds and the margin impact of that sale, that's control."[4]

Discounters have also prompted whole new shopping patterns that are hurting traditional brands. While there will always be those who prefer to shop traditionally, a large percentage of consumers are scanning traditional outlets for information and pricing, then actually buying the products and services at discount centers such as Wal-Mart, Home Depot, and Circuit City, and membership/warehouse outlets like Price Costco.

The huge and growing catalog industry and the in-home electronic shopping phenomenon are also calling into question whether we ever have to leave home again to shop. Upwards of $50 billion worth of merchandise and services are purchased from catalogs alone by check or credit card, representing as much as 6 percent of all items bought from retail outlets.

■ *Consumer distrust is mushrooming, making it tougher for brands to create customer loyalty.* Fueled by uncertain economic times and a stream of broken promises by our leaders, Americans have raised cynicism to a cultural standard. The 1993 DDB Needham Worldwide Life Style Study reported that a record 53 percent of men believe that an honest man could not get elected to high office. The 1993 Yankelovich Monitor reported a continued decline in consumer trust: 28 percent of their sample in 1988 said they had a great deal of confidence in "consumer information from corporations." By 1993, that figure had fallen to 12 percent.

At a time when we're supposed to be going back to the basics, we are even questioning them, starting with the brands we grew up with. Consumers are demanding more information about virtually everything they are asked to buy. They no longer simply mimic their parents by buying premium brand names because "you can trust them." Trust is harder to come by, and harder to hold, resulting in more discriminating shopping and more skepticism about brand claims.

Branding is the art of trust creation; with trust on the run, brands cannot be far behind.

■ *Commercial cacophony is becoming the cause of as much deafness as rock band loudspeakers, prompting more Americans to tune out brand messages.* The din of commercial messaging is pushing the limits of endurance, leading more and more consumers to pay whatever it takes to shut out the noise.

Ads are appearing on the ceilings, aisles, checkout stand dividers, and floors of supermarkets, on ATM screens, computer screens, kiosk screens, theater screens, school monitor screens, airport screens, scoreboard screens, and sunscreens. It's been estimated that typical Americans are exposed to about 250 ads per day, but for every ad they see, they are taking in untold numbers of logos, packaging, theme lines, theme music, endorsers, and other forms of brand messaging.

Contributing to the commercial clutter have been sports sponsorships, event marketing, merchandising, and sales promotions that abound in virtually every conceivable setting. In 1985, for example, about 1,700 companies were involved in sports marketing. Today, that figure has tripled and now represents nearly $3 billion in sponsorship spending.

While those dollars provide much-needed financial support to professional and amateur athletics, and represent important communications channels to advertisers, each new wave of commercial media makes it that much more difficult for individual brands to be heard above the din. (A 1993 study by *Advertising Age* magazine and the Roper Organization found that brand marketers were even more likely to be offended by clutter than the general population. That sentiment has not stemmed the tide.)

■ *The splintering of conventional media and the advent of inter-active communications has presented marketers with a two-edged blade: New media offer more opportunities to seed brand messages via narrow targeting, but they will also make it more difficult for many brands to efficiently reach large enough audiences to create profitable volume levels.* Americans are now receiving their information and entertainment through an explosion of new communications channels, including ultra-narrow cable networks, in-home shopping programming, distributed CD-ROMs, interactive kiosks, hard copy and electronic catalogs, and eventually a whole new world of in-home video alternatives. These new communications options will improve marketer targeting accuracy; but they could also make it *more* difficult to create a broad customer base because a complex mosaic of media will be needed to reach a sufficient number of prospects.

■ *Most disturbing of all, brand equity itself is being diluted by marketers who have the most to lose.* Brand assets are being undermined by managers who know that such actions, sooner rather than later, will catch up with their brands. It's more common than ever for managers to methodically strip marketing support from brand-building efforts to fight tactical fires, or to use funds as reserves to offset shortfalls in brand or corporate profits. This habit-forming ritual can be harmful in normal times, but disastrous in an age when the marketplace punishes brands that fail to establish and sustain a sturdy identity.

Just as common, competition has lured brands into continuous promotion or discounting that end up deflating more than just the price. Larry Light, chairman for the Coalition for Brand Equity, has described the dangers this way:

> Brands do not have to die. They can be murdered. And the marketing Draculas are draining the very life blood away from brands. Brands are being bargained, belittled, bartered and battered. Instead of being brand-asset managers, we are committing brand suicide through the self-inflicted wounds of excessive emphasis on prices and deals.[5]

It's time to recognize how valuable—and how vulnerable—brands will be in the coming years.

Our Economy's Atomic Core

Brands have become the atomic core of our consumer-driven, capitalistic economy. They have interacted with one another in a dance that has fueled our commerce. They are the nucleus of product and service categories toward which consumers have been attracted in search of benefits that will make their lives more pleasant.

A brand has been defined as the name, logo, and other outward symbols that distinguish a product or service from others in its category. But a brand is much more than that. It's the owner-employees who rent you an Avis car or the owner-employees who book you a seat on a TWA flight. It's DHL's flying vans, the voice of Jack Lemmon for Honda or Eli Wallach for Toyota, the prices you find at Office Depot, the no-spill spout on a Clorox bottle, the lifetime guarantee on Tumi luggage, and the select locations where Ralph Lauren is sold, and not sold. These characteristics and many more make up the totality of a brand, and contribute to what is referred to as its "identity."

On a deeper level, a brand is an assortment of expectations established by the seller that, once fulfilled, forms a covenant with its buyers. A brand covenant is an implicit guarantee that what consumers see is what they get. It's the *brand* of Miller Genuine Draft that promises and provides a crisp-tasting amber liquid that refreshes a football fan while watching his favorite team on a Sunday afternoon. It's the *brand* of General Electric that promises and provides a reliable, reasonably priced clothes dryer to the teenager who has to fluff-dry a blouse before the big date.

Superior brands promise and over-deliver, and are in the best of all possible positions because they have consistently exceeded the expectations of their prospects and users. Snapple, Gillette, Honda, MCI, Kleenex, Hewlett-Packard, CompUSA, Federal Express, Motorola, Doritos, Tylenol, Campbell's, Cover Girl, Hunt's, Southwest Airlines, and Disney are all examples of this higher order of brands.

Consumers around the world think of the stable of brands on which they depend as packages of trust and performance, based largely on the perceived value of the brand, that is, its performance-to-price quotient. Brand performance that matches or exceeds brand promises has the highest probability of harvesting brand loyalty. That's how Acura, for example, built an early lead in its category, by delivering on its promises (despite skepticism about a Japanese luxury car), thus earning three J. D. Powers consumer satisfaction awards during its first three years of existence.

On the flip side, brand performance breakdown means that all bets are off and a brand's user becomes the rightful prey of competitive brands that are seen as more trustworthy. Such was the fate of the doomed Yugo automobile.

Creating and sustaining trust within a franchise requires the matching of what is expected with actual performance. A formidable brand identity is the end product of that process. The closer expectation and performance match in form and substance, the stronger the brand identity. The poorer the match, the weaker the identity and the greater the risk that the brand will be vulnerable to any number of debilitating threats from competitor and marketplace alike.

The Meaning of Brand Identity

Brand identity is not a new concept, although it's only recently been explored in depth. Within the last few years, more strategists, notably the French academic and consultant, Jean-Noel Kapferer, have begun to think of identity as a key component of branding. In his 1992 book, *Strategic Brand Management*, Kapferer summarized brand identity this way:

> though all things are possible when a brand is first created, after a time it acquires an autonomy and its own meaning. Starting as a nonsense word attached to a new product, year after year, it acquires a meaning, composed of the memories of past emergent communication and products. It defines an area of legitimate possibilities, yet appreciates its own limitations.[6]

In the broadest sense, brand identity is the configuration of words, images, ideas, and associations that form a consumer's aggregate perception of a brand. The identity is a brand's unique fingerprint that makes it one of a kind, what Kapferer called its "meaning." The identity is the whole fabric of how a product or service is seen by its constituencies, the integrated composite of how it's perceived to perform. That includes the strategy that dictates how it will be sold, the strategic personality that humanizes it, the way in which those two elements are blended, and all those tangible and intangible executional elements that ideally flow from their joining, such as the brand name, logo, graphic system, and so on.

Perhaps the most important thing to keep in mind about a brand identity is that it lives entirely in the mind of the beholder. An identity is not what a marketer creates, but *what consumers perceive has been created.* That, in turn, hinges on who consumers are as individuals, the environment in which they live, and the signals sent from the brand itself. A brand's messages are received through a series of filters that exist within each consumer's life. What settles into his or her brain is the only true identity the brand has created. The rest are only intentions and wasted messages.

The Whole and Its Part: Brand Equity and Brand Identity

What has been called "brand equity" refers to a brand's net worth, financial and otherwise. Dr. David Aaker of the University of California at Berkeley, one of the leading authorities on brand equity, has defined the term as "a set of brand assets and liabilities linked to a brand, its name and symbol, that add to or subtract from the value provided by a product or service to a firm and/or to that firm's customers."[7] Professor Aaker has clustered those assets and liabilities into five categories: brand loyalty, name awareness, perceived quality, brand associations, and other proprietary brand assets (patents, trademarks, and so on).

A brand's total equity can have a direct influence on, among other things, a parent company's potential selling price, its absolute revenue, the profit it generates in the marketplace, the

THE LEXICON OF BRANDING

In recent years, as brands and branding have commanded more attention, marketing researchers, consultants, and academicians have created a complete vocabulary to describe various aspects of a brand's makeup. Here's a brief glossary:

- *The brand "equity"*—The total accumulated value or worth of a brand; the tangible and intangible assets that the brand contributes to its corporate parent, both financially and in terms of selling leverage.
- *The brand "identity"*—Part of the brand's overall equity; the total perception of a brand in the marketplace, driven mostly by its positioning and personality.
- *The brand "positioning"*—What a brand stands for in the minds of customers and prospects, relative to its competition, in terms of benefits and promises.
- *The brand "personality"*—The outward "face" of a brand; its tonal characteristics most closely associated with human traits.
- *The brand "essence"*—The core or distillation of the brand identity.
- *The brand "character"*—Having to do with the internal constitution of the brand, how it's seen in terms of its integrity, honesty, and trustworthiness.
- *The brand "soul"*—Related to the brand character, defined as the values and emotional core of the brand.
- *The brand "culture"*—The system of values that surround a brand, much like the cultural aspects of a people or a country.
- *The brand "image"*—Generally synonymous with either the brand's strategic personality or its reputation as a whole.[8]

incremental retail price it can support compared to competition, the degree to which it must promote itself in its category, even its parent's corporate debt rating.

For the purposes of our discussion, we have divided brand equity into two regions: "brand valuation" and "brand identity."

1. *Brand valuation* refers to those factors that have a direct bearing on the worth of the brand, including its financial assets—both tangible and "goodwill"—that the brand contributes to its parent. The valuation side of equity is directed toward the company's stakeholders and other parties interested in the financial worth of the company, such as shareholders, vested employees, financial analysts, and the like. [9]

For the past several years, *Financial World* magazine has attempted to quantify the financial value of the world's largest brands. According to *Financial World*'s 1994 study, the world's most valuable brands are, in this order: Coca-Cola, Marlboro, Nescafé, Kodak, and the fast-rising Microsoft. (Note that several major global brands were deleted from the *Financial World* analysis due to lack of data, including Sony, Rolex, Mars, and Michelin). At the bottom of this list was IBM, to which *Financial World* assigned a negative value because of (in their opinion at the time) its ineffectual recovery efforts to date in the mainframe and PC businesses (see Exhibit 1-1 for a recap of the ten most valuable brands according to *Financial World*).

2. *Brand identity*, on the other hand, refers to that part of the equity that reaches outward to offer benefits that make it more attractive as the object of a possible purchase. Brand identity is a product of the melding of a brand's positioning and personality, and is played out in the product/service performance, the brand name, its logo and graphic system, the brand's marketing communications, and in other ways in which the brand comes into contact with its constituencies.

The identity facets of the brand are directed toward its customers and prospects. The parent company's employees are also important audiences who can have a significant effect on a

EXHIBIT 1-1

Brand	Value (mil.)	1994 Rank	1993 Rank
Coca-Cola	$35,950	1	2
Marlboro	$33,045	2	1
Nescafé	$11,549	3	4
Kodak	$10,020	4	7
Microsoft	$9,842	5	8
Budweiser	$9,724	6	5
Kellogg's	$9,372	7	6
Motorola	$9,293	8	13
Gillette	$8,218	9	11
Bacardi	$7,163	10	14

The world's ten most valuable brands.
Source: Financial World, August 2, 1994.

brand's identity, particularly in service industries (see Exhibit 1-2 for an illustration of brand identity/equity relationship).

Using an analogy, if you think of a brand as a house, the total financial worth of the house is its equity. Part of that equity is its identity: its attractive architecture, the color it's painted on the exterior, the landscaping, how cozy its interior looks, how well it's been maintained, and how it compares to its "competitors," that is, neighboring houses. If the house's appearance becomes shabby, its identity (in the minds of the neighbors, let's say) degrades; it was once a showplace that made the neighborhood proud, but now it's an eyesore. The financial value of the home—its "equity" (not to be confused with the real estate term)—has also declined.

Looking at one example of brand equity/identity in the marketplace, Volvo has accumulated a substantial amount of brand equity in the form of its revenue and profit contributions, its effects on the holding company stock, the loyalty of its customers who represent future sales, and so on. The brand's equity has

EXHIBIT 1-2

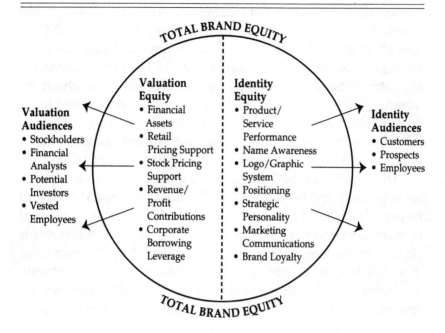

The relationship between brand equity and brand identity.

been built by a good many factors, including its reputation (part of its identity) as a brand of safe automobiles.

When it was discovered a few years ago that a television commercial the company had aired had included a faked torture test, the Volvo brand identity became tainted. Volvo's brand stewards saw their brand equity begin to decline because their identity as a leader in safe transportation had eroded. The brand's equity was ultimately restored as its identity was repaired, with the help of even more elaborate safety equipment such as a side airbag, and persuasive advertising that reinforced its safety positioning.

In late 1994, a similar, but far more devastating identity trauma stunned Intel, the world's leading microprocessor manufacturer, when its popular Pentium chip was discovered to have a subtle flaw that could influence complex mathematical calculations. The company was rocked by a series of events after a mathematics professor at Lynchburg (Va.) College discovered the problem, and his discovery was broadcast on CNN a few weeks later. Two percent of Intel's total stock value disappeared in one trading day, and one of its major customers—IBM, no less—halted shipments of its Intel-driven hardware until the problem could be resolved. Intel's famed CEO, Andy Grove, felt obligated to issue an apology on bulletin boards throughout the Internet. The escalating PR debacle ultimately forced Intel to offer to replace all flawed chips, which triggered a huge $475 million charge against earnings. Here was an unfortunate case of brand identity damage causing massive brand equity damage.

This distinction between brand equity and brand identity is an important one because a brand's identity, while still part of its overall equity, deals specifically with how a brand is viewed by its current and potential purchasers. While all brand stewards should be working to increase a brand's total equity over time, it is their brands' identities that may have the best opportunity to routinely influence customers. If their brands' identities are successfully sustained, their brands' equities will strengthen and grow.

The Misleading Image of "Image"

One term used to describe a brand's general reputation—its "image"—has had a somewhat checkered history. On the positive side, the phrase "brand image" has been the focus of a large amount of important academic and field study. In that context, marketing researchers have equated "image" to a wide range of physical and attitudinal brand associations that have to do with how people view a brand's outward characteristics.

Unfortunately, most of us also think of the word "image" in a way that implies a fleeting facade. That's not surprising, since the word was first used widely to describe the reputations of stars in Tinsel Town. Still, even theatrical agents would admit that the most outrageous image is only the surface camouflage for a real person. For instance, the queen of image, Madonna, has carefully constructed a controversial persona for her fans to adore. Yet her *Truth or Dare* film revealed that there is a lot more to her identity than her "image" conveys. The same is true of virtually any celebrity you name; very few project an image that is totally consistent with who they really are.

In the same way, the term "image" can suggest a shallow reflection of a brand rather than a brand's more essential qualities. As a result, when "brand image" and "brand identity" are used interchangeably, it can trivialize the importance of a brand's positioning and personality components. This can be much more than a semantical difference, because when it comes time to justify the use of marketing funds, "image campaigns" simply don't sound like they are substantive enough to justify marketing spending. When the same argument is made about fortifying the brand's "identity," everyone involved will likely better understand the need to invest in the brand.

Names and Logos as Identity Mortar

The names we are given can have a great influence on our lives. Every time we write our names or hear them spoken, it reinforces who we are. Thousands of people legally change their names every year, and millions more reconsider which of their given names they want to be known by. Parents-to-be often spend months considering names for their newborns, including every variation or nickname that might be stamped on their future five-year-olds on their first day of kindergarten.

Remember Picabo Street, the lightning-fast, free-thinking American skier who bagged a silver medal at the Lillehammer Olympics? Picabo was named after the town in Idaho where she was raised, with the idea that she could change her name when she found one she liked. In the end, she liked Picabo just fine, as did every sportswriter in the country. It had a positive effect on the amount of press she received and the endorsements she reaped.

The foundation of a brand's equity, and the most enduring aspect of its identity, is its name. In the case of brands with immense power (Coca-Cola, McDonald's, Marlboro, Levi's, AT&T), the brand name can help propel a brand through the marketplace. In other instances, particularly with younger brands, the descriptiveness of a name can have a strong influence on how well it's accepted (Aleve, America Online, Performa). For still others, the brand name might have no effect at all until it's given greater meaning through identity-building programs (Era, Foster's, ESPN).

According to the Name Change Index of Publicly Traded Companies, during one recent 12-month period 107 major firms changed their names to better reflect their core businesses, a 24 percent increase from the year before. That included mergers (for example, the Chemical Bank and Manufacturers Hanover marriage, which resulted in Chemical Banking Corp.), and those that dropped terms that were hurting their identity, such as Horizon Gold Corporation becoming Horizon Resources because gold had lost its sheen among investors.

Closely related to the identity message sent by a brand's name is that conveyed by its logo and graphic identity system. The 1994 Logo Value Study by The Schecter Group tested 27 well known logos and found that 17 actually detracted from their brands' reputation. Schecter's research indicates that identities can be significantly influenced by the graphic that symbolizes the brand.

One of the most effectively publicized logo/name changes was orchestrated in 1994 by Federal Express. The overnight express company converted its planes, vans, and office signage to read "FedEx," using a bold new logo design that changed its moniker to match how the public had already been referring to the brand. FedEx management reasoned that becoming the generic for the category has been of tremendous benefit to its brand equity. They believe that whatever confusion exists when businesses say they will "FedEx" a package—even when those firms use another express company—will only reinforce FedEx's superiority in the field.

A few months after the FedEx announcement, an even more venerable generic also underwent identity surgery. Xerox has become "The Document Company—Xerox." The idea behind this change was to lead the company into a new era in which document copying will be part of a much larger vision that in-

THREE BRAND NAMES AND THEIR INFLUENCE ON BRAND IDENTITY

Here are three well-known brands whose names have had a significant effect on their overall brand identity and their business success:

- *Pampers*—A typically succinct, descriptive Procter & Gamble brand name that says it all in as memorable a way as possible, that is, with minimal syllables, virtually impossible to mispronounce, positively evocative, directly linked to the product performance. Anyone who understands English understands that Pampers must be soft and gentle to human skin. Just as important, during the 1960s and 1970s when the brand was rolled nationally, the name helped mothers live with the guilt of switching from cloth diapers to disposable, a crucial psychological leap that might have been much more difficult if the brand had been named "Easies."

- *Bank of America*—Arguably, the best bank brand name in the country. The bank's founder, A. P. Giannini, changed the name of his Bank of Italy in 1930 when he foresaw the huge opportunities for interstate banking. That name change helped Giannini transform a moderate-sized bank into a formidable financial services brand, with a much more powerful brand identity. Interstate banking is now a reality. As the Bank of America seeks to become America's first nationwide bank, it has a headstart with the name that best represents our country and its people. Strictly from a name standpoint, if you're a grocer in Des Moines or a school teacher in Portland or a bookkeeper in New Orleans, what better bank to do business with than Bank of America?

- *Natural Light*—Light beer as a segment has been a roaring success, now representing about 30 percent of the $4 billion-plus sales among the top ten suds brands. The heavies in the light group are those with names that are variations on their mother brands: Bud Light, Miller Lite, and Coors Light. Natural Light is about half the size of the others and,

> while there are a number of reasons for that, it's no accident that the leading lights are the ones communicating their parentage in their name. The Natural Light brand name connotes an identity that's not all that relevant to the category and that has no connection whatsoever to its genealogy. Mind you, the Anheuser Busch organization has managed to build Natural Light into a $165 million-brand, but you wonder how much larger it might have been with a more powerful name.

cludes faxing, computing, printing, and television ventures. The move has raised at least three important questions about the company's identity: Can Xerox achieve its leadership objective in all of these disparate businesses? Is it smart to place all your identity eggs in the "documents" basket when we appear to be heading toward a paperless society? And, will "The Document Company" appendage be too bulky, or more memorable, or both?

Names and logos are part of the mortar that bonds together the bricks of a brand's identity. They are the most frequently seen and heard facets of a brand, with a powerful influence on how a brand is viewed by its users and prospects. Yet, as critical as they are in symbolizing a brand, they are not at the core of what a brand *is*. For that, we need to look even deeper than the brand's name and graphic symbols.

The Positioning/Personality Core

If you're a working marketeer, it's unlikely that you have the time or the inclination to ponder all the elements of brands that have been so carefully dissected by marketing theorists. While serious brand stewards certainly should be aware of these important building blocks, the pressures of their workaday lives often demand that they act quickly, and examine the fine points of branding only after they're sure they still have a brand to worry about.

Realistically, brand teams may only have the time and energy to concentrate on the two most crucial variables that dictate a brand's identity: 1) how a brand is "positioned" within the minds of customers and prospects; and 2) what kind of living personality the brand projects into the marketplace.

Brand positioning and personality are hardly new concepts although, as we will explore in later chapters, they are often misunderstood. Even so, they remain the most critical components of the brand identity because they dictate how users and prospective users judge the attractiveness and the necessity of a brand. In other words, people buy brands mostly because of the way they can fit those brands into their own lives, and because they like the personalities projected by them.

Brand positioning is the strategic genesis of the marketing mix. Freudians might call the positioning the "ego" of a brand and, like the human ego, it's not created by the individual brand itself, but by how others perceive it. A brand is positioned by consumers in their own lives based on their own perceptions of the brand, including how it performs compared to other brands and other purchase alternatives that compete for their affections.

If a marketer wants to change the positioning of its brand, it sends out signals into the marketplace, signals from this point forward we will be calling "positioning prompts." Any time that the positioning of a brand is changed, it has a significant effect on that brand's identity. For instance, BMW was the archetypal symbol of the go-go 1980s. The company sold a record 97,000 cars in 1986 in the United States when its [reputed] yuppiness was lapped up like mineral water. Five years later, BMW was selling just over half that many units, as potential customers reportedly were reluctant to accept what the brand stood for. Then, with the more recent introduction of the sensible 320 series and the freezing of prices on the high-end 700s, BMW sent out positioning prompts that characterized the brand as the common-sense luxury car. The brand's repositioning efforts appear to be making a positive impact on the overall brand identity, not to mention domestic sales.

The *strategic personality* is the set of external qualities of each brand, its public face, which is a direct extension of its positioning. (We refer to it as a "strategic" personality as a reminder that it flows from the strategic center of the brand). The strategic personality is the brand brought to life, its way of relating to current and future customers on their own plane, providing the attractiveness and emotional linkage that cements relationships with them (see Exhibit 1-3 for graphic representation of the brand identity "core").

Johnson's Baby Shampoo, for example, was created solely for babies with a "no more tears" support for its gentleness positioning. Its brand personality was played out for years through its name, its labeling, its product performance, and the gentle executional approach to its television advertising. That personality also allowed the brand to try a secondary positioning along

EXHIBIT 1-3

The core of the brand identity.

the way as a good choice for adults who wanted to "baby" their own hair. In that case, a brand's personality enabled it to veer from its original positioning, without endangering either.

At the Core of the Core—The Brand "Essence"

The identity of a brand is largely formed from the confluence of its positioning and strategic personality, that is, from the singular way in which those two core components stream together, and outward toward the prospect. The identity is a brand's DNA configuration, a particular set of brand elements, blended in a unique way, which determines how that brand will be perceived in the marketplace.

In his fascinating book, *Mythmaking on Madison Avenue*, researcher Sal Randazzo points out that a brand sometimes even has a "soul," defined by Randazzo as "its spiritual center, the core value(s) that defines the brand and permeates all other aspects of the brand."[10] Closely related to the brand soul concept is the idea of a brand's "essence," meaning the central nature of what it represents to all those who come in contact with it. The essence of a brand is the core of its identity.

Michael Llewellyn-Williams, director of account planning at Ketchum/San Francisco, helps clients distill a brand or product/ service proposition down to such a single word essence, after completing an exhaustive analysis of the brand's targets, positioning alternatives, and personality opportunities. This is sometimes referred to as the "-ness" of the brand. What single words, for instance, describe "Coke-ness," "Delta-ness," or "Compaq-ness?" Scan Exhibit 1-4 to see whether you agree about the essence, or "-ness," words proposed for a number of famous brands; the words are divided between one-word associations as consumers might see them and as marketers might see them, based on advertising and other prompts they send into the marketplace.

The brand essence can originate with its form, such as the creamy texture of Snack Pack pudding, or the unmistakable profile of a classic Jaguar coupé. Or, the essence can be based in its heritage, as in the purity of Ivory soap, or the flavorful history of Life Savers candy. The brand essence can also reside in its founder, which gives Fords something Chevrolets don't have, and gives the Dean Witter brand an edge over other, Johnny-come-lately brokerages. The essence of a brand can sometimes even be represented by a single word association. Take a look at Exhibit 1-4 and see if you agree with the one-word essences of the brands listed there.

Beyond single word associations, the essence of a brand extends to include everything the brand hopes to register with prospects and customers about why it is the preferred choice: its brand vision, its name, its performance standards, its signage, its packaging, its pricing philosophy, its marketing communications, its community relations policy, its sales force activities, its promotion strategies, and so on.

To repeat, however, the positioning and strategic personality of a brand—and the essence of the brand that is the product of these elements—are proposed by the marketer, but can exist only if those on the receiving end actually buy into the proposition.

EXHIBIT 1-4

Brand	Association as Consumer Might See It	Essence as Marketer Might See It
Excedrin	Headache	Relief
Marlboro	Cowboy	Independence
Tide	White(r)	Clean
Levi's	Cool	Cool
Visa	Get-away	Ubiquitous
Wheaties	Jordan	Champion
Sprint	Candice	Technology
Gillette	Razor	Men
Disney	Magic	Magic
Marriott Courtyard	Mid-priced	Businessperson

Brand "essence" (or "-ness") words.

In order for a successful identity to be created, a brand's optimum positioning and strategic personality must drive the marketing program. Harley-Davidson motorcycles are considered by their owners to be a companion as much as a vehicle because consumers have affirmed the brand's positioning as a motorcycle that will change your view of life, and its strategic personality as an American-style, machismo original. Allstate Insurance sells itself as a financial safety net that people can count on because Allstate is a friendly, caring company. The Gap epitomizes hip in retail clothing. Its positioning and personality are so closely aligned that they appear fused into one statement of continually updated casual chicness, a reflection of the individual its customers might like to be.

These brands were provided with positioning and strategic personality prompts that have been enthusiastically accepted by their many users and that have created almost tangible brand identities (see Exhibit 1-5 for a comparison of identity compo-

EXHIBIT 1-5

Brand	Apparent Positioning	Apparent Strategic Personality	Brand Identity Summary*
Harley-Davidson	The authentic motorcycle experience	A trusted friend and companion, with a dose of machismo	The proud original; the all-American tradition of quality and pride
Allstate Insurance	We'll be there to help when disaster strikes	A friend in need; caring, helpful	The safety net that protects you from financial ruin
The Gap	The place to buy what fits you as an individual	Casual, chic, direct, and confident	The reflection of who I am and would like to be

Brand identity components of three selected brands.

*Note: A brand's identity cannot be adequately captured in a phrase or sentence, but a summary statement can be helpful as a target to work toward.

nents of these three well-known brands, based on the messages they send into the marketplace).

Building the Identity Fortress

Building the right brand identity can be the single most efficient way to protect and nurture a brand's equity, although there are many different routes to establishing strong brand identities. Benetton, the Italian clothing giant, mounted an identity offensive with the help of its "United Colors of Benetton" campaign, which takes provocative stands on controversial issues. The company has been criticized for its controversial work, which has attracted both positive and negative attention to its label, but the campaign has also established its clothes as those worn by the socially conscious set. See Exhibit 1-6 for one well-known Benetton ad.

MetLife Insurance has been working on a completely different kind of identity using Charles Schulz's "Peanuts" gang. Their multiyear campaign is designed to offset the reputation of insurance companies as distant and uncaring, and has reportedly helped make MetLife a friendlier corporate giant in the eyes of its customers and future customers. Exhibit 1-7 shows one of the "Peanuts" ads.

Speaking of friendly, McDonald's first became the fast-food outlet for families looking for inexpensive fare at friendly, clean, well-run restaurants. The brand's family identity is still seen in everything from its menus to the jungle gyms out front. McDonald's eventually expanded its appeal to include teens, young adults, mature adults, and so on, but the core of its identity—and the continuing strength of the franchise—remains with families.

Hewlett-Packard, as another example, could easily have fallen by the wayside as a mainstream hardware manufacturer during the fearsome computer wars that still rage on. Instead, HP has remained true to its identity as a technically superior supplier to engineers and companies that seek the precision and speed that engineers require. That identity has also enabled the

EXHIBIT 1-6

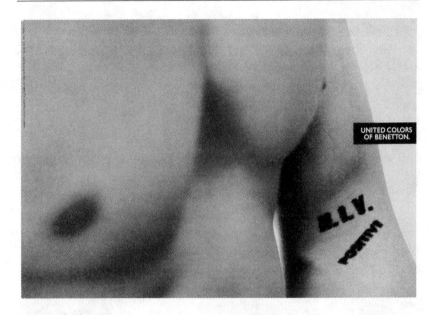

A print ad from the controversial "United Colors of Benetton" campaign that helped establish the brand's identity as being from a socially conscious manufacturer.
Photo by O. Tosiani for Benetton.

brand to attract consumers who need a dependable computer printer for home or office.

What these brands are doing is building a strong brand identity "fortress." A franchise will weather the slings and arrows of marketplace fortune in significantly better shape if it has a sturdy brand identity in place.

An identity fortress can also help protect a brand against the avalanche of communications that continuously bombard consumers. The more cluttered the marketplace becomes, the greater the need for a reinforced identity fortress that envelopes a brand and keeps its equity intact.

Consider the jumbled over-the-counter analgesic market. One brand remains above the fray: Tylenol, with retail sales approaching $1 billion, well over twice that of its nearest competitor, Advil. Tylenol stays far ahead of the pack because consum-

EXHIBIT 1-7

WE'RE THE OLD MASTERS OF FINANCIAL SECURITY.

GET MET. IT PAYS.
✿ MetLife®

MetLife "Peanuts" campaign helps reinforce a positive, caring identity for a huge insurance company.

ers have a clear understanding of where it should be positioned in their minds (effective pain reliever with no side effects), and that stance is reinforced with smart advertising at spending levels commensurably ahead of other category advertisers. (Tylenol's lead is now being challenged by the new Aleve brand that is using Tylenol-like techniques to build a strong identity.)

As the Tylenol success story implies, however, simply building a brand identity fortress is not enough. The brand must be managed so that it is continuously reinforced with new identity replenishments that maintain and build on its strengths as a brand. These come in a variety of forms: Sega keeps the pressure on Nintendo with rapid introductions of new games and new channels for their games. Campbell's Soup makes sure that it will never run out of ideas for new flavors. Home Depot relentlessly expands and rotates its inventories, leaving the impression that anything necessary for living can be found under its roofs.

Among other things, these moves are investments in brand identity. The brand stewards involved are knee-deep in identity management, the planned and deliberate fortifying of a brand's total meaning in the marketplace.

Identity's Effect on Value

The term "value" once referred to the compromise struck between price and performance. The lower the price in relation to acceptable quality, the better the value, and sometimes the quality wasn't all that acceptable. A "value brand" was lower priced in the absolute, and the consumer had to be ready to sacrifice quality, at least compared to premium brands, in order to save money on the purchase.

Premium brands were built on the assumption that a large percentage of the population is willing to pay more for a product that lasts longer, or tastes better, or a service that is more luxurious. That assumption held up well until the country experienced its most recent recession. The abrupt end to endless expectations redefined value in our lives. Today, Americans lean toward premium brands if, and only if, such brands can justify their pricing with evidence of substantive quality. The brand identity carries that substantive quality message.

Levi's, Sony, the *New Yorker*, Lexus, and Microsoft are often considered good values despite their higher pricing. In contrast, the premium airlines have had a tough time justifying their higher ticket prices in recent years because they cannot easily demonstrate why one airline seat is all that different from another. One set of brands has created the right form of identity and the other has not.

Price, of course, will remain an all-important factor in virtually any purchase, regardless of the state of the economy. However, it's being relied on less today as a measurement of quality because good quality is available at virtually all price tiers. In the past, price has been a critical part of the identity only for those brands at the extreme ends of the spectrum—the very expensive and the very cheap. With the value of "value" changing, it will be mandatory for every brand to communicate good value in some way.

The Uncertainty of Brand Loyalty

Some say that brand loyalty is becoming an endangered species. There's good reason to be concerned about its decline, considering it's estimated to take more than five times the marketing spending to get a new customer than it does to hold onto the one you've got. It's also been proposed that a 5 percent increase in customer loyalty can yield increases in profitability ranging up to 85 percent.[11]

Brand loyalty is a much rarer commodity than in the past for a number of reasons: First, brand inertia—the force that keeps consumers in their habitual purchase pattern—is weakening. Brand switching is becoming an easier decision to make as product/service parity grows more common, and as consumers are being offered greater incentives through competitive price cutting and short-term "switch" promotions.

Also, as pointed out earlier, the leveling of technology has permitted even small companies to provide products and services that can effectively compete against their larger rivals, encouraging consumers to check out whether the grass may be greener elsewhere. Ten years ago, there were only a handful of computer hardware companies in business, whereas now there are so many IBM clones that they have become the single strongest segments in the category, all because technology enabled them to compete with Big Blue (as prompted by IBM's open architecture).

Still another reason for the shakiness of brand loyalty is that the consumer is significantly better educated than ever before about the goings-on in the marketplace. Labels are being studied more closely, the fine print of disclaimers is actually being read, consumer magazines, television shows, and newspaper articles keep all of us up to date on what product or service works and what doesn't. If a brand fails to deliver on its promises, the consumer is more likely than in the past to know it, and be better equipped to look elsewhere.

Among durables, marketers of historically strong brands face uphill battles in retaining repeat customers. Consumers used to remain loyal to companies such as General Electric and Frigidaire because they trusted the brands and did not want to risk making a mistake on large-ticket items. But the volatile economy and the availability of more lower-priced, quality brands through discount outlets has weakened some of these businesses.

It hasn't helped any that some old favorites have reportedly fallen in esteem, at least according to the Total Research Equi-Trend survey of perceived brand quality. The General Electric appliances brand, for example, has slipped from 20th in rank to as low as 40th in just three years. Although, several more expensive brands such as Lexus and Mercedes have all shown new strength as the economy has rebounded (see Exhibit 1-8 for a comparison of selected quality rankings among the top 100 brands).

Service marketers are finding that they must invest in more and more costly continuity programs to retain customers, often loading up their books with long-term liabilities that come back to haunt them. American Airlines reported that, in 1993 alone, its frequent-flier liabilities increased by one-third to a staggering

EXHIBIT 1-8

Brand	1991	1992	1993	1994
GE Major Appliances	20	27	40	36
Lexus	65	59	26	19
Mercedes	3	8	8	5
Marriott Hotels	45	41	54	37
Hilton Hotels	42	34	45	42

1994 EquiTrend® Survey: Selected quality rankings among top 100 brands. (The lower the rank number, the higher the relative quality.)
Source: 1994 EquiTrend® Survey, courtesy of Total Research Corporation.

$380 million. United and other airlines restructured their bonus programs to include expiration caps, extensive "black-out periods" on customer credits, and a miles depreciation program starting in 1995.

Service companies are in even greater danger of losing otherwise loyal customers because they are selling intangibles that make it more difficult to provide users with visible reasons to repurchase. Among service providers, the Marriott and Hilton brands experienced some quality erosion, according to the EquiTrend® Survey, possibly as part of the long-running slump in the hospitality industry.

Identity Building Is Loyalty Building

There are at least four proven ways to build or sustain brand loyalty, even given the tumult in the marketplace. The first approach is still the best—that is, to ensure that the product or service represented by that brand lives up to (or, better yet, exceeds) its customer's expectations. The way the product/service performs reinforces (or detracts from) the brand's identity. If a Mercedes is positioned as the best mass-produced car in the world, and its users feel that way each time they drive one, then its identity has been assured. That's loyalty building at its best.

A second tried-and-true method is to build innovation into existing products/services and to introduce innovative new entries as often as is feasible. Apple's PowerBook, Gillette's new series of male toiletries, Gerber Graduates, Frito-Lay's Rold Gold, MCI's 1–800-COLLECT, and AT&T's various "True Savings" promotions, are just a few examples of existing brands that have built new wings for their brand identities with product/service innovations.

Third, more brands are designing loyalty-building programs into their marketing activities, ideally activities that don't turn into ledger liabilities like the airline mileage programs. The expansion of automobile leasing programs in the first half of the decade not only made cars more affordable, it also allowed dealers to sell those vehicles just as the lease expired. GM and Ford also have successful credit card programs that earn rebates on new vehicles, a strong brand loyalty device. Ford created the Mustang Club, which offered members a chance to participate in the relaunch of the model. And Saturn held a well-publicized "homecoming" of 44,000 Saturn owners in June 1994 which was essentially a celebration of brand loyalty.

A fourth and powerful way to build loyalty, is to invest in marketing support to strengthen the brand's identity. An NPD Group study a few years ago revealed that total brand loyalty for all brands measured had fallen to a "brand equity index" of 95 from a benchmark index of 100 in 1975. But brands with lower advertising spending saw loyalty drop even further, to an index of only 84. Brands that received uneven or no ad support at all fell to an index of 82. Obviously, advertising is only one form of brand identity support, but it's one form of commitment marketers must consider making to maintain brand loyalty, and build a stronger brand identity.

The Brand Identity Strategy

By strengthening a brand identity, or creating a formidable one from scratch, the perceived value of the brand to prospects and customers can be significantly enhanced, better equipping it to cope with potentially destructive forces in the marketplace. For example:

- Lower-priced brands are less threatening opponents to a brand that enjoys a powerful brand identity. At a minimum, a strengthened identity offers a brand more options in the face of a significant price disadvantage. Oscar Mayer, Minute Maid, and Pepsi are all examples of brands with strong identities that registered sales gains in 1993–94 in the face of significant pressure from price brands.
- The growing prowess of the retail trade can be counterbalanced with a strong brand identity that gives a retailer pause before reducing facings (packages visible on the shelf) or choosing to de-list one or more SKUs. Snapple and Healthy Choice brands have built brand identities with enormous marketplace clout. Both brands continue to command extensive shelf space despite the onslaught of new competitors, including those introduced by the trade chains themselves.
- When the economy goes sour—and it will again—the shield of choice will be a brand identity that registers strong value at any and all price tiers. Premium brands like Hertz, Nestlé, Hewlett-Packard, Nabisco, Vicks, and Cheer have weathered many economic hard times and survived intact, if not in better shape.
- A brand with a reinforced identity gives its customers and prospects something substantive and trusting to believe in, even as trust wanes in the marketplace as a whole. A prime example: Campbell's "Never underestimate the power of soup" category sale has registered big gains for that brand, indicating that consumers still believe what the soup expert says about soup.
- A memorable identity with sufficient marketing support can help a brand rise above the noise and fractionated messaging that is apparently going to be part of the new media revolution we will all be participating in. The pizza business, for instance, is as crazy as the Little Caesar's character, yet the brand from the wild side is the most talked-

about item in the category, thanks to a brand identity that's hard to forget. If Little Caesar's ever introduces an Internet pizza ordering business, its existing brand identity will make it *the* fun place to order on the Net.

■ Finally, a strong brand identity provides the ultimate benefit that every consumer seeks—peace of mind. Brands— at least brands that we can count on—are small signposts of stability in our lives. When a consumer decides that she likes Westinghouse light bulbs or prefers to rent cars from Budget or to use Microsoft software, she is reducing the number of decisions she has to make each day, and she is signaling that there are some brands she intends to count on until they lose her trust. The first step in building and holding that trust is to establish a trustworthy brand identity.

Given this evidence, why do brand handlers regularly abandon identity-building efforts to fight brushfires? Possibly because the most immediate problem often appears to be the most important. But fire can burn those who use the wrong weapon to fight it, and experienced brand people will admit that battling solely with short-term tactical weapons can ultimately do long-term harm to their brands (although there are many tactical marketing tools that do a fine job of building brand identity).

Marketers may also feel they must concentrate on the day-to-day running of the brand and simply choose to ignore some fundamental flaws in their brand's identity. They may mislead themselves into believing that brand identity and its component elements are theoretical in nature, something to be discussed occasionally in off-campus meetings, but not as part of the day-to-day real world in which they must compete. Or they may be concerned that changing their marketing programs could do more harm than good. Identity building may also appear to be a "luxury" in which they cannot afford to invest until business is better . . . or the category becomes more stable . . . or the company's new management is less jumpy, or . . .

If this rationalizing sounds familiar, then consider this: a robust brand identity is no more of a luxury than a name or a logo.

The right identity will provide a brand with its point of differentiation from competitors, a compelling reason for preference for would-be customers, and a rationale for shaky believers to stay loyal.

Those brand marketers who wish to increase their probability of success in these times of danger to all brands should consider adopting what we call the "Brand Identity Strategy," summarized as follows:

> Brand teams that are fighting to maintain healthy franchises in an increasingly hostile marketplace will concentrate their marketing efforts on building the strongest possible brand identity by:
>
> - conducting periodic, objective analyses of where the brand stands at the present;
> - learning where a brand's opportunities lie by getting to know its customers and prospects *as individuals*;
> - blending the most relevant positioning cues with a unique and attractive strategic personality;
> - driving the brand's identity through all possible brand identity contact points; and
> - readying the brand for full participation in interactive marketing programs
>
> This on-going process must be given the highest priority on the brand team's agenda.

The Brand Identity Strategy is an attitude and a framework for action. As an attitude, identity building can be the edge that a brand needs to survive and excel in a hostile marketplace. It can help brand teams focus on how to retain and build those brands under their care. The Brand Identity Strategy is about being honest regarding what assets and liabilities a brand carries with it, and about looking for every opportunity to capitalize on a brand's strengths. It demands full-time concentration, the same kind of concentration that good parents are willing to commit to their children.

As an action plan, it calls for brand marketers to understand their customers and prospects as they understand themselves, and to use that perspective to create irresistible marketing programs that are operating at capacity every time the brand is in contact with those individuals.

No brand identity is perfectly built or entirely secure. Consequently, every brand, regardless of its position in its category, should be in some stage of identity building. The best managers are never completely satisfied with their business performance to date, nor should they ever believe that their brand identity is ideal.

Executing the Brand Identity Strategy

The Brand Identity Strategy offers a multistep approach to identity building that also forms the structure for the remainder of this book:

1. *Evaluating the Brand Reality*—If a brand has been around for any length of time, it's likely that its handlers have become less than objective about its assets and liabilities. The first step in implementing the Brand Identity Strategy is to objectively analyze the images, associations, and vital statistics that make up the brand. If a new product is being planned, this "identity interrogative" can also help to prepare a future brand for its trial by fire in the marketplace.

2. *Indivisualizing the Customer*—Smart brand marketers rethink who their targets are by acknowledging that they are not "targets" at all, but individual human beings who must be understood in the same way that marketers understand themselves. This process we call indi*visual*izing, the profiling of prospects as individuals and how individuals think about brands.

3. *Prompting the Power Positioning*—The only position with real power is the one in the mind of the prospect, positioned by that prospect. Everything in the brand's marketing program emanates from its positioning, and the positioning must emanate from marketers' accurate visualizations of their individual prospects. What's most relevant to the prospect—and, therefore, what's most relevant to a brand—is what's going on in that individual's life.

4. *Humanizing the Identity*—A brand's identity is most vividly manifested in its strategic personality, its external extension into the customer's world. Once all the strategic pieces of the

identity have been assembled, a marketing team can identify the optimum strategic personality that flows from the positioning in order to bring the brand to life in an utterly unique and persuasive way. When the strategic personality and positioning have been successfully blended, the result is a brand essence that is hard for prospects to ignore.

5. *Managing Identity Contacts in the Real World*—A brand is only as effective as the success it has in communicating its identity on the "street," that is, within the real world of the real marketplace. The emerging discipline of "brand contact analysis" will help marketers project their positioning/personality prompts into every available contact opportunity. We are now in an exciting age of brand relationships, thanks to the early work of direct marketers. This new era bodes well for brands that know how to create two-way communications that lead to user loyalty and user dependence.

6. *Analyzing Those Brands that Succeeded and Failed at Building Strong Identities*—Creating the right brand identity is like most marketing tasks—it becomes a lot easier to understand when you can study others that did it right. In chapters 7 and 8, we will examine the stories of four very successful brand identities, one enormous stable of brands that is undergoing fundamental identity changes, and one brand that still hopes to create an identity that will lead it past the golden arches into the promised land:

- Disney—The strongest brand of its kind in the world, a story of identity magic and riches even Aladdin's genie would have a hard time matching. Disney is now facing its toughest challenge in a generation as its parent company molds new leadership;
- Nike—Everywhere you see the Nike "swoosh" logo—and that's just about everywhere—you know that there has been some brilliant branding going on. Nevertheless, this brand still has some steep hills to climb.
- Procter & Gamble—Not one brand, but a huge cluster of classics whose managers are learning to cope in a tough new world where premium-priced packaged goods have to justify their very existence. It's an identity shift for many brands under one large corporate umbrella.

- Southwestern Bell Yellow Pages/Swbyp's—A mid-America yellow pages company that has revived interest in a product people habitually take for granted;
- Saturn—One of GM's newest real brands, a unique young division that taught America how to take pride in what's made by Americans; and
- Burger King—the fast-food runner-up that has had as many marketing directors as ad campaigns. Turnover in both categories, plus fractious franchisees, have prevented the creation of the strong brand identity that BK deserves. But there are some good things happening to change all that.

7. *Gauging What Lies Ahead in Interactive Marketing*—The so-called information superhighway is upon us, regardless of what the cynics say. The new interactive, multimedia options that will soon be offered to American consumers will change our lives in untold ways, as they will change brands that participate in them. Brand stewards must begin participating now in this brave new world of opportunity and risk.

8. *Minding the Brand Identity*—With the systemic changes in the economy and the increased importance of brand identity, there is also a change happening in the triad relationship between the customer, the marketer, and the brand. These changes are reshaping branding's future, making outcomes less certain, yet providing exciting new opportunities to build brand identities. The way we market after the turn of the century will largely depend on how well we manage this transition.

Which brands will survive and prosper in the coming years, and which will not? There are never any guarantees when it comes to branding. The happenings in the marketplace have made the tough job of brand building that much tougher. Yet by carefully managing the care and feeding of a strong brand identity, stewards will minimize the risks that lie ahead, and increase their chances of achieving their ultimate goals. The journey starts with objectively analyzing the brand.

2

Evaluating the Brand Reality

The best brand stewards are accomplished detectives, constantly searching for what works, and what works against, the cause. They regularly dissect their brands, honest to a fault about a brand's strengths and shortcomings, and about what's needed to keep the brand strong.

This is not the fun part of brand building, its the heavy lifting, the hard thinking that must be done with precision and perserverance, the patient analysis that opens the door to brilliant positionings and engaging brand personalities. But when it's done right, all the pieces fall into place.

The 3-D Brand

Brands are complex animals that live in their own ecosystems of economic, social, and competitive realities. The most important realities of all are the realities that they share with their customers. Evaluating a brand's reality is the first step in creating and managing the optimum identity. One way to begin that process is to take a photograph of a brand using a brand "diagnostic," basically a thorough checklist that helps stewards prepare for the decisions they must make about their brands' identities.

Three realities are important to understand: the *customer's individual reality*, as will be described in the next chapter; a brand's *internal reality*, that is, how it's managed and viewed by those in charge of its care; and its *external reality*, the environment in which it is being sold in the marketplace. By weaving all of this information together into workable formats, a marketing team can obtain a full, three-dimensional view of its brand.

Knowing When to Take a Temperature

Brands are continuously sending messages about their own health, one time as a spike in customer traffic, the next as a drop in sales-per-point-of-distribution, or maybe as an unexpected flurry of calls into the customer service center. There never seems to be enough time to consider the long-term ramifications of these signals, but when share or volume or revenue head south, there's always time for the problem to get immediate attention.

Veteran brand stewards look for telltale signs that indicate when a brand's identity may be in need of inspection and repair:

1. *Low or fluctuating "top-of-mind" brand-name awareness*— Prospects aren't likely to buy a brand if they can't remember its name without working hard. Top-of-mind (or unaided) aware- ness is a rough indicator of how prominent a brand is in the minds of the respondents surveyed. Strong unaided brand awareness is the trailhead to a strong identity. No manner of insightful strategizing or creative copywriting will move the needle if awareness is limited to a small group of loyal users.

As obvious as that may sound, there are a good many mar- keters who hope to be big players in their respective categories but who cannot, or will not, ante up the marketing support nec- essary to create sufficient top-of-mind awareness. In California, First Interstate Bank tried without luck for years to attract new customers by competing with Bank of America and Wells Fargo using a fraction of their advertising and promotion budgets. The Nature Valley Granola brand, the Gaines dog food brand, and the Volkswagen brand have all fallen on hard times, at least partly due to reduced marketing support. In contrast, the Crest toothpaste brand has gained a 3-to-2 advantage in share of market against Colgate due partly to a consistent share-of-(advertising) voice advantage over time.

Similar parallels between shares of market and consumer spending can be found in a huge range of categories, including long-distance telephone service, beverages, shampoo, overnight package express, photographic equipment, electronics, and fast food. Each product/service category has its price of entry and cost of survival, including appropriate marketing support levels necessary to maintain adequate brand awareness. Drop below those levels and a brand's chances of creating and sustaining a strong brand identity drop as well.

2. *Unfocused attribute ratings*—Well-informed brand marketers carry in their heads ongoing assessments of how their brands are evaluated against the competition according to the most leverageable criteria for the category. For cruise lines, that may be a "fun index"; for dishwashers, it may be a "scours rating"; for analgesics, a "speed-of-relief" comparison. Whatever the measure, the brand should be seeking a crystal-clear set of attributes against which it can be evaluated.

3. *Fuzzy brand associations*—A brand may be seen in a good light or bad, but its worst enemy is the darkness. People have a hard time identifying with a brand that doesn't seem to be sure what it is all about. Crystal Pepsi hasn't been clear whether it's a cola or an uncola. Sears' management struggled for a decade as they tried to determine if they wanted their stores to be discount outlets, a village of boutiques, or a mainstream department store. In the hotel industry, Ritz-Carlton means top-drawer service and properties that are unerringly elegant. Motel 6 units equate to clean and Spartan. Hyatt Regencies are known to be luxuriously contemporary and dramatically designed. So, what are Hiltons like again?

The exceptions are those rare brands that use intrigue to

stimulate trial, such as Coors' mysterious Zima alcoholic beverage, which refuses to be defined, and the Chrysler Neon, which used teaser ads to play peek-a-boo marketing during its first few weeks of introduction.

A brand's associations must not only be clear, but positive. It used to be prestigious to say that you worked for Exxon, but now it can mean to some that you are not concerned about the environment. The Kentucky Fried Chicken identity was hurt by the word "fried," which has been removed by creating the KFC brand.

4. *Subpar product/service performance*—If a product or service fails to live up to the expectations of its customers, sooner or later its brand identity will be devalued in their minds. Before Ford rescued it, Jaguar nearly killed itself off, buried alive under its legendary repair bills. Not all that many years after GM extended its lead during Ford's Edsel debacle, GM began a slide of its own on an even more epic scale, stimulated by a parade of poor performers like the Chevrolet Vega, the Pontiac Fiero, and various trouble-ridden Oldsmobiles and Cadillacs. All of these brands had perfectly sound brand identities at one point, but when part of their product lines faltered, their identities suffered as well. (Most of the GM brands have since made good recoveries.)

The reverse is also true. The McDonald's brand has few broad-scale product failures because its stewards would rather test too much and forego a preemptive introduction than to introduce an item that would damage the brand's identity. Häagen-Dazs would never dream of bringing out a product that was anything less than superior; if it did, the brand's identity would weaken, resulting in a loss of valuable brand equity. Honda's Acura and Toyota's Lexus divisions have consistently produced cars that provide minimal-maintenance driving for the first several years of ownership, resulting in strong brand identities, particularly among current owners.

5. *Consistent customer complaint levels*—The smartest companies are the best listeners. What people think of a brand is right there for all to hear. It shoots through telephones in customer service centers, it echoes through salespeople's ears when they're in the field, it stacks up in the CEO's outer office in the form of

letters and postcards from customers and rejecters. Consumers frequently speak with their pocketbook, but the boldest are even more direct. When they call or write, they are doing more than giving feedback, they are doing the brand a great favor by giving an early warning that its identity could be in jeopardy. The crumbling of a precious brand identity can begin with a single disgruntled customer.

Preparing for a Brand Reality Analysis

A question: How much time does the typical brand team spend thinking about the brand's identity, and the environment in which that identity exists? Answer: Not nearly as much time as they may spend trying to correct problems caused by a faulty brand identity.

A Brand Reality Analysis identifies those factors that can be used to build a strong identity, and those that cause unexpected problems down the line. It all starts with setting up the right objectives for the Analysis, so the brand team can focus on information that will be of maximum use. Some questions that may help the team determine the objectives for a pending Brand Reality Analysis:

- Is the team clear on its business objectives, marketing strategies, and customer targets?
- Is there potential for growth that should be capitalized on, or potential for major business losses that must be dealt with?
- Are there going to be changes in the brand (line extensions, core or auxiliary service introductions, marketing spending cutbacks) that could have a significant impact on the identity?
- Are one or more of the brand's competitors showing a vulnerability that can be capitalized on, or a new strength that could threaten the business?
- Is the category showing unusual signs of weakening, or robustness that might call for some forthright action on the brand's part?

■ Specifically, what problems on the brand will the Analysis help eradicate?

Before embarking on a major identity review process, the brand team may also wish to consider these suggested operating guidelines that will make the analysis as useful and actionable as possible:

1. *Be ruthlessly objective*—Marketers are expected to observe the marketplace objectively, and they should be doing the same when reviewing their own brands, no matter how painful that might be. If a brand has some elemental flaws or untapped resources, it's best to get that information into the daylight as soon as possible so it can be dealt with by the team. All involved should agree to "call it as they see it," as opposed to how they might like it to be.

2. *Research & re-search*—A Reality Analysis calls for a thorough search of what's known about a brand, without necessarily spending a fortune on new research. There's probably some valuable information hiding in the corporate attic, particularly if the brand in question has been around for a while. Start with the most obvious—existing marketing research that has been conducted within the last several years, both quantitative and qualitative.

There may also be some useful insights residing in the heads of some veteran company executives. Alex Haley, the author of *Roots*, once toured the country speaking about his life and discussing the origins of his landmark book. The key point he made in those talks was that *Roots* is not a book about African-Americans, it's a book about how he found his own identity among the origins of a family that just happened to be African-American. To search for and understand ancestors who came before you, Haley used to say, is to better understand who you are. He recommended that those in the audience go home, get a tape recorder, and spend as much time as possible taping the memories of their oldest living relatives.[1]

If the brand is more than a few years old, spend time with those individuals who have a sense of its history. Ask anyone who might know where there could be other bits of information about the brand that could have a bearing on what users and nonusers think about its identity.

3. *Look beyond marketing communications*—A brand's identity is influenced by literally hundreds of communication avenues and contact points, including advertising, consumer/nonconsumer promotions, merchandising, direct marketing, and public relations. But a Reality Analysis should not be confined to marketing communications alone, for two reasons. First, although they may be the most visible expression of a brand's identity, marketing communications often represent a *minority* of total brand impressions. Packages of nationally distributed brands on a shelf, or colorful buttons on retail employee uniforms, may be seen more times by more people than network advertising.

In addition, because of their visibility, marketing communications get so much attention from management that the marketing team can end up spending an excessive amount of time on the obvious forms of identity communication. Those may or may not be as important as more subtle brand messages to the people who count—the brand's prospects and users.

4. *Don't start what can't be finished*—Any major brand analysis will tax a brand team, its company, its communications agencies, and even its company management. Those involved need to consider how committed they are to getting some answers about their brand's identity. Are they willing to stretch beyond their already tough schedules to do the homework and take part in the discussions necessary to truly understand what their brand represents in the marketplace? Are they willing to make a personal commitment to get the job done thoroughly, and within a reasonable time frame?

The Brand Reality Analysis

Context Branding

No man is an island, the poet John Donne reminded us, and no brand exists alone in its own world. Anthropologist John Sherry coined the term "brandscape" which is the literal landscape of brands that we see in every facet of our lives.[2] To that, we add the concept of "context branding," the idea that what surrounds a brand—whether it is other brands or any other immediate environment that hovers around a brand—is nearly as critical to the success of the brand as the specific cues that its sponsors send out to their constituencies. The Sears Auto Centers is a brand (or sub-brand, in this case) that benefits from being found in shopping malls where customers can drop off their cars while they shop. Yet its locations and name also suggest that the centers are a spin-off of a company whose primary business is not automobile accessories. The Sears Auto Center brand lives in a mixed context.

The Reality Analysis is divided into four sections that focus on both the brand itself and its surroundings: the **Internal Brand Environment,** which gauges the enthusiasm and commitment of the marketing and management teams; the **Selling Environment,** which sets the scene for the identity exploration by establishing the brand's in-market context; the **Identity Interrogative,** which is a series of questions that enables the brand team to candidly describe and evaluate its brand's current (or proposed) identity; and the **Identity Composite,** which synthesizes all of the collected information and interpretation into a bottom-line assessment of where the identity stands.

The Internal Brand Environment

Although a brand identity lives within the lives of its users and prospects, it is born among the people of its parent company. This is where the brand was created and where, ideally, it is sustained with continuous and enthusiastic support from every company employee who has a role to play in its development and marketing. All of those in a company that markets a product or service are real or potential "brand ambassadors," representatives of the brand who can leave strong impressions of the brand wherever they may go. Company employees are conveying something about a brand's identity every minute they communicate with outsiders and with each other in any way that relates to the brand—in a casual conversation at a cocktail party, through their body language in a selling situation, in their responsiveness on a service repair call.

■ *Brand Connections*—The brand support system is like a family of individuals, each of whom believes that he or she is part of something strong and lasting. Talk to someone from FedEx or Saturn or Hershey or Motorola—the chances are they know what their brands are all about. They won't necessarily be able to recite the brand positioning, but they know that they are working for a winner, and that their brand's winning is no accident.

This contagious sense of confidence, of the inevitability of success, is crucial to the care and feeding of brands. Manufacturing this feeling is not easy, but all things are possible if the marketing team embarks on an intentional planning process that seeks to learn how close employees feel to their brand, and how much more must be done to fully integrate them into the marketing program. Here are some questions that can help get at these issues:

—*Has anyone ever conducted marketing research among company employees to determine what they think of the brand, and how that compares to what consumers believe?* Employees are almost always one of the primary audiences of any brand effort, and that's particularly critical in service companies where the employees can have the single greatest impact on a brand's identity.

—*Do employees feel emotionally connected to the brand, or is it just another product or service sold by the company? Is the brand's health a common topic of conversation among employees who are <u>not</u> on the marketing team?* Either the brand is just a name attached to a job, or it is a part of the employees' own lives. A brand must be a companion in employees' lives if they are expected to represent the brand and provide it with their best possible support.

—*Has the marketing team ever held brand "rallies" (not meetings, <u>rallies</u>) to keep company employees informed and enthusiastic about its brands?* There's nothing corny about showing open support for a brand that helps pay your wage. Is that something that would be consistent with the corporate culture, or out of place?

—*Are members of the so-called staff departments (for example, marketing research, manufacturing, R & D, service quality control, and so on) invited to participate in marketing planning?* Despite the obvious complications this might cause, it would be an important symbolic move, even if offered only occasionally.

—*Are ideas solicited from the ranks about how the brand's marketing efforts could be improved?* Anything from a brand suggestion box to more formal channels could make employees feel more like brand ambassadors. Asking employees how *they* might market the brand would give them a feeling of involvement, without committing the marketing team to implementing anything they didn't feel was appropriate.

A brand is a collectively supported institution, just as is a city or nation. When support wanes among its creators, or never fails to materialize, the brand is put at jeopardy. Employees who are not committed to a brand are less likely to go the extra mile and more likely to make mistakes.

▪ *The Brand Vision*—Brands are companies themselves, whether they are individual selling units or a corporate brand. They require clear direction about what their stewards hope to accomplish and what management expects employees to contribute in order to achieve those goals. A brand "vision" might be defined as: "where we'd like to be ten years from now." Some questions that can help assess if everyone is signed up for the same thing:

—*Has the marketing team or company management ever articulated a "brand vision," that is, where you see the brand going in the short-term and long-term future?* Sometimes the brand vision has been made clear through advertising (for example, MCI's "Friends & Family" campaign clearly communicated that the brand would be people-oriented), or through other marketing methods (for example, Taco Bell's very aggressive price promotions demonstrated that they were geared for a long price war). But the most important place for the brand vision to be articulated is within the host company itself through clear employee communications.

—Do the nonmarketing employees share your vision for the brand? Does anyone share that vision with new employees? Does anyone ask veteran employees if they can contribute special perspective on the vision? Keeping a brand vision within the marketing team alone is a little like keeping your birthday a secret, then wondering why no one threw you a party. Again, a brand can only be an internal focus of enthusiasm if the marketing team's hopes for its future are shared by others in the company.

—Do employees know why the brand was created, how it's doing in the marketplace, how and why it's superior to the competition? The more explicit the brand team can be with the company's employee force, the more likely the employees are to actively support the brand.

—Are the company's employees able to articulate the kinds of things that should be repeated about the brand outside the company? Each employee talks to dozens of people a day; he or she could be saying something good about the brand to help spread positive word-of-mouth. Their comments may only reach .01 percent of your prospects, but they may solidify the commitment of those employees and make a difference in how well your brand is sold.

—Does the executive management of the company endorse and support the brand vision? Have they articulated a company vision that is compatible with the brand vision? Obviously, it would be to everyone's benefit to ensure that where the brand is heading is completely compatible with where the company as a whole is being steered.

The Selling Environment

The environment in which a brand is sold is not literally *its* selling environment, but rather the environment that customers are experiencing which, in turn, affects how they perceive the brand.

Not all that long ago, alcoholic beverages were evaluated by partygoers according to their taste, color, potency, and badge value. Today, they are also chosen based on their effects on the drinker's ability to drive home. In the 1970s and 1980s, your only questions about ordering a steak might have been "how big?" and "how much?" In the 1990s, you might want to think about the fat level of various cuts before you order. A credit card used to be selected according to where and what you wanted to charge, or by its prestige value. Now, your decision is more likely based on its current and future interest rates and what extra benefits come with it.

The reality of the everyday American consumer is the reality a brand is evaluated within by that consumer. For better or for worse, that reality contributes to a brand's identity. Here are some important consumer realities to be considered:

■ *The State of the Economy*—More than ever, how economically healthy the nation is can have a profound effect on how individuals spend their money. Depending on the category, these perceptions influence the desirability of particular brands, especially if they are premium priced.

—*Where does local unemployment stand? How does it compare to national and state levels?* This could be one of the most important factors in the purchase of many brands. Even when deeply discounted, most products and services just won't sell as well as in more stable periods if consumers are unsure of where their next paycheck is coming from or if it's coming at all.

—*At the time of the analysis, is the U.S. economy growing, stagnant, or declining in real terms? In general, how are the local/regional economies doing where the brand is being marketed? How much play is the economy getting in the press compared to recent periods?* Even the healthiest of brands can suffer when the general impression by residents is that bad times still lie ahead. Conversely, if the economy is strong and growing, consumers may be more likely to take a chance on a new product or pay a little more for a service they wouldn't indulge in during tougher times.

—*What are the consumer and general business confidence levels, as being reported by the University of Michigan and the Conference Board, and how are the levels trending?* These reports are now widely reported monthly or quarterly by most major news media, and have a real influence on a wide spectrum of opinions from Wall Street to Main Street.

—What are the current and projected trends for inflation? What have been the Federal Reserve's recent actions and public statements regarding short- and long-term interest rates? These announcements from Washington are watched by many more people than just stock analysts. Consumers are at least vaguely aware that their ability to borrow money is ultimately affected by the Fed, and how much discretionary income they can spare after they've paid the rent or mortgage.

—How much talk has there been in local/regional news media about the national debt? The trade deficit? Housing starts? Talk may be cheap, but it can be devastating to some categories—luxury cars, travel, the hospitality industry—that depend on consumer confidence to perform well.

Taken as a group, these general economic indicators paint a fairly clear portrait of the general selling environment in which a brand competes. The net effect of these elements may vary considerably according to category, as noted in Exhibit 2-1.

■ *The Selling Place*—There's a world of difference between how a brand's identity is perceived if, for example, it is primarily distributed through membership chains versus conventional supermarkets. Consumers' mental pictures of a brand often hinge on what kind of selling place they are in when they encounter it. Watchmakers can realize more margin per unit in jewelry stores, but sell more units at lower prices through discount houses. Is that a good tradeoff in terms of the effect on the watch brand's identity? Yes, if the brand is Timex; maybe not if it's Omega.

—Evaluate where the product/service is sold, gauging the degree of quality communicated by the selling environment. If wholesalers or distributors are involved, how do these agents define the brand's position in the category? More than ever before, a manufacturer loses a tremendous amount of control over its brand's selling environment once the product leaves the distribution center. This is less of a problem for service marketers who often have greater control over the selling environment.

—If the brand is sold through retail channels, how supportive or challenging to work with are its selling agents? Are they considered marketing partners? Positive factors in the selling process, depending

EXHIBIT 2-1

Category	Degree of Sensitivity	Possible Causes
Automobiles	High	Recession, unemployment reduces disposable income; inflation decreases buying power
Clothing	Moderate	Consumers need clothes regardless of economy; type/price of clothing purchased may vary
Travel/ Hospitality Industries	High	Often considered a luxury that can be postponed
Health/Beauty Aids	Low	Low out-of-pocket; considered a necessity, although price brands may do better in poor economy
Electronics	Moderate/High	Postponable luxury; usually involves moderate/high out-of-pocket expense
Ice Cream/ Desserts	Low	Often considered affordable indulgence, even during tough economic times
Beverages	Low	Lower out-of-pocket; discounting common

Category sensitivity to economic uncertainties.

on the region? Generally nonfactors? Necessary evils? Company-owned sales forces are the most easily controlled but the most expensive to maintain. Brokers and other freelancers are tougher to control, but generally cost less.

A marketing team and its management might consider the "net cost" of a sales force, defined as payroll and benefits, plus gross out-of-pocket costs, adjusted for the positive and negative effects on the brand's identity created by the performance of the sales people.

—*How many people, places, or things can interfere with the brand's selling environment?* The visibility of a brand is directly affected by the obstacles standing between it and a direct connection with its customers. A brand identity grows and flourishes much more quickly if a customer can have as many positive, direct contacts as possible with the brand. Is a brand sold where there is a high degree of commercial clutter, for example, a bank branch in a grocery store? Where there is a great deal of distracting activity by other shoppers, for example, a fragrance in a department store? Where there is another activity unrelated to what a brand is all about, for example, a confection sold in an office building's concession stands?

—*Does the brand break through these clutter barriers and stand out as a singular brand, or is it constantly fighting for attention among many other competitors?* At supermarket checkout stands, Beecham's gum may have a hard time being seen among the myriad of other gum and candy brands on the shelf. A few feet away, however, Schick razor blades may be more visible because they are sold on jobber racks where there are rarely more than a few brand alternatives.

—*In the case of a service brand, is the service offered within a fully controlled environment (for example, a company-run rental car facility), one with limited control (a rental car counter among many others in an airport), or virtually uncontrolled location (a rental agency housed in a parking garage)?* These restrictions should be calculated into the net impact a brand can have in its servicing surroundings.

—*For a business-to-business brand, are customers called on in person at their premises or the company's, or primarily by phone?* Business-to-business brands often have more riding on the sales force than consumer brands because the products/services tend to be higher in cost, and tied into establishing personal relationships with customers. The environment in which the brand is presented can be one of the most crucial factors in generating sales.

■ *Communications Clutter*—The most visible form of consumer distraction is communications clutter caused by overlapping messages from competing media noise. The new, more narrowly targeted media may assist a brand in homing in on audiences who are more likely to be interested in the message, assuming such a message can be seen and heard amid all the other equally intrusive commercial messages out there.

—*Starting with the basics, what is the brand's share of voice, not only in advertising, but in all marketing communications arenas?* For example, its share of attention among consumer promotions, re-tail discounting programs, retail signage, and wholesaler incentives could have a significant effect on the health of its brand identity. Although there are few competitive spending monitoring services available beyond advertising tracking, competitive clutter scenarios can be constructed based on "educated guesses." While they may be speculative, they will help the brand team to begin thinking about all the opportunities competitors have to crowd out the brand's message, and what can be done to prevent that from happening.

—*What is the brand's relative impact vis-à-vis its competition?* Take a realistic look at the marketing communications material created by the brand team. Look at competitors' messages that have the most influence on category behavior, regardless of how much money is spent behind them. How much of what is purchased in the brand's category can be attributed to its marketing programs? In other words, how much "bang" is the company getting for the brand's marketing spending relative to competition? (You can count on the category leader to be more efficient by almost all measures compared to trailing brands.)

—*How much control does the team have over the communications clutter in the selling environment?* Are there actions that could be taken to reduce it or to increase the brand's ability to rise above it? The team may have more control than they realize over competitive clutter.

—*Have any tests been conducted in the past that have significantly raised or lowered the brand's share of voice or relative impact? What have the results of those tests indicated about the amount of leverage the brand has in the marketplace?* Some brand teams fail to run "what if?" tests because they don't believe the test plans will ever be broadly implemented. That may not be the point. High/low support tests may help the team to understand the general responsiveness of the brand to variations in spending, regardless of whether the test plans will be literally translated as tested to larger geographical areas.

■ *Category Analysis*—Like it or not, the category in which the brand competes can have the single greatest effect on how it is evaluated by its prospects. Even if you sell the leading brand of microwave french fries, you're in for a challenge because most people don't believe you can get good fries from the microwave. In contrast, such successful brands as Sunkist oranges, California raisins, and Evian water have convinced dubious consumers that there really are superior brands in so-called generic categories.

—*How well defined is the category? Do consumers have a clear understanding of where the category stops and others begin?* What exactly is the difference between an analgesic and an antihistamine? Between an HMO and indemnity health insurance? Between a sports van and a sports utility vehicle? The distinctions may not be all that clear in consumers' minds.

—*How often is the brand's category consciously considered by consumers as they go about their daily lives?* Is the brand in a category of staples such as toothpaste or paper towels that are used and purchased frequently, or among durables that are bought only every few years? Do consumers think about the category when the product is in use, such as golf clubs, or do they tend to take it for granted, such as dishwashers?

—*How relevant is the category to consumer needs and wants?* Does the brand team have to work hard to stay on top of consumer whims such as in the toy business, or do they just need to check in from time to time because consumer needs evolve slowly, such as with facial tissues?

—*What is the core "essence" of the category?* Categories have rational, emotional, and sensory core values, just like brands. If you're selling a snack food, you're probably dealing with strong consumer needs for salt or sugar. If you're in the hardware business, you've got to be thinking about the male needs of being the "fixer/provider" in the household. If you sell telephone equipment, you must be concerned with specific time/efficiency standards set by your industry.

—*How healthy and dynamic is the category? Are the current trends old and unchanging, or have they taken a recent turn? Are there any root problems or upsides that could have a long-term effect on the category?* Concerns about saturated fats, for instance, have negatively affected the dairy industry, yet have had little effect on candies. Declining retail prices of PCs have triggered higher demand for those products, yet rising prices on some on-line service brands have not seemed to dampen consumer enthusiasm.

—*How volatile is the category in terms of movement in share rank of the brands?* Is the category mature with established competitors and relatively stable shares, such as among coffee and soup brands? Is it a newer category with a great deal of instability, like computer peripherals? Or is it an older category with new volatility such as in the beverage industry, which is being turned topsy-turvy by the "new age" drinks?

—*Does the category seem to have a life of its own, or do the fortunes of a few dominant brands influence how consumers look at the category as a whole?* The category of ready-to-eat cereals has a few strong leaders, but it reshapes itself regularly depending on the needs of consumers and the responsiveness of the sellers. In rental cars, however, the moves of Hertz and Avis alone can have a significant effect on all other brands.

—*What images and emotions are currently associated with the category?* For example, beer = good times; cars = comfort or speed or exhilaration; athletic shoes = hard exercise or "hipness."

—*Describe the dominant characteristics of the category.* Is the category considered contemporary (for example, salsas) or traditional (tomato sauces)? Younger (jeans) or older (slacks with elastic waistbands)? Topical (telecommunications) or rarely in the news (dish-washing detergents)? Luxury/indulgence (premium ice cream) or a staple (milk)?

—*What are the tangible and attitudinal competitors to the category?* Is the category like salty snacks that are clearly competing for a share of the stomach? Or like insurance companies that appear to be offering financial security but, in fact, are competing with other financial service companies to attract investment funds?

—*What is the structure of the category?* Is it the more common "hierarchical" type, with one to two strong category leaders, followed by several also-rans, such as is typical in packaged food? Is it the less typical "balanced" category, such as the airlines, where four of the top eight brands each have a 12 to 20 percent share of the business? Or the "fluid" type where share positions can change from year to year, such as toys or the movies/entertainment categories?

■ *Competitive Analysis*—Marketers routinely study the spending, pricing, promotion, and distribution strategies of their competitors. But competitors are more than rivals for shares of market, they are a key part of the brand's immediate environment.

—*How well-defined are the competitive brand identities?* Can the marketing team succinctly state what each competitor stands for in the marketplace, and what personality it projects?

—*How clear are competitors' strengths and weaknesses?* For example, if the targeted competitor is Sony, it may be relatively easy to discover its vulnerabilities, but the weaknesses of lesser known brands such as Toshiba or Fujitsu may be more difficult to uncover.

— *How much is known about the CEO of competitive companies and the individuals who run the brands that represent the greatest threat?* Remember Malcolm Forbes's view: the single most accurate indicator of a company's approach to business is the personal philosophy of its CEO.

— *What are the marketing support patterns of the competitors?* Do they advertise heavily? Do they spend consistently or sporadically? When they increase or curtail spending, do they do so for what appears to be logical reasons, or is there no apparent method to their madness? How closely is their spending related to their business performance?

— *If they advertise, do they concentrate their support in broadscale or direct-selling media or both?* Are they showing any real interest in the new media, such as interactive or infomercials?

—*To what degree do they rely on consumer sales promotion, merchandising, public relations, event marketing, interactive media?* Has their emphasis on promotional support increased or decreased in relation to advertising in the past year, and compared to the previous three years? Do they buck the trend in these and other marketing support areas as opposed to the usual approach in the category?

—*What nonconsumer support do they use? Are they dependent on it for ongoing share maintenance or short-term volume/revenue stim-*

ulants? In packaged goods, a competitor who is wedded to retail trade dealing might be vulnerable to consumer programs that generate more "pull" than they can muster. In service industries, brands that fail to invest in consumer programs have a more limited ability to establish new positionings or evolve their strategic personalities.

■ *What Type of Brand Is Being Marketed?* Consumers understand so much more now than they did in the past about what's happening in the marketplace. They know when a brand is "hot," or hasn't been heard from in quite a while. They know brand families, although they may not call them that. They judge a brand like they judge people, by the company it keeps.

—*During the past few years, has the brand steered a steady course (Seven-Up), sent new positioning prompts into the marketplace (Coke, Pepsi), or has it been relatively inactive (Mountain Dew)?* Brands carry identities that consumers must be able to count on, yet without taking them for granted. Is the brand giving its constituencies a clear look at what it is, or changing positioning and personality cues so often that it risks confusing even its most loyal users?

—*Has the brand traditionally been considered a loner (Beefeater gin), or part of a larger family (Seagram gin)? If so, how much does it borrow or depend on the other brands?* This can be a good gauge of the breadth of the total brand identity, which can be enhanced by being part of an overarching family or subordinated by the presence of other family members.

—*Is the brand identity an umbrella for a variety of other products and services (the Charles Schwab brand that casts a halo over mutual funds, stock trading, and bond buying) or even other brands (Ford's halo over Mercury, and Lincoln's halo over all of the Ford Corporation cars)?* The more products or services that a brand must encompass, the more complex the identity building process. Exhibit 2-2 is a Schwab ad promoting some of the products and services under the Schwab "umbrella."

—*Is there a corporate brand that stretches over a wide range of products or services (AT&T)? If so, how much of the brand is related to the fortunes of the corporation (for example, financial performance, stock movement, community relations issues).* Consumers could care

EXHIBIT 2-2

SOME OF THE BEST THINGS IN LIFE ARE FREE...

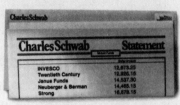

Maintain a Schwab One® asset management account with at least $5,000 and enjoy **no monthly fees.**

Choose from over 250 mutual funds and pay **no loads or transaction fees.**

Reinvest dividends for free with our new Schwab No-Fee StockBuilder Plan™.

Move $10,000 or more into a Schwab No-Annual-Fee IRA by September 15, 1995, and **pay no annual fees for life.**

WHEN YOU TRADE UP TO SCHWAB.

With products, services and values like these, there's never been a better time to trade up to Schwab.

Investing Made Easy.

With the Schwab One account you can trade stocks, bonds and mutual funds through a single account, free of monthly fees. You can also access your money through unlimited checkwriting or a no-fee Visa® debit card.

A Better Way to Buy Mutual Funds.

Now, with just one telephone call, Schwab's Mutual Fund OneSource™ service lets you choose from over 250

well-known mutual funds and pay no loads or transaction fees.¹ And, you can hold them all in one account and receive one easy-to-read statement.

Reinvest Dividends for Free.

Schwab's No-Fee StockBuilder Plan can turn your cash dividends into stock— free. You can reinvest the dividends, even in your IRA, from over 4,000 eligible stocks and pay no commissions?

Free IRA for Life.

The Schwab No-Annual-Fee IRA is guaranteed free of annual fees for the life of the account if your balance

reaches $10,000 or more by September 15, 1995.³ To make more of your retirement money work for you, transfer it into a Schwab No-Annual-Fee IRA.

So, trade up to Schwab today. For more information about these and other Schwab products and services, stop by one of our more than 200 local offices or call:

1-800-472-4922 ext. 64B

CharlesSchwab
Helping Investors Help Themselves®

1. Prospectuses available upon request. Three funds are also available without transaction fees, but are not no-load funds. Mutual funds have management fees. Schwab reserves the right to change the funds available with no transaction fees (NTF) and reinstate the fees on any funds. NTF shares purchased may always be sold without transaction fees. However, if you paid a fee to purchase a fund, you will be charged Schwab's normal transaction fee to sell it as well. If you make 5 or more short-term redemptions of NTF funds (shares held 6 months or less) in a calendar year, you will be charged fees on all of your future mutual fund trades. 2. Dividend reinvestment does not assure profits on your investments and does not protect against loss in declining markets. 3. Maintenance fees for special assets such as limited partnerships and promissory notes still apply. ©1994 Charles Schwab & Co., Inc. All rights reserved. Member SIPC/NYSE. (10/94)

A Schwab print ad promoting its range of services under a single brand identity.

less if the maker of their favorite salad dressing is having trouble because it had to write off the cost of discontinuing an aging manufacturing plant. But they may be very concerned if an airline they must use files for Chapter 11.

—Is it an older established brand that carries a lot of good and bad baggage (Cunard Cruise Line)? Or is it a relatively new brand that still has considerable built-in flexibility about where its identity can go (Carnival Cruises)? How much flexibility does the brand's current reputation carry with it, meaning, how much has the brand team got to work with in attempting to build the business?

By completing this analysis of where and how a brand is sold, the category in which it competes, and the type of brand it is, the marketing team is now better equipped to directly address the issues surrounding the brand identity itself.

The Identity Interrogative

As discussed in chapter 1, a brand's identity is an amalgam of images, opinions, and impressions carried by all those aware of the brand. The Identity Interrogative is a method of evaluating what signals the brand is sending into the marketplace, signals that ultimately mold the brand's identity.

■ *The Brand Name: What Associations Does It Generate?* We mentioned earlier the importance of linking a brand name to positve associations. The brand name is a word or phrase that sends out messages each time it is seen, heard, discussed, or recalled. The name most likely operates on at least two levels: 1) what the word(s) itself means to people, and 2) what the brand name "cluster" means, that is, the group of meanings and associations that have come to be attributed to the brand name.

The word "mustang" means a wild horse, but if used in a conversation today, the listener would likely think of fast cars. The coined word "Tylenol" could only mean one thing. You would think that Ivory and Zest were better names for a bar soap, but the upstart with the ultracontemporary name, Lever

2000, is right up there among the leaders of that part of the pack. If you are introducing a new line of tents or butane-fueled anything, what better name than Coleman?

—*What does the brand name mean as a word by itself, unrelated to what has been established in the marketplace?* Sometimes it's tough for a marketing team to step away from the brand meanings of a name and look at it as just another word in the language. Yet, that may be how some prospects are viewing it. The word "Tombstone" does not necessarily conjure up pleasant images of mouth-watering pizza toppings or scrumptious cheese-pulls, but Clearly Canadian does send out positive signals about its water.

—*Does the brand name have multiple meanings? Are they all positive or can some be harmful to the identity?* Yoplait yogurt may sound light and tasty to some, but foreign and odd to others.

—*Is the brand name working as hard as it could for the brand identity?* Burger King is a great name for a "Get Your Burger's Worth" advertising program, but it may not be the best name for a dessert promotion. The Edge shaving gel name might connote a close shave, but work against an identity of a smoother shaving experience.

■ *The Brand Icon(s): How Well Does It Convey Who You Are?* The brand logo and related icons often can have nearly as important an effect on the brand's perceived identity as its name. The Betty Crocker portrait; the Prudential rock; the Texaco star; the Reebok union jack; the Apple apple; the script typeface of Kellogg's, Campbell's, and Sara Lee; the Ralston-Purina checkerboard; the CBS eye; the NBC peacock; the Gerber's baby; and the Breck girl—they each contributed at least as much to their respective brand's distinctiveness as virtually any other elements in the marketing mix.

—*Does the brand have an established icon or simply a logo? How important is it to the total marketing program?* Is it an integral part of the promotion programs and public relations efforts, or simply relegated to the lower right-hand corner of print ads?

—*What has been done to analyze the logo's worth, and exploit its strengths?* Should it be reintroduced as an updated version that might provide some new interest in the brand? Or should you find ways to celebrate the stability that continuity as a logo?

—Do the competitors' logos have more impact in the marketplace? Why? Has that learning been incorporated into the brand's own logo evaluation?

■ *The Brand's Physical/Perceived Attributes: What Messages Are Being Sent?* If the brand represents a physical product, it's already way ahead of the game. Human beings can most easily relate to, and recall well, those tangible items they experience with their senses. How something looks, tastes, feels, smells, and sounds provides them with clues about how they should place it in their lives.

For brands of intangibles, the problem can be considerably more complex. Virtually all of the attributes attached to a service brand are really perceptions created by the service itself and the people and things that provide that service—in other words, the service *experience*. An airline brand is not a thing, it's the cumulative impressions of how the employees treat the passengers, what the ticket costs, how bumpy the ride was, how good the food tasted, whether the passenger was treated courteously, and so on. While all brands have a potential relationship with their customers, that relationship is on multiple, subtle levels when it comes to service brands.

—What are the physical signals that the brand sends out to its customers and prospects? How many different ways does the brand come in visual contact with the user? Are the signals potentially positive unless something goes wrong, or is the opposite likely to happen?

—In what ways can the brand's physical attributes be improved to convey a stronger, more positive identity? Are the physical aspects of the brand, or its representatives, consistent in tone and content with what they are conveying to customers? Are the variations helpful or hindering to the goals set by the brand team? Are they fixable, or something you must live with?

■ *The Current Positioning: Where Does the Brand Stand?* Define the current positioning of the brand in no more than one paragraph. As a reminder, a positioning is defined as what the brand stands for in the consumer's mind vis-à-vis the competition, not necessarily the signals the brand team believes they have communicated to their prospects.

—*Is the current brand positioning clear in the minds of the marketing team?* Has it been articulated, both verbally and in written form, and reviewed on a regular basis within the marketing team, or has it been filed away in a brand summary book and not reviewed more than once a year before annual plans are created?

—*How often and how thoroughly has the positioning been examined and reevaluated?* Nothing is sacred in the brand's marketing mix, particularly if the team believes that a stronger brand identity can be created.

—*How accurately can the team determine the brand's positioning against the competition, and its relevance in relation to customer/prospect needs?* Positioning analysis is like any sport; the more you practice it, the better "muscle memory" you develop.

■ *The Current Strategic Personality: What Kind of Person Is the Brand?* Describe the current strategic personality of the brand.

Traditionally, a brand personality has been defined as how a brand would be described if it were a person.

—*"Who" is your brand?* A brand is a living being, so start there and describe who that person is in as great a detail as possible.

—*If you had to consider the brand personality as one trait at a time, how would you go about it?* Is the brand "angry" or "contented"? Is it "passive" or "aggressive"? Is it "friendly" or "standoffish"?

—*How would you describe the brand, using only a series of adjectives?* For example, Coors beer might suggest adjectives such as "cool," "fresh," or "golden," while Colt 45 Malt Liquor might suggest "bold," "powerful," "macho."

■ *The Brand's Overall Identity*—A brand's identity is the accumulation of impressions that are reactions to a series of cues sent out from the many facets of the brand. In general, the identity is the synthesis of the brand positioning and strategic personality, come together in a unique way.

Here the brand team should ask: What is the "essence" of our brand? One way to approach this challenge is to try and synthesize the core of the brand in one word. For Jergens, that word might be "soft." For Kodak, it might be "color." For *Time* magazine, it might be "news." (Refer back to Exhibit 1-4 in Chapter 1 for more examples.)

While the full identity of a brand is not easily summarized, the brand team needs to develop a succinct summary statement as a tool in identity management. An identity statement is only a recap of what the marketing team hopes to convey about the core of the brand, not an effort to capture literally all that the brand represents in the marketplace. Take a look at Exhibit 2-3 to compare the apparent positionings, strategic personalities, identity statements, and communications theme lines that are commonly associated with several well-known brands.

■ *In What Emotional Context Is the Brand Considered?* Consumers carry a certain set of emotions with them into the marketplace as they consider buying a brand. Spend some time considering how consumers *feel* about the brand as they are considering its

EXHIBIT 2-3

Brand	Positioning	Personality	Identity Elements	Brand Themeline
Honda	More advanced than the competition	Friendly, accessible, sophisticated in a simple way	The helpful car that helps me without complicating my life	"We Make It Simple."
U.S. Army	Where you can reach your full potential	Challenging, demanding, exhilarating	A mentor who will show me how to succeed	"Be All That You Can Be"
Little Caesar's	Fun, cheap pizza and lots of it	Wild and crazy	Party food that doesn't need a party	"Pizza, Pizza"

Selected brand identity elements.

purchase. For example, there are emotion-laden products/services such as soup (nurturing), lingerie (sexiness), and entertainment parks (excitement); and less emotional products and services such as chewing gum, air conditioners, and car waxes.

However, there are few, if any brands that have no emotion whatsoever attached to them. Chewing gum may translate to relaxation because it reduces stress for some people. Air conditioners may remind others of the hot, sticky nights when, as a child, they slept in the backyard. Car waxes might give users a feeling of accomplishment as they wipe away the dried wax haze to reveal a shiny finish beneath.

—*What specific emotions are likely to be part of a purchase decision?* What emotions will the buyer experience when considering, buying, and using the brand's product or service? Will those emotions change over time? For example, I may feel anticipation while I shop for a new car, anxiety while I negotiate the purchase price, elation while driving it home, and pride when I show it off to a neighbor.

—*What effect does the brand have on the emotional set of the prospect?* Is the brand set up—purposefully or unintentionally—to deliver certain emotions or to be associated with emotions of a particular kind? *Essence* magazine sounds as if it delves into the souls of the people it reports on. The Club sounds like it means business, either as a protector of cars or people.

—*Or does the brand represent a product or service that is largely functional?* Even so, does its functionality mean that it is literally unequipped to generate some emotion on the part of its users? In what ways can the brand imbue the product with emotion? There's nothing particularly emotional about salad dressing, but Hidden Valley adds as much homey mystique as possible to its advertising. Wheaties has always been just a good-tasting cereal, but it's also been successfully linked with the emotions felt by sports heroes.

—*Describe the emotional set that surrounds the category it competes within.* Is it highly charged, laid back, boring? Does the brand team have to work at getting people excited about the category, or is it difficult to control the emotion that's wrapped up in what you sell? Levi's first set the emotional tone for jeans with its famous "501 Blues" campaign, then Calvin Klein followed with its study of male and female posteriors. Neither of these pioneers meant to set the stage for Lee, yet that brand's "Jeans That Fit" campaign has very successfully introduced a whole new emotional set to the category by playing off of consumers' frustration with chic jeans that hug a bit too tight.

—*Do the users feel passionate about the brand (whether or not they are literally brand loyal)?* If not, why not? Be specific. Who would have guessed that a new toothpaste in an ultra-mature and already crowded field would generate a loyal, passionate following? But that's just what's happened in the last few years as Rembrandt toothpastes are reportedly doing well in a highly competitive category.

■ *How Far-Reaching and Consistent Are the Contacts that Potential Buyers Have with the Brand?* In order to understand the impact of a brand, a marketer needs to gauge the scope of its contacts with consumers, employees, and other interested parties. There will be an in-depth discussion of brand contacts in a later chapter, but for now, think about how the brand identity is being distributed throughout the marketplace.

—*In what places and under what circumstances does the brand come into contact with users and prospects?* Consider a contact to be any time or any place that people experience the brand in any way. Delivery trucks, brochures, business cards, prime-time commercials, shelf signage, word of mouth—all are examples of brand contacts.

—*How positive are the impressions left by the packaging, signage, labeling, advertising, sales promotion, retail employee contacts (where appropriate), and others?* How contemporary do they appear in relation to the competitors? Is the brand a Bud or a Zima? A Home Depot or an Ace Hardware? A Warner Brothers or a Touchstone Films?

—*What kind of good/bad publicity has the brand or its parent been subjected to in the past year or two?* Has the marketing team had good/moderate/poor control over whatever publicity the brand has received?

The Identity Composite

Brand teams live everyday with what they regard as the reality of their brands, yet it's only after considering factors such as those listed throughout this chapter that a team can begin to conceive of the totality that comprises the brand, the entire brand experience that customers encounter.

Using the information from the Reality Analysis, create a "model" of the brand, the sum total of the findings about the brand identity. Express the brand's identity as simply and lucidly as possible, first in a listing of identity components, then in a core identity statement, composed of the positioning and strategic personality.

Sample Brand Reality Composite Outline Example: A Leading Prepared Spaghetti Sauce Brand

(Note: This is an outline only, based on in-market observations of leading spaghetti sauce brands. Proprietary information would be substituted when an actual analysis was conducted.)

Internal Brand Environment
Strong loyalty to the parent company. But employees have more knowledge of, and commitment to, brand itself.

Selling Environment

- State of Economy: Steady growth, with a Fed-dampered recovery from 1991–93 recession.
- Selling Place: Primarily supermarket and memberships chains. Increasing distribution in mass merchandisers. Heaviest skew in Northeast and Mid-Atlantic.
- Communications Clutter: Network advertising clutter levels high compared to mid-1980s, but unchanged since early 1990s. Print advertising clutter in women's service books slowly returning to prerecession levels. In-store merchandising curtailed by retailers except for private labels. Continued severe clutter from packaged goods brands, particularly in canned/jarred foods categories.

- Category Analysis: Category continues to grow by 2 to 5 percent per year, fueled by near-universal appeal of base dish and convenience of prepared spaghetti sauce. Anticipate declining growth rate in 1996 and leveling off by 1997–98 due to increased siphoning of category business from cooking sauces and ethnic food dishes.
- Competitive Analysis: Category leader's line continues to hold 33 percent share, but share eroding because of strong pressure from other brands in several price tiers. Continuous trade dealing keeps everyday low pricing on all major brands. Private labels are a relatively small factor, but growing at a good rate, now representing nearly 5 percent of category. Total category advertising spending has increased steadily in the past three years due to cross-attacks between two leading brands, plus the introduction of new brands and line extensions.

Identity Interrogative (Example Outline)
- Prospect:
—Demographic Profile—Women 25–45, married, with children at home, household income $35–$45K+, suburban neighborhood, Northeast United States, works part-time.
—Psychographic Profile—Neo-traditionalist.
—Indi*visual*ization Profile (See hard copy and videotapes on file with Brand Marketing Team)
- Positioning: Full of all the high-quality, good-tasting ingredients you'd add yourself
- Strategic Personality: Helpful, understanding, knowledgeable
- Brand Identity Summary: A busy cook's best friend (See Brand Marketing Team for full identity profile)
- Emotional Context:
    Primary: Even with all the pressures on working parents, they still want to prepare dishes their families love, but don't have the time, and still do have the guilt, associated with most convenience foods. Our brand allows them to provide all the good ingredients they normally would add, but much more conveniently.

Secondary: Anyone seeking to have a hearty, but simple meal will find that our brand offers the warmth and comfort of home cooking without the hassle.

- Brand Contact Summary: Advertising, sales promotion pieces, labels on shelf, chats with other mothers, shopping carts, etc.
- New Product Opportunities: Continues to be good potential for line extensions with new flavors/textures. Also opportunity for flanker products in several strategic directions (for example, dry pasta, refrigerated pasta and/or sauce, other cooking sauces, and so on).

The Identity Prospectus for New Products/Services

Much of the analysis of existing brands that should be completed by marketing teams is also important for new product groups as they are preparing to introduce a new brand. New product teams can use the Brand Reality Analysis to envision what the brand-to-be will be like, and what impact it may have on the category involved. This requires a somewhat different approach than that taken for existing brands.

The Existing Brand Mindset

It's human nature for marketers who plan to introduce a new product to think of it as just that—the interjection of a new entry into the market. But a new product or service, whether it's another version of what's already out there or an entirely new concept, may also be a natural extension of the marketplace in which it will compete.

It was a surprise to many when Healthy Choice frozen dinners galloped to extraordinary volume and share levels so shortly after its introduction, but consumers were primed and ready for a low-fat/low-calorie product line that really delivered on taste. Snapple natural beverages started slow, but eventually tapped into existing needs for a huge variety of delicious drinks.

The Ford Explorer seemed to come out of nowhere to take a commanding lead in the sports utility segment but, in fact, it was simply filling a need that had been there for several years—the need for a premium-quality 4×4 at a price well below the Jeep Cherokee. None of these brands was an accidental success. They were envisioned successfully by their creators, who saw the same needs as consumers did in their own lives.

New brands in development can be treated as if the future brand already exists, visualized by marketers in the same way that they have ind*ivisual*ized the customer (see chapter 3). The brand team can project out to the time when they will be doing a review five years *after* the brand has been established in the marketplace. How quickly did it catch on? Who turned out to be its most loyal followers? What effect did the new brand have on the category? Which competitors successfully defended their franchises against the brand, and which did not?

Some of the benefits of this approach:

- If they can begin to live the future, the marketing team will carry a confidence that comes from success rather than an anxiety that can seep into any speculative venture that's just hoping to get off the ground.
- The team can more successfully envision how the market and its competition will react to their introduction because they are—at least attitudinally—already in the fray. They can anticipate what has not yet happened. They can feel more comfortable dealing with future events because they will be theoretically living the future in the here and now.
- The brand identity that the team hopes to create with its introduction will be easier to envision. Pulling together the disparate pieces of an identity can be a full-time job, and one that makes it difficult to see the finished product. But, by acting as if the brand has already been introduced, it's easier to act as if the brand identity is already in place.

The Internal Brand Environment

How a new brand is created within a company is as important as how it's launched externally. The "existing brand" perspective is critical here. Those who work on a future brand must have the kind of focused commitment that you find in NASA space projects. Everyone must be made to feel that he or she is a key midwife in the birth process. The goal set by the brand project leader should be to overcommunicate as much as possible to employees about the new brand (recognizing certain necessary security constraints), and to get them motivated about making this new entry a success before it's even launched.

The New Products Selling Environment

This is a projection of the selling environment you are likely to encounter. Review the current brand subjects discussed earlier in the chapter and project out from there into "Ideal" and "Most Likely" scenarios. Will private labels and discounted services still be growing in importance? Will commercial clutter still jangle the nerves and distract the senses? Will advertising exist at all, or only in interactive long-duration formats? Will the new brand be in a "selling" environment, or will it be an "information" environment in which products and services are on display but backed by no partisan communications, just information modules?

Category Analysis

This would be similar to that for existing brands, except that the marketing team must describe what effect the new brand is expected to have on the category. Take into consideration that future categories may have merged (computer hardware and software?) or disappeared altogether (the vegetable shortening category?) by the time the new brand hits the market.

Competitive Analysis

Again, many of the same issues encountered by existing brands should be considered here. But with the introduction of a new brand, there is usually a more active jockeying for share, some-

MAKING A BIG SPLASH WITHOUT DROWNING

If you have the money, it's relatively simple to introduce a new product in most categories. Alas, the 90 percent failure rule applies today even more than in the past. Some new products made a splash in the last two or three years that threatened to soak some of the old timers in the category, largely because they made such good use of existing brand identities. Others dove in with an entirely new brand, squeezing out a fresh new identity. Here are three examples:

1. *Hershey's Hugs*—Located somewhere between cute and adorable, Hugs is as natural a line extension as you'll find anywhere. This one turned out to be a keeper because it offers virtually unlimited cross-merchandising possibilities and because it further strengthens the Hershey's identity as the premier American chocolate. The brand is making it that much more difficult for competitors to increase their shares of the sweet tooth.

2. *Zima*—Coors' malt entry into this yet-to-be-defined adult alcohol beverage category has been micro-marketed and has attracted a crowd of curiosity seekers prodded on by unusual Z-rated advertising and promotion that's intriguing even the skeptical. It's not yet clear what effect Zima will have on its competition, mainly because it's not yet clear exactly what category it's competing within. Very ztrange.

3. *Taco Bell Products*—Armed with deep pockets and a well-known Mexican-food brand name, Taco Bell got the attention of competition with its 1993 introduction of a line of grocery store items. The Taco Bell brand name, and the halo effect from a huge fast-food ad budget, will give this new line a serious kick start. Something it will need against such category stalwarts as Pace Picante Sauce and Rosarita Refried Beans.

> An existing brand franchise is no guarantee of success for its offspring, and a from-scratch brand will not necessarily face impossible odds. What's crucial in both cases is that the brand handlers carefully erect a brand identity (either borrowed or new) that carves out a unique and credible place in prospects' lives.

times involving the surface aspects of competitive identities, such as the changing of an ad campaign.

In other instances, more fundamental changes may occur, up to and including the alteration of strategic positionings in order to better defend against a new entry. Two examples: Citicorp's introduction of credit cards with the customer's photo triggered several other successful photo cards, and a new emphasis on security for card holders. With the arrival of Entenmann's fat-free line of pastries, competitors had to concede that fat-free claims were a force to be reckoned with in what was previously an indulgence-only category.

Brand Contact Analysis

It's critical that all brand contact points be managed as thoroughly as possible. Every possible communications channel should be considered. For example, if a new chain of arts & crafts stores is opening, flyers could be put in every elementary and middle school surrounding the outlets to tell funds-starved teachers that they have a new place to send parents to stock up on supplies. Such seemingly minor brand contacts can be disproportionately important to new brands, particularly if those brands are supported only with limited marketing support budgets.

The Future Identity Composite

You have done all the work necessary to create a new brand, you might as well enjoy the satisfaction of seeing the accomplishment fully laid out before the uncertainties of the marketplace bring you back down to earth. The new-product team can now create a full identity composite of the brand-to-be and search for flaws. Take this opportunity to envision the ideal positioning, personality, and associated imagery for the future brand.

Look for the Role Model

They say that there have been no truly new ideas since Shakespeare, and he got most of his from the Greeks. Brand marketers should never be too proud to borrow ideas from successful existing brands. Which brands within the category successfully introduced their entries, and precisely how did they do it? Which brands with similar issues have introduced successfully outside of the category? Which brands in other categories might have some characteristics that you admire? The brand team might consider these previous successes, and even more so the past category failures, as cases that can be combed for valuable lessons learned.

When thinking ahead to the Taurus, Ford certainly learned about the importance of a reliable sedan by studying the remarkable success of the Honda Accord in the 1980s. IBM's PC division owes a debt for insights learned from the success of clones. The positioning of Saturn as "A Different Kind of Company" with vignettes from Spring Hill, Tennessee, clearly influenced the Mazda people as they created a campaign in 1993 to tout their own American manufacturing roots, this time in Flatrock, Michigan. Any number of banks borrow promotional ideas from fast food, department store, and other retail categories.

Questions Remain

Before going on, look again at the information gathered to date about the brand and ask the marketing team:

1. Do we really know the category and where it is going, or have we mostly relied on the usual trending data without really exploring the tough questions about what lies ahead?

2. Have we done everything possible to understand the selling environment our identity must be created and refined within?

3. Have we unearthed every possible fact about the brand's current makeup that could be useful in carving out a new/improved brand identity?

4. What have we *not* investigated about our internal goals, our category, or our competitors that might come back to haunt us somewhere down the line?

This further stretching prepares the marketing team for the ultimate question: Now that we know as much as possible about our brand and its surrounding environment, how can we build a better brand identity? That work continues in chapter 3 by getting to know a brand's customers and prospects as well as marketers know themselves.

3

*Indi*visualizing the Customer

Citizen Kane explores the life of Charles Foster Kane, a fictional newspaper publisher, multimillionaire, and would-be politician roughly patterned after the larger-than-life William Randolph Hearst. The film traces the efforts of newsmen to understand what the real Kane was all about, and particularly what was meant by his last dying word—"Rosebud." No one ever discovers that Rosebud is the name of a snow sled that Kane loved as a boy, at a time when he was poor, yet carefree, long before he had inherited the wealth that would cause him more pain than pleasure. Rosebud represented the last time Charles Foster Kane was truly happy. It was at the core of his identity, but it was buried too deep for anyone to find.

Marketers must search for the Rosebud in each customer if they hope to understand the power and the flaws in their brand's identity. They need to learn all they can about their prospects *as individuals,* to get to know him or her as they know themselves. It will not be easy because marketers and their customers can look at life in very different ways.

Who Do We Think We Are . . . The Customer?

Several years ago, the DDB Needham advertising agency asked 200 of its employees to fill out a lifestyle questionnaire, then compared the results to those from a survey of consumers. The findings of the survey were released in the agency's in-house publication under the headline, "I Have Met the Customer & He Ain't Me" (see Exhibit 3-1).

While the DDB Needham staff were not necessarily representative of the marketing industry as a whole, the huge disparities between their responses and those of typical Americans underlines how large a gap can exist between seller and buyer.

EXHIBIT 3-1

	Percent Agreeing with Statement		
Finding	**General Public Response**	**Agency Response**	**Difference**
Job security is more important than money	75%	52%	23 pts.
My greatest achievements are still ahead of me	65%	89%	24 pts.
Couples should live together before getting married	33%	50%	17 pts.
TV is my primary form of entertainment	53%	28%	25 pts.
My favorite music is classic rock	35%	64%	29 pts.

DDB Needham/Worldwide 1991 lifestyle study.

Source: Reprinted with permission from *Advertising Age*, January 20, 1992.

When marketers are in the process of creating or sustaining brand identities, the differences between their views of the world and their prospects' views can dramatically influence how those identities are constructed. The old bromide is too often true: Marketers and their agency partners hop into airplanes and *fly over* the people they're selling to, but rarely get to know them on a one-to-one basis.

One way to begin grappling with the differences between a marketer's view and that of the individual customer is to compare how the two might look at the same business situation. Marketers are concerned with the dynamics of the marketplace, the health of the category, and their brand's business trends relative to competition. Their customers, needless to say, have a much narrower perspective. Generally speaking, they are uninterested whether a brand is achieving its business objectives, they care only how it might relate to their personal lives. That distinction may appear obvious, but not so obvious that businesspeople remember it every time they make a marketing decision (see Exhibit 3-2 for a comparison of the marketer's and consumer's perspectives in various marketing situations).

A lack of product news might be considered the beginning of the end by a marketer, or it also might be reassuring to users that the brand can always be counted on. A "war" between brands to see which can provide the most stocking fees to the grocery trade could be seen as a survival test by the brand manager, while the customer might see it as a windfall.

Marketers and consumers even look at basic products and services in entirely different ways. In their book, *Why They Buy*, Robert Settle and Pamela Alreck point out that "business managers and executives operate on the basis of the physical realities associated with the goods they sell. Consumers in the marketplace operate on the basis of the *psychological* and *social* [italics are theirs] images of the goods they buy. The distance between the two is often great, and marketers have to bridge the gap."[1] At a time when Americans' trust in brands is dwindling, that gap must be narrowed by assessing why customers do what they do and think what they think.

EXHIBIT 3-2

Situation	Individual Marketer's Perspective	Individual Customer's Perspective
Brand has had no product improvement in the last five years	We need more "news."	"Why try it again? It's the same it's always been." *Or* "I stick with it because I know I can always count on it."
Competitors have forced escalating trade allowances	We have to match them or face de-listing by the trade.	"Isn't it great to see prices head down for a change?" *Or* "It seems like all these brands are just about the same."
Service technology is out of date	It's only a matter of time before we lose customers.	"Everything seems to move faster when I use that other service." *Or* "It's slower, but I'm more comfortable with that pace."
Brand outspent by 50% in advertising	Our share of voice is too low.	"I never pay much attention to advertising." *Or* "Whatever happened to that brand, anyway?"

Comparing the marketer's and consumer's perspectives.

Mass Marketing, Mass Research

In April 1985, the Coca-Cola Company announced that it was reformulating its mainline product. This extraordinary step was taken only after one of the most extensive and expensive marketing research programs ever conducted. The company had talked to nearly 200,000 consumers at a cost of $4 million. The introduction eventually cost the company many times that amount in futile marketing expenses and excruciating share loss, not to mention a heart-stopping blow to the Coke brand identity.

To this day, there is still much debate about whether Coke's research design was flawed, or the results misinterpreted, or whether research could ever have really gotten at the issue at all. That issue was whether the taste of Coca-Cola is so familiar and reassuring to Americans that they themselves could not predict how they would feel when its formulation was changed. Regardless of the cause, it was a mistake that very smart marketers thought they had avoided by talking to enough consumers beforehand. No doubt, the current set of smart marketers in Atlanta still remember that day in April, and consequently find good comfort in their most recent positioning line, "Always Coca-Cola."

The old concept of mass marketing, as executed by Coca-Cola in the mid-1980s, was a simple one: the marketer conducts as much consumer survey research as possible, determines what the largest number of consumers want or need, designs a product or service to meet those needs, then notifies prospects of its availability through one-way marketing and communications efforts. Occasionally, of course, something went wrong, such as attempts to sell a product no one really wanted (New Coke, LA beer), or a service no one needed at the time (various home banking programs, various ultra-premium airlines). Still, if accurate, projectable survey research was done, a marketer could count on a reasonably large section of the consumer universe to at least try the new entry.

The Never-ending Search for Quantitative Cocoons

Things have changed or, more accurately, people have changed and there are new and better ways to dig for what really motivates human beings to buy. It appears as if a good many marketers have accepted that mass marketing is dead or dying, but they continue to have considerable faith in mass-market research. But large statistical samples are only as valuable as consumers' willingness to follow the crowd. To supplement valid large-scale statistical studies of behavior, marketers need to better understand how their prospects think as individuals. This means holding off on reaching conclusions based on quantitative research until more intimate research techniques can be employed.

Perhaps the most important reason that qualitative research should take precedence over more numbers-oriented approaches is because, by talking to consumers in small groups or one-on-one, a brand team can get a better fix on critical emotions that drive purchases. It's hard to see emotion in a table or a chart, but it's written all over the face of an individual respondent.

Why is it difficult for many of us to look beyond quantitative support? For one thing, logic says that the more people you talk to, the more likely you will be able to predict what the universe as a whole will think, assuming that what is being asked can be accurately detected using large-sample research. Businesspeople need numbers to support decision making. There are times when such quantitative support is critical, usually at the beginning of the marketing planning process when the parameters of the "playing field" need to be carefully measured, and near the end when recommended approaches need to be validated.

Regrettably, it's also easy to use broadscale measurements as quantitative cocoons to protect those involved from failure. The cocoons come in the shape of segmentation studies that are touted as the ultimate descriptors of users (such as the $64,000 study that predicted that Absolut vodka would never sell because few consumers were interested in Swedish vodka in a funny-looking bottle) or as blind testing that is thought to be the last word on consumer preferences, or as copy research that incorrectly assesses the long-term impact of an advertising campaign on business. Too often, the size of a sample base is used to indicate how accurate the research is.

Quantitative goals and analysis make business a workable system because they appear to provide a precision that more qualitative approaches cannot. In fact, the flurry of numbers marketers must manipulate can obscure the significance of the single consumer, and with it, issues that all consumers believe are important. As businesspeople in the 1990s, it's all too easy to become creatures of our computers, addicted to their speed, confident in their faultless accuracy, comfortable with the reportorial-like way they help us to manage. But precision of this statistical type is not always desirable when it comes to one very important aspect of customer targeting—the inherent humanness of the "targets" themselves.

In his book, *Stephen Hawking's Universe,* biographer John Boslough describes the moment when he asked the brilliant cosmologist to compare himself to Albert Einstein. "It's never valid to compare two different people . . . ," Hawking replied with a smile. ". . . People are not quantifiable."[2]

Quantum Targeting and Segmenting

Many believe that segmenting can reveal the innermost reasons why people buy what they buy. But, as segments of groups are gradually preempted by what's being called "the segment of one," brand stewards should consider future purchasers as individuals rather than just whatever segment *du jour* is popular at the time.

Thanks to the tireless efforts of research suppliers, marketers now have more target segments to choose from than Baskin Robbins has flavors. A lot more. To name just a few: Emulators and Achievers, Dieters and Hedonists, Strivers and Actualizers, Desperate Singles and Sensitive Men, New Middle Americans and New Traditionalists, Savvy Shoppers and Trendy Savers, Aging Hippies and Displaced Homemakers. Not to mention the alphabet soup gang—the DINKS; the SINKS; the DIWKS; the YUFIES; everyone's favorite whipping boys, the YUPPIES; and some newcomers, the PEWNEPS, or "people who need people" (presumably including Barbra Streisand).

Segmenting represents legitimate efforts to break down masses into chewable chunks. Unfortunately, segments can also describe theoretical groupings without really providing the marketer with a genuine understanding of how consumers think as individuals. In addition to whatever segment analysis makes sense, marketing teams should also direct their energies toward what Stephen Hawking might call "quantum targeting," that is, the study of prospects on an intimate, one-on-one basis.

Certainly, marketers must develop strong statistical photographs of their targets, but they must also learn how to translate those numbers into human terms or they will forever be thwarted by customers who have a habit of being capricious, inconsistent and irrepressibly, well, human. Consultant Judith Langer sees it this way:

> A main reason insights into lifestyles are often missed in qualitative research is that most researchers and marketers are trained to think in terms of numbers. Unless there are statistics (in the case of quantitative research) or many respondents (in the case of qualitative research), they assume what they hear is just an isolated, unrepresentative response. Some of the valuable insights about consumers, however, come from the "telling comment," the remark of just one or two people.[3]

Undoubtedly, quantitative decision making will continue as a mainstay of marketing, as well it should, in order to ensure there are enough genuine prospects out there to justify the mega-million-dollar commitments many brands face. Nevertheless, in this age of the empowered individual, quantitative analysis may be helpful in many situations, but should be dictatorial in few.

Rediscovering Your Customer

Happily, a good many marketers are gradually weaning themselves of a total reliance on statistical consumer analysis. As evidence, about 100,000 focus groups are now being held each year, involving roughly one million respondents.

There are, of course, a bundle of caveats that should be packaged with every focus group to avoid taking the findings too literally. Still, groups can be an important first step in beginning to hear the individual customer's voice, leading to an entirely new and better way to market.

Large-scale one-on-one interviews can sometimes offer the best of both worlds: a look at how individuals think and a large enough sample to provide statistical predictability. For instance, in researching their "Just How I Feel" non-occasion line in 1990, Hallmark Cards needed to probe deeply with individuals about sensitive emotional issues. Quantitative research simply could not get at the object of their search, and focus groups would have required the respondents to bear their souls in front of nine strangers. Instead, Hallmark conducted 6,500 personal interviews to determine which emotional situation held the most opportunity for one of their non-occasion products. (The greatest consumer need, by the way, was to support individuals who were experiencing an emotional roller coaster in their lives.)

An updated version of one-on-one interviews is on-line focus groups, which have been called "virtual research." New York-based BKG America conducts on-line research using America Online's one-million-plus subscriber base. It's an inexpensive way to collect massive amounts of qualitative data, and respondents seem to be willing to open up more about their inner feelings than in focus group settings. Of course, the interviewer cannot see the respondent, so some researchers are concerned that emotional nuance will be lost.

There are many other ways to research to help marketers understand how the individual consumer looks at brands. To cite just a few:

■ The Color Research Institute has had good luck with "PhotoSorting," a technique in which respondents are given pictures of various types of individuals, then asked to sort them according to their perceptions of different brands. Using this approach, General Electric discovered that their corporation tended to be associated with older, conservative businessmen, leading them to seek a new brand identity that has been successfully portrayed in their "We bring good things to life" campaigns.

More recently, *Fortune* magazine commissioned a PhotoSort qualitative study of beer drinkers to determine how they imagined the users of various brands. Fewer than half of the respondents liked the looks of the types they figured Budweiser and Coors attracted. People who were assumed to like Miller scored better, with a 66 percent affinity rating.

■ Ad agency D'Arcy Masius Benton & Bowles has recently used "collage research" to enhance their focus group research on behalf of client Cadillac. Respondents are given "homework" prior to the sessions, usually involving the cutting out of pictures from magazines and pasting them down for show-and-tell the next day. The collages are used to help describe how consumers see themselves and their relationships with their cars. In one instance, respondents described their Eldorados in scenes on vacation and other times away from the office. The perspective was used to develop that year's Eldorado television campaign.

■ Ketchum Communications relies on emotion sketches by focus group participants to help nail down their real feelings about cooking dinner, shopping, or entering a bank branch. The respondents are given time to think about the core emotion that drives their attitudes about a product or service, then provided with all the crayons and sketch pads they need to color in their feelings. Ketchum also asks groups to imagine that a brand or category has "died"; they're then asked to write "obituaries" or "eulogies" to help determine how emotionally connected users are to the subject (see sidebar).

■ One of the most unique examples of customer profiling has been made possible by the advent of home video. In 1993, Chilton Research Services launched the Right There Research project, which asks respondents to videotape themselves as they go about living their daily lives. The Bugle Boy company has used the technique to guide the development of recent television advertising.

■ An even more direct approach to understanding the individual consumer's perspective was borrowed from a branch of anthropology known as *ethnography*, meaning the direct observation of subjects in their own cultural environment. Since the 1950s, marketing researchers have been practicing ethnography by spending time in consumers' homes, recording their every move. One fairly recent example: ad agency Young & Rubicam conducted survey research indicating that many Americans felt vaguely hostile or indifferent toward the U.S. Postal Service. Some ethnographic research, however, revealed that there were actually some positive feelings about individual mail carriers

PERSONAL REMEMBRANCES: BRAND EULOGIES

There's an old theater story about Nelson Eddy that has kicked around backstages for decades. Eddy and Jeanette MacDonald were a famous silver screen singing duo in the 1930s and 1940s. Every movie they made together spawned gossip about a rumored romance that reportedly mirrored their love in front of the camera. Eventually, their careers took different paths, but the world preferred to assume that they had remained close, even as time and circumstance pulled them apart.

Years later, as the story goes, Nelson Eddy was sitting in his dressing room in a small theater, putting on his makeup, when a stagehand burst in. "Mr. Eddy! Mr. Eddy!" the stagehand exclaimed, "I have terrible news . . . Jeanette MacDonald has just died!" Without even looking up, Eddy replied, "So?"[4]

How broken up would your customers be if your brand suddenly died? To find out, for the past several years Ketchum Communications has run a series of focus groups and one-on-one interviews using an unusual format. After the preliminaries, the respondents are given a pen and paper and told that the brand in question has just "died," and that it will never again be part of their lives. They are asked to write a brief "obituary" or "eulogy" to help gauge what the loss means to them as individuals. Below are a few samples of some candid and revealing obits:

For a regional telephone company on the brink of new competitive attacks:

"The funeral has been canceled, since Ma Bell's body has been carved up by his loyal relatives, Mr. AT&T, Ms. Sprint and Ms. MCI. . . . Several million people regretted the loss—a year later."

In remembrance of fresh fruit:

"We grew up together—since early childhood. You were my constant companion. We shared happy days in the sun as well as quiet moments on long winter evenings. You helped me over frustrations and shared happy times. You were there for me when I was bored. Without you, life will never be the same. You will be sorely missed."

For a major fast-food chain:

"This is a sad time. A time to say good-bye to old faithful. A friend. A meal, a savings. A part of our childhood. So long old friend, we will see you in hamburger heaven."

Last words for their local bank:

"You were always there for me, but you never cared."[5]

The relationships that individuals have with brands or products are not always clear until the marketing team can devise ways to break down the inclinations of consumers to deny their emotional involvements. Once those barriers are lowered, some very revealing insights can emerge, insights about a brand's identity and about the people who will miss the brand when it's gone (or not even notice that it's left).

who became more of a family friend when delivering regularly to a given route. That insight led the agency toward the successful "We Deliver For You" campaign.

■ If ethnography is the direct observation of subjects, then what might be called *brand ethnography* could be that approach applied toward building a link between the individual consumer's identity and a brand's identity. Such was the case a few years ago when Creative Research Associates in Chicago delved into the Harley-Davidson identity. After spending a lot of time with motorcyclists, they discovered that there was a sort of "weekend warrior" mentality that gripped one type of nine-to-fiver. The Harley bikes were part of the way these people found release. Their motorcycles allowed them to become someone else. That insight was the result of in-depth investigation into how individual users identified with the brand. It has led to a huge array of marketing programs that have refocused the Harley brand identity and helped reestablish it as a leader in the category.

The modern marketing team has a number of research avenues available to help understand consumers as individuals in order to create a stronger brand identity. Depending on the resources of the company involved, a team can: 1) tap a quantitative survey of a statistically representative sample for behavioral and attitude data (for example, usage and attitude studies), and to create demographic segments, 2) field motivational research in the form of syndicated or customized psychographic studies, 3) conduct standard qualitative interviewing (focus groups and one-on-one's), and "virtual research" previously described which probes into the psychological meanings of certain consumer preferences, and 4) delve into brand ethnography, the tracking of the daily routines of consumers in search of insights about how a brand's identity might match those of its users.

Each and all of these methodologies can be important contributors to the knowledge about customers. The more individual-driven the research can be, the more likely that an optimum brand identity can be created because the most complex relationships can often be better understood when telescoped to the individual level.

The Quiet Revolution Called "Account Planning"

Account planning began as an experiment in English ad agencies in the 1970s, and has been practiced in the United States only during the past decade or so. The purpose of account planning is to learn why people buy what they buy, and what makes them respond to certain types of marketing communications, then to help agency creative teams make their work more persuasive, using those insights. Key to making all that happen is the account planner's ability to represent the customer in agency discussions and idea generating.

Planners stand in stark contrast to traditional marketing researchers in that they are not primarily hired to obtain marketing research data, but to focus on specific consumer issues that can help create the most persuasive advertising possible. Unlike traditional researchers whose responsibility largely ends with delivering the information requested, account planners are held personally responsible for the creative product, along with the creative teams.

Jeff DeJoseph, head of account planning at the Deutsch agency in New York, once described account planning as being like method acting: "The planners must immerse themselves in the character, in this case the target, and *become* that person in the agency."[6] This personifying of the customer forces agency and advertiser alike to look at the consumer eyeball to eyeball, to become intimate with the person who is scurrying through life without any pressing need to buy the brand you're selling.

Arrow shirts was a beneficiary of account planning. For years, the company labored under a strictly white-shirt identity, although it had been making colorful shirts for years. By spending quality time with more than 200 shirt wearers, planners at the Chiat/Day/Mojo agency in New York helped the creative team to understand that Arrow would not be credible to its prospective customers if it tried to make a fashion statement. It was far more important for Arrow to be "hip" than to be high fashion. The result was a series of television ads that perfectly captured the changing Arrow identity, using the transformation of a staid men's choir into a let-it-loose gospel group, tagged with the theme line, "We've loosened our collar."

Account planners are, among other things, a conduit through which marketers and their agencies can view prospects as individuals living their individual lives. Planners can then extrapolate from what they learn from these people, and apply it to the creation of effective marketing communications.

Individualism Makes a Comeback

The increased demand for personalized products and services in the United States can largely be traced to a resurgence of individualism that is our heritage as Americans. Personal freedom—

that is, the right to celebrate who we are as singular human beings—is one of the underlying reasons why we fought a war to
extricate ourselves from Mother England. Those first shots at
Lexington and Concord did more than start a revolution, they
announced to the world that there was to be a limit on the constraints that could be levied on individuals in this country.
Americans were then, and have remained, fiercely independent.
As a nation, we would sooner return to the forest than sacrifice
our rights as individuals.

With the loosening of social and economic constraints, individualism has made a comeback in America. Some of the reasons
why individualism is making a comeback: Better technology permits us to buy what suits us best as individuals; buying what
we personally like is a way to "treat" ourselves and to buffer us
from stressful life situations; and buying individualized products can be a statement of self-esteem, a way to say we're special.
Marketers can capitalize on the renaissance of individualism by
learning how to project their brand identities into each individual's world.

Cheryl Russel, former editor-in-chief of *American Demographics* magazine, has described in her book, *The Master Trend*,
what she calls "free agents." These people are at the forefront of
individualism, and will form the foundation of fundamental
changes in our economic and social framework. They are also
the people who will be the first to use the ultimate in personalized communications and interactive media.[7] They may also be
the first to respond to brand identities that recognize the importance of individual customers.

The unpredictable economy notwithstanding, the quest for
personal fulfillment is apparently driving an increasing number
of decisions in individuals' lives, up to and including what
brands they choose to purchase. Brands that respect the environment, for instance, or that balance style with substance or that
emphasize value, speak to these people about what's important
in their individual lives. Consumers choosing what's right for
"me" as an individual, instead of what others pursue or what
makes a statement, is a sea change that will have a lasting impact

on branding. A brand is just another name on the shelf or a service among scores of other services until prospects internalize what the brand stands for and decide to incorporate it into their personal routines.

Some marketers have a better understanding than others about how consumers view the brands in their lives. Gillette, for instance, has kept its heritage alive as the leading men's toiletries brand with strong product innovation and dominant advertising, merchandising, and distribution support. (A few years ago, Gillette was averaging 8 new products a year. In 1993–95, it will have introduced more than 50.)

Each of Gillette's marketing communications demonstrate the company's understanding of how a man goes about leading his life, including how important shaving is, what kind of scents and looks he's comfortable with, and so forth. Gillette's brand teams have taken the time and effort to think about their prospects as singular human beings with specific needs and wants. In a 1993 *Harvard Business Review* article, consultants Michael Treacy and Fred Wiersema proposed the concept of "customer intimacy," defined as the investment of time and money necessary for a seller to understand precisely what a buyer needs in terms of products and services.[8] Gillette's brand identity reflects that kind of sensitivity to the individual's perspective.

We also see more brands than ever focusing on the individuality of their prospects to carve a niche in terms of positioning and personality. Subaru off-road vehicles portray their owners as having their own minds about how and when to drive the narrow path taken by others. Levi's 501 and Dockers campaigns have emphasized the uniquenesses of their users. RC Cola, Dove soap, Dove Bar, Reebok footwear, Taco Bell, Fox network, Old Spice toiletries, Jose Cuervo—all are brands celebrating what makes their users different (and, by implication, better) than shoppers who turn toward the conventional.

Marketers need to refocus their marketing lens from a mass/ statistical point of view toward a more individualized perspective. To do that, they must be willing to stretch beyond conventional customer analysis and into customer visualization.

Indi*visual*izing the Customer

Glance through any newspaper and you'll find feature articles that focus on individuals. Here are the leads from three articles in a single edition (July 12, 1994) of *The Wall Street Journal*:

> Tung Choy shines the shoes that guests leave outside their rooms at the elegant Four Seasons Hotel in Manhattan. As he makes his rounds of the hotel between 11:15 P.M. and 7 A.M., Mr. Choy also checks the housekeepers' carts and the equipment in the hotel's fitness center. (story on U.S. immigrants).
>
> Michael Bennett's research team blows something up or sets something afire almost every day. The technicians aren't accident-prone—just conscientious. (story on quest for new fire fighting chemical agent)
>
> Adam Nathan seems to have an idea of the problems Columbia/HCA Healthcare Corp. is giving his father. Playing Monopoly one day against James Nathan, the chief executive of Lee Memorial Hospital here, the nine-year-old warned Mr. Nathan that he was going to buy every property he landed on, "just like Columbia." (story about hospital chains' acquisition policies)[9]

News editors know that an article about complex social or political issues is more likely to be read and understood if it can be encapsulated into a profile of individuals who are directly affected by such issues. *American Demographics* magazine, a leading purveyor of consumer statistics, has also seen the value of personalizing the consumer. The magazine's "Demogram" feature profiles individuals and families who represent particular demographic trends (see inset). Rather than relying solely on statistical bracketing, *American Demographics* probes beyond the numbers to dig for key insights about human beings that can be obtained only from close observation.

What's happening in these individuals' lives is part of a much larger socioeconomic pattern, and most people—including marketing executives struggling to understand their customers better—can more easily grasp the bigger picture by first looking at the micro level. What marketers need as much as the data itself is a way of packaging the information so that it can be used productively, on a daily basis if possible, as they make tough decisions about how to best nurture their brands' identities.

An Indivisualizing Tool: The *American Demographics* "Demogram"

For the past ten years, *American Demographics* magazine has run close to 500 feature profiles that demonstrate the value of dimensionalizing segments and mass audiences as individuals. Called "Demograms," these profiles of individual Americans help put a face on the cornucopia of statistics the magazine provides its readers each month. As in the case of indi*visual*izing, the profiles are not meant to be statistically representative of an entire universe of consumers, but to add texture and meaning to comparatively lifeless quantitative data. The following excerpts are from two issues:[10]

> Jeremy's room is more oriented toward his position as captain of the football team at Bethesda Chevy Chase High School. Football and soccer trophies line his dresser; stacks of *Sports Illustrated* sit next to a guide to American colleges. But the media blitz hasn't passed him by. On one wall is a poster of sexy Kathy Ireland selling light beer.
>
> *—From a Demogram exploring how the Himelfarb family of Chevy Chase, Maryland, deals with sex in advertising*

> Forty-one years ago, Peter Loomis married Sally Black in her hometown of Corning, Arkansas. Their honeymoon was a drive to his hometown of Denver. On the way, the newlyweds passed through Taos, New Mexico. "None of the streets were paved," says Sally. "We liked it." [After moving to Taos] . . . "We're not in heaven, but this is a very interesting place," says Peter. . . . The Loomises can't say exactly why they chose Taos as the spot for their retirement. "We're demographic aberrations," says Peter. "We don't watch much TV, and we don't do things for clear-cut reasons." But that's typical. After all, the West was settled by people who had a vague feeling that a better life was waiting just over the next ridge.
>
> *—From a Demogram about the Loomises, who migrated to a rural retirement location in Taos, New Mexico*

These profiles are one way to help marketers understand the people behind the numbers they are exposed to daily in their brand management roles. By studying customers and prospects on this level, each marketing decision is seen more clearly as an act of persuading individuals to buy, rather than simply exposing populations to communications messages. There is a place for both perspectives in marketing planning.

All of which brings us to "indi*visual*izing." Put simply, indi*visual*izing is the discipline of continuously visualizing the customer or prospect as an individual rather than as part of a mass population, group, or segment. It concentrates on an individual's identity, both self-perceived and as seen by others. Its purpose is to train the brand team to think on the individual's level, just as they think of their own lives. Even more, it helps teams to vividly bring these people to life in discussions and work sessions, and to "see" what their prospects see, much like a professional athlete is encouraged to visualize a difficult feat before performing it. Finally, indi*visual*izing helps marketers better understand the identities of their customers, so they can match customer identities with those of the brand.

It's very easy to fall into the habit of thinking on more mass levels, partly because all marketers are judged by their ability to see "the big picture," meaning what's going on in the marketplace as a whole. But it is by indi*visual*izing that they can bring their eyes back down to the world where the purchase decision is made.

Indi*visual*izing can be accomplished in four steps:

1. Gathering as much factual information as possible about target prospects and customers from all available quantitative and qualitative research;
2. Reconfiguring that information into profiles of individuals who are considered to be prototypical of the brand's targets;

3. Using those profiles to help visualize the daily lives of those against whom the marketing programs are directed; and

4. Integrating the indi*visual*izing process into the marketing planning process, using target models as living symbols of the team's marketing partners in the establishment and sustaining of a powerful brand identity.

Don Peppers and Martha Rogers, in their book *The One to One Future,* lay out a future for marketers that revolves around their knowledge of consumers as individuals. They believe that those changes will bring about what they call "collaborative marketing," in which buyer and seller consider themselves members of the same team.[11] The authors assume that collaborative marketing will primarily involve direct selling, but there is no reason that marketers can't establish a collaborative-like environment among their customers even when more broad-scale selling of goods or services are involved. That can only be accomplished if the marketer is planning with the individual customer in mind, in addition to whatever macromanaging of group- and mass-oriented programs is called for.

The act of indi*visual*izing itself encourages marketers to create a living, fluid visualization of their individual customers that keeps their personal perspectives uppermost in mind. Indi*visual*izing is a commitment by marketers to move onto intimate terms with individual consumers in such a way that they are not only studied, but also literally and figuratively incorporated onto the marketing team as partners in the selling process.

What If We Indi*visual*ize the Wrong Person?

Researchers who conduct quantitative studies are rightly concerned about whether their respondent samples are representative of all of their customers. Major marketing decisions can turn into major mistakes if responses from a non-projectable subject base are extrapolated to the population as a whole. That's why qualitative research has traditionally been looked on as a weak sister to survey studies.

Yet a growing number of marketing and advertising decisions are based on patterns of responses from qualitative research. For example, it's increasingly common for important creative strategy components to be evaluated based on the responses from four or five focus groups, even though 40 or 50 people may not even come close to being a statistically reliable sample base.

To that point, doesn't indi*visual*izing run the risk of misleading a marketing team if the subject turns out to hold opinions that are not shared by fellow consumers? Absolutely. That's why care must be taken to construct indi*visual*ized profiles that have been validated by as much projectable quantitative data as possible. In fact, the process of indi*visual*ization begins with a bracketing of statistical information about the people who really are the broad base of customers or prospects. Who they are in terms of age, income, family size, residence, location, and so on, forms the superstructure of information that tells marketers what general characteristics are shared by the brand's users and potential users.

Remember that the purpose of the profiles is to encourage the marketing team to consider how the brand identity is viewed on an individualized basis. It's not meant to imply that all purchase decisions are made exactly the same way, or even that the profiles reflect the majority of the other members of the franchise.

Kept in their proper perspective, indi*visual*izing profiles are thought-provoking, directional exercises, not rigid etchings of the target. Above all, the profiles should help the team *think* differently about their targets as individual human beings.

Descriptive and Indi*visual*ized Profiling

The research methodolgies mentioned earlier describe the customer as vividly as possible in two different ways: First, marketers construct the strongest possible foundation of quantitatively supported facts and qualitative insights that serve as the undergirding of knowledge about customers and prospects. These represent what has been called "descriptive research," meaning research that describes consumers as they are seen by others.

Descriptive findings contrast markedly with indi*visual*izing profiles, which are detailed portraits of how individuals see themselves within the context of a purchase decision. Indi*visual*ized profiles portray how a respondent identifies him- or herself with a specific brand or the context surrounding that brand (see Exhibit 3-3 for a comparison of the two perspectives).

Indi*visual*ized profiles help marketers envision how individual customers might observe and participate in what goes on in the marketplace. Using the examples in Exhibit 3-3, if a pricing increase is planned for the Acura Integra, how might Eric react to the news that his "cost for speed" has just gone up? If Charles Schwab wants to create a new mutual fund product, what type of yield/risk ratio will Alice be most interested in? Should FedEx consider making marketing decisions (for example, naming service programs) based on what Curt and other secretaries prefer, since it is they who are likely to steer their companies away from a shipper that does not cater to their individual needs?

While indi*visual*izing is a better way to package information, it is actually a *de-packaging* of the consumer, a reshaping and refocusing of descriptors to reveal the individual human being beneath. The indi*visual*izing process forces marketers to think of any marketing decision on the same level that they themselves are operating—the individual level (see Exhibit 3-4 for an example of an indi*visual*izing profile).

Using Indi*visual*izing to Build a Better Identity

The marketing team needs to think the way their customers think as individuals, with their own peculiar needs and expectations. That's a little like asking airline pilots to visualize themselves as passengers while also flying the airplane. One way to help make it happen is to give the marketing "pilots" of the company in-

EXHIBIT 3-3

Brand	Descriptive Profile	Abridged Indi*visu*alized Profile
Acura Integra	"Generation X," 20–29, unmarried, urban, East/West coast, young professional, $25–35K income, drives Acura Integra	"My name is Eric. I don't trust much of what I read. I want value as I define it. The Integra was the right choice for me because it's a no-BS kind of car that gives me speed I can control. I don't have anything to prove to anyone but myself, so I bought what was right for me."
Charles Schwab	Middle/upper-middle income, married, children in high school or college, suburban, some discretionary investments	"I'm Alice. I'm feeling the burden of my responsibilities more than ever. I don't want to waste money on commissions for advice I'll just end up having doubts about. Schwab is run the way I would run a brokerage."
FedEx	Secretarial/clerical, $20–32K income, unmarried, high school education	"I'm Curt. I refuse to be held responsible for a lost shipment. I'm happy to help out my boss, but I can't work miracles. FedEx has state-of-the-art tracking and tracing which means I can prove who screwed up. I think whoever runs that company has me in mind."

Examples of customer/prospect profiling.

di*visu*alizing training that they will look forward to and, consequently, learn from. Here are some ways to accomplish that:

1. *Selecting the Customer or Prospect*—Indi*visu*alizing candidates need not be the fabled "everyman." You are not looking for a single composite person so much as a representative(s) of a large group of known targets. In the beginning, select study

EXHIBIT 3-4
Sample Indi*visua*lizing Profile (Abridged)

"You know how we judge a bank? By how well they understand that it's *our* money, not theirs."

My name is Jim Runyeon and my wife is Joan (my wife's name looks like "Joan," but it's pronounced Jo-ann"). We live in San Rafael, California, north of San Francisco, in a nice little area in the eastern part of town called Glenwood. We're in our sixties (no need to go into details) and in the old days we probably would have been retired by now. Frankly, it hasn't even occurred to us to slow down that much.

I'm a financial advisor during most of the day. I work out of my home and have for years. I guess that makes me ahead of my time. I'm also the moderator of what's called the Presbytery of the Redwoods, a fancy name for the governing body of the Presbyterian churches in Northern California. It's a big job that takes a lot of time, mainly because Presbyterians like talking about doing things almost as much as they like doing things.

Joan works in leadership roles on the Peacemaking and Social Justice committees for the national church. She travels a lot, and the work keeps her going 'round the clock, but it's important work that could change the world. She's just the person to do it, too.

Three of our four kids have left home; the last is a senior at the University of Oregon in Eugene. We're proud of all our children. They've ended up with happy lives, common sense, and a good feeling about other human beings.

Joan and I aren't rich, but we're okay financially. We've got some investments and will have some Social Security coming. Our house and cars are paid off. Rather than run up big debts, we tend to save for particular things, like a trip to Vancouver or a small addition to our house. We have a pool, and that takes extra money to maintain, but it's worth it because we both like to swim, not to mention entertain out back during the summer. We watch our money pretty carefully, though, because we worry about having enough left over for our "real" retirement in a few years. We talk regularly to various banks to keep up with what they offer in terms of CDs and so on.

You know how we judge a bank? By how well they understand that it's *our* money, not theirs. If we have to go through a lot of red tape, or get hassled by a teller or bank officer just to move our money around, then we figure they don't get it. The way we look at it, they're sitting behind that counter to serve *us*, to be courteous and helpful with *our* money. Some banks figure that once you give them the money, it's theirs and they're doing you a big favor to even let you see it!

Joan and I tend to like most people we meet, and we're not the type to be really demanding. But when it comes to handling our hard-earned money, we just want to do business with an outfit that really believes that the customer is the most important person in the building at any given time. We may not be the folks who own the bank, but we figure that we deserve to be treated like the people who own the money we put in the bank. Because we do.

individuals the brand team would want to learn more about. If you consider a candidate who is an insurance broker and one who is a firefighter, choose the firefighter. If you are considering the owner of a pet store versus an accountant, go for the pet store owner. Eventually, you will not discriminate because all customers and prospects are important, but as you get started, team members may find it more intriguing if you select people with lives that are most unlike their own.

2. *Naming the Prospect*—Indi*visua*lizing can begin at the simplest level, by giving the prospect a name. Not just any name, but a name that precisely fits the personality of the individual you are tracking.

If you are marketing an airline that caters to vacationers and businesspersons who avoid higher fares—an airline like Southwest, for instance—then you select names that fit your vision of people who like a good time and don't have all the money in the world to find it. For Southwest, names like Rebecca and Theodore probably wouldn't fit; names like Becky and Ted might. The specific names you select are not all that important except in what they connote. (You'll notice, by the way, that the chairman of Southwest, who regularly rides with his passengers and serves them drinks, introduces himself as "Herb"—not Herbert—Kelleher. "Herbert" just wouldn't fit Kelleher, and it wouldn't fit the rest of the Southwest identity.)

3. *Living the Life*—Ethnography, the branch of anthropology mentioned earlier in this chapter, is the science of cultural observation. Using the same observation skills that have been honed while studying foreign cultures (it's possible the "language" of your customer may be as foreign to your brand team as the language of another country), the marketing team should be prepared to observe their prospects close at hand, to "live the life" in the settings in which they live.

Ethnography gives marketers an opportunity to see what similarities and differences exist between how they live and how they think, and how their customers do the same. When a decision must be made to raise pricing or run a promotion or change advertising media, a marketer who has vicariously experienced the lives of her prospects will have a more authentic context in which to make a decision.

Close observation also forces members of the team to put specific faces and names on prospects who, until that time, have been faceless numbers and quantified profiles. This is not all that different than what is done in theory in marketing conference rooms throughout the country. (How many times have marketing teams discussed "what the customer is telling us," or "how the consumer feels.")

Marketers can arrange to live the life of prospects in any number of ways. Members of the team can visit consumer homes during times when purchase decisions are made, or follow a consumer family around with a videotape camera to record their daily activities, including shopping or the use of certain services. Or they can use the field anthropologist's approach and actually reside for a limited time in individuals' homes. Obviously, the behavior of a carefully scrutinized individual or family is likely to be different than when they are alone. Nevertheless, researchers have found that most subjects return to mostly routine behavior soon after their observer has settled in.

4. *Acting It Out in "The Purchase Theater"*—There may not be many Laurence Oliviers on staff, but consider trying to act out what can and does happen in the lives of prospects. The Purchase Theater is essentially role playing, the periodic reenacting of what goes on in the customer's house, supermarket, or any other venue where a purchase decision is made. The purpose of the theater is to help identify emotions that cause buyers to buy the way they do.

These are not elaborate productions, but more like a "readers' theater" where the players sit in a circle and "act out" various scenarios in the life of the consumer. Have fun with it. Encourage creativity in how the consumer is represented. Don't put members of the team in embarrassing positions, but do suggest that everyone find a role to play, no matter how small. Focus on vignettes that, based on your observations, are representative of how individuals might think about a brand and incorporate it into their lives. This technique can help everyone sharpen their intuitive abilities, gently forcing them to think more frequently about what it really would be like to be on the customer's side of the fence in a transaction.

5. *Tapping the Panel*—One easy and relatively inexpensive way to tap into consumers' views and emotions about a brand is to maintain a permanent users' panel with a rotating membership.

This should not be a glorified focus group, but a set of carefully selected individuals who appear to be representative of who you have learned is your core group of users and prospects. Ideally, these people would be considered part of the marketing team and periodically brought in to talk and interact with team members. The team can pose real and hypothetical questions to panel members about why they buy or reject certain brands, how products affect their lives, what expectations they have from certain services. The panel should be rotated periodically to ensure that the team does not get overly swayed by the strong personality of one or two panel members.

6. *Viewing the Video*—During the course of a busy business day or week, it's too easy for marketing executives to forget what the consumer looks like. A piece of research is completed, a report issued, maybe a presentation is made by the research supplier, but sooner or later the information and the insights are filed away along with the other reference material that is pulled off the shelf annually, if that.

After conducting some ethnographic studies of customers and prospects with the help of a videotape camera, set up a permanent VCR display in the marketing department which can play regularly updated tapes designed to remind everyone what their individual customers believe, what they look like, and how they live their lives.

7. *Driving Indivisualization throughout the Organization*—It's important that *all* people in the company who are involved in marketing in any way be exposed to indi*visual*izing training. Regularly going back to talk to customers is a critical process that should be practiced by those in customer service, sales, and any other area that has a direct impact on the marketing of a brand identity.

Again, those studied by the team are not meant to represent the entire population of customers, but they should help those who manage the brand to think on an individual level as they make marketing decisions.

Indi*visual*izing within Multitier Relationships

As we've discussed earlier, brand marketers are in the customer loyalty business. The success of the brand identities they build will be judged by how many customers they can attract and how long they can keep them.

Increasingly, brands need to connect with their constituencies by establishing relationships on several levels: *broad-scale relationship-building* through more traditional marketing communications, *direct relationship-building* via direct selling to identified households and individuals, and *interactive relationship-building,* the burgeoning extension of direct marketing that will be discussed in detail in chapter 9 (see Exhibit 3-5 for a graphic that illustrates the multitiers of brand relationships).

Until recently, broad-scale marketing (often supported by what is called "general" marketing communications) and direct marketing have been seen as rivals for the same marketing budget. More often, they are close allies that are both essential to the construction of an effective brand identity because they are seeking the same goal: to establish a long-term relationship with customers.

Despite the popular view that "relationship marketing" applies only to direct selling, brand relationships can and do exist on a more broad-scale basis as well. One reason, for example, is that broad-scale advertising and other communications can cre-

EXHIBIT 3-5

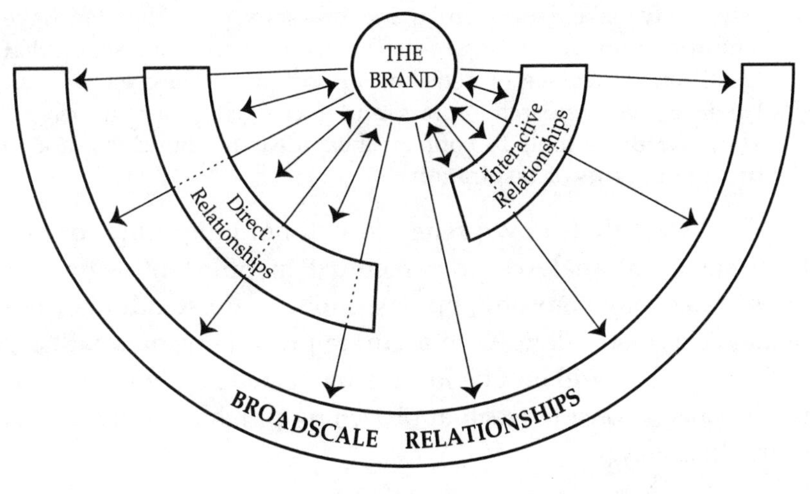

Multitier relationships with customers and prospects.

ate pride in what a brand stands for. When Chevy car ads use the theme "What else would you expect from the country that invented rock 'n' roll?" and Chevy truck advertising talks about being "like a rock," they are sending out mass messages that have a definite effect on those who may buy the products and those who may influence the buying.

Marshall Field's, The Limited, Tiffany, Nordstrom, Bloomingdale's, even the discount chains, all have clientele that have relationships of sorts with those stores. Perhaps you like Tiffany for the cachet, or Nordstrom for the service, or The Gap because of its "narrow-deep" way of stocking merchandise (narrow style choices, deep in sizes). Consumers might not describe their feelings in those terms, but the relationship definitely exists and carries important emotional overtones that bond individuals to brands.

It's more and more difficult for marketers to use quantitative data alone to accurately predict what prospects will think and buy in a turbulent marketplace. Not only does that mean that brand stewards must rely more on personal-level research; it also implies that a higher percentage of decisions will have to be based on judgment and instinctive understandings of how consumers think, rather than solely, or even largely, on the conclusions of empirical data. As author Paul Brown wrote in his *Lessons in the Art of Marketing:*

> What truly makes [successful marketers] stand out is that they have a thorough understanding of their customers and they act on that "feel" once they see or sense an opportunity. They act without laboring over research reports and focus-group summaries. . . . They use those tools to confirm their ideas (or hunches), not to provide insights or inspiration.[12]

The "feel" that Brown refers to will not jump fully-formed from statistical analyses or perceptual mapping of segments. Those tools may be useful, but a genuine understanding of potential customers, along with accurate predictions of what they will respond to, will best be located by visualizing how individual prospects consider each approaching purchase in their own individual way.

4

Prompting a Power Positioning

Richard W. Sears was a 23-year-old entrepreneur who employed railway station agents to sell his watches to patrons, then became one of the country's first direct-mail marketers, selling his wares via postcards and newspaper ads. He ultimately "retired" at the ripe old age of 36 with the $60,000 in proceeds from the sale of his company.

A few years later, Sears used what he had learned in the watch business to create one of the great retail brands of the twentieth century. He decided that his new company would stand for something that people could count on—a single source for a wide range of low-priced merchandise. He formed a new firm called Sears, Roebuck and Company in 1893, setting prices for his products well below national brands by eliminating middlemen and achieving extraordinary volume through his mail-order catalogs. By 1908, just 15 years after starting his new business, Sears was selling $40 million worth of merchandise, an astonishing revenue stream in those days, and not all that bad even by today's standards.

The success of Sears's ventures can be traced to his understanding that people needed moderately priced, reliable merchandise to live the lives they aspired to in the industrializing United States. Richard Sears realized that growth and profitability did not solely depend on new product innovation or large capital investment. Success in selling could be achieved, as it can today, by persuading people to favorably position your brand in their lives.

That philosophy helped create Sears, Roebuck and Company at the turn of the century, and it was when the same company wandered from that principle almost 100 years later that it encountered serious marketing problems.

Positioning as the Identity's Compass

Every brand, no matter how large its marketing budget, is as homeless as a waif until it's invited into someone's life. An invitation isn't extended until there's a place in there somewhere for the brand. Without such a place, a brand is just another product or service in search of a customer. With it, the brand becomes a helpmate that answers some practical or emotional needs and desires that, once fulfilled, may form the basis for a long-term relationship with the customer.

A brand's positioning is the compass of its identity, pointing it toward the place where it can leverage the most power in the category in which it competes, and establish the most powerful leverage within the lives of its potential users.

How a brand is recognized in the marketplace is based largely on its personality, but what it means in someone's life is derived from its positioning. As has been pointed out by Howard Schultz, the cofounder of the remarkably successful Starbuck's coffeehouse chain, "Marketing . . . is the ability to deliver, over and over, a strong level of trust and confidence that the customer comes to expect . . . (customers) must recognize that you stand for something."[1] What your brand stands for is generally reflected best in its positioning. In the case of Starbuck's, for example, it is a very good cup of coffee, and an inviting place to enjoy it.

When people think about brands, they think of them within a sea of associations that form the mental set that surrounds and includes the brand. Its positioning is its "location" in and among those associations.

The Toys 'R' Us brand might be associated at different levels with toys, kids, fun, value, stores, crowds, Christmas, wide selection, birthdays, money, colors, playing, and so forth. These concepts do not have equal value in each prospect's life. If the person happens to have very little discretionary income, the "value" and "money" associations may predominate. If the shopper happens to be childless and only buys toys for a niece, the word "kids" might have a different meaning. Importantly, these associations also include alternative purchases that the consumer might select instead of the brand. If Toys 'R' Us tends to bring up a stronger associative link with the words "money and "wide selection" than it does with "value," the consumer in question may be thinking that Toys 'R' Us is a slightly pricey store but with a wide range of shopping options.

Meanwhile, if a local toy store is aware of Toys 'R' Us's positioning, then advertising "All the selection of Toys 'R' Us—but at lower prices" might create a strong competitive position in a shopper's mind. (By the way, Toys 'R' Us is well into a successful campaign to help reinforce its good value positioning.)

Only One Positioning Has Real Power— The Customer's

The term "positioning" was made popular in 1972 by admen Jack Trout and Al Ries, who wrote a series of articles on the subject, followed by a book. They speculated that inside the mind of every buyer can be found a full-fledged battle between warring brands seeking attention and loyalty. Positioning, they said, is the way in which a customer thinks of a brand relative to its competition. As they wrote at the time, "Positioning is what you do to the mind of the prospect. That is, you position the product in the mind of the prospect." [2] Within a few years after Trout and Ries first wrote about positioning, the term became a part of the vocabulary of every self-respecting marketing strategist.

What makes the positioning concept so irresistible is its innovative angle of approach. Positioning focuses both on what the marketer *thinks* is important, and what the consumer *perceives* is important, ideally two views that link up along the way.

This was semirevolutionary thinking at the time. The positioning theory spotlighted how consumers were involved in the selling process as individuals, not just as masses who were the targets of marketing and media efforts. In the same way, it reminded marketers that they were not the center of attention. The Trout and Ries book was one of the earliest to insist that marketers must be customer-driven, and beyond that, customer *mind*-driven. (Similar ideas had been proposed years earlier by the famed consumer psychologist Dr. Ernest Dichter, among others, but largely ignored by marketers who felt more comfortable dealing with a marketplace they could see and track, as opposed to the psychological space that Dr. Dichter explored.)

The irony in all this is that the same marketing community that has come to adopt the positioning premise has largely failed to buy into the underlying assumption of the concept, specifically, *that it is ultimately the customer who positions a brand, not the marketer*. Or, more accurately, it is the customer who implicitly agrees to a positioning that is proposed by a marketer.

In 1972, Trout and Ries said that marketers should be "positioning" a brand in consumers' minds. While that was certainly a breakthrough way of thinking about it at the time, the reality is that marketers cannot force consumers to do anything; marketers are not literally creating the positioning, they can only create strategic and tactical suggestions to encourage the customer to adopt a particular positioning in his or her mind. Not even the most formidable brands can persuade consumers to accept a positioning prompt if they refuse to play the game.

Crystal Pepsi has failed to convince cola drinkers that cola doesn't have to be brown, or noncola drinkers that a drink called

"Pepsi" is not a cola. Subaru could not talk car shoppers into believing that they were selling an upscale brand. Despite hundreds of millions of dollars in advertising, the various dairy boards around the country have never succeeded in increasing branded milk consumption by focusing on nutrition. Try as they might, these marketers could not position or reposition their brands successfully because their prospects simply refused to let it happen.

Marketers may plan to "position" a brand against their competitors by running advertising that compares the performance of two products, or by designing packaging to carry a competitive superiority statement, or by asking their customer service reps to emphasize that they are the best in the business. But, a brand is not literally positioned until customers have agreed to buy into those propositions. Holiday Inn, for instance, may take its name off of the Crowne Plaza signage, but if guests still think of it as a Holiday Inn property, no repositioning will have been accomplished. The actual act of positioning is left for the consumer to consummate. Sellers can only suggest a positioning with what we call "positioning prompts."

In the long run, what difference does it make whether the positioning is created by the marketer or by the customer as long as the positioning is successful? Just this: marketers are only suppliers of alternatives from which the consumer selects. They can influence, but never literally control, how a brand is positioned within a consumer's mind. That's an easier concept to understand than to accept. Until it's accepted, a marketer runs the risk of underestimating the power of the purchaser, which can lead to overestimating the power of the brand. Both roads can lead to disaster.

Indifference and the Circle of Relevance

A brand is rarely one of the most important things in a consumer's life. How a Diet Pepsi tastes is not likely to change my view of the world. Still, there's a reason I choose Diet Pepsi instead of another brand, and that choice has something to do with how I think, how I use my senses, or how I live. I may be concerned about my weight, but prefer a sweeter-tasting drink than Diet Coke. I may like to think of myself as young at heart and feel a closer affinity to parent Pepsi's enduring "Choice of the New Generation" identity. Or I might have always had a soft spot for Ray Charles and his "Uh-huh" advertising. Whatever the reason, I have "positioned" Diet Pepsi in my mind based on how my own realities, reconciled with the marketing prompts launched by the brand team.

When the concept of positioning was first popularized in the 1970s, marketers were most concerned with the immediate category in which they competed. Now, however, brand stewards must look to a much wider field.

In a roiling marketplace that annually produces approximately 20,000 new products, services, flanker spin-offs, line extensions, private labels, and an overload of commercial messaging, it's that much harder for a brand to own much of my attention, let alone loyalty. Only those brands that can persuasively and realistically demonstrate their relevance within my life are likely to become my regular choice. At any given time, indifference or distractions can be the most formidable hurdles for brands in establishing long-term relevant positionings.

The health of a brand identity is a direct function of its perceived relevance in its customers' realities. In a healthy franchise, the brand-to-customer relationship is symbiotic, a continuous circle of relevance bonding the seller and the brand to the buyer. A brand team does its homework and consistently delivers relevant benefits to its brand's customers. That, in turn, creates a trust in the brand, hopefully leading to an ongoing relationship between buyer and brand. As the relationship continues, the marketing team understands more about the buyer's needs, enabling them to deliver more relevant benefits (see Exhibit 4-1 for schematic of this circular relationship).

Why has the company that Richard Sears founded so many decades ago struggled through such difficult stretches in the last ten years? Among other reasons, because Sears stores became less relevant in Americans' new shopping reality, and there was sufficient indifference to Sears that the brand identity lost its

EXHIBIT 4-1

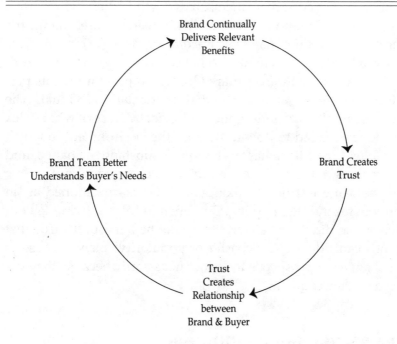

Brand Continually
Delivers Relevant
Benefits

Brand Creates
Trust

Brand Team Better
Understands Buyer's Needs

Trust
Creates
Relationship
between
Brand & Buyer

The circle of relevance.

power in peoples' lives. The new reality for Sears shoppers suddenly was filled with discount mass merchandise chains like Wal-Mart, membership warehouse outlets like Price Costco, discount appliance chains like The Good Guys, quick-service oil change chains like Jiffy-Lube, home improvement chains like Home Depot, and trend-driving clothing chains like The Limited. You could say that competition just got tougher, or that Sears was poorly managed, or that the company didn't know what it wanted to be when it grew up. All of those observations might be true, but the precipitating cause of Sears's fall from grace was that its brand identity became less relevant within the changing reality of customers' daily lives.

When the attributes of a product/service are relevant to the customer's life, the customer is inclined to trust the brand that symbolizes that product/service. It's not enough to simply analyze impressions that customers may have of a brand; the brand must be evaluated within the context of how it has been positioned—by the customers themselves—within their own worlds.

Americans may believe that Rolex watches are among the finest made, but if a man feels uncomfortable wearing a $12,000 watch when he walks by the homeless everyday, then the product superiority of Rolex is markedly less important than its perceived relevance, at least to that particular individual. The brand's identity has undergone a shift, not because of what Rolex has done or failed to do, but because the environment in which the Rolex brand lives has undergone a substantive change, and perceptions of the brand's identity have changed with it.

The same is true of Alka Seltzer. It was positioned as an antidote for indulgent living. But when indulgent living fell out of favor, so did Alka Seltzer. It may not be fair, but it's true that brands can ride a roller coaster of popularity solely because of the changes in prospect's lives, not necessarily because they deserve fickle treatment.

The Positioning Equilibrium

Prospects walk into possible purchase situations with a set of assumptions, or a particular *mindset*. That mindset has a direct bearing on how the brand will be viewed. Included in the mindset is a group of *needs or wants*, waiting to be satisfied by product or service *benefits*. Marketers have specific goals in mind about how they would like their brands to be seen in the absolute, and how they would like them compared to whatever might compete with their brands in the purchase decision. That is the marketers' *positioning objective*. To achieve that objective, marketers must deliver benefits that prompt the prospects to position brands in their minds in such a way that they appear capable of meeting consumers' needs or wants.

Regardless of what prospects expect, or what the marketers want to happen, those products and services will perform in a certain way, delivering benefits derived from their actual level of performance. That is their *absolute performance*, which is cognitively filtered by prospects into the *perceived performance*. That perceived performance then prompts customers to create the *positioning* in their minds.

Brands that are successfully positioned achieve a delicate balance between the goals of the marketer, the needs/wants of the prospect, and the absolute and the perceived product/service performance (that is, delivery of benefits). While marketers do not literally position brands, they can have a significant influence on how they are positioned. To do so, they need to skillfully maneuver the various elements to achieve a state of equilibrium in which the positioning objective set by the marketer is achieved because the perceived performance of the brand matches perfectly with the mindset and needs of the prospect.

Such a successful positioning can be said to be both relevant to the needs of the customer, and credible coming from that particular brand.

For years, Gallo has been known as a brand of good-tasting wine for a low price, a positioning encouraged by the Gallo family and its marketing and sales teams, and largely accepted by consumers. The marketer had achieved a positioning equilibrium, and prospered to become the largest wine maker in the world, without even a close second. Then, during the 1980s, Ernest and Julio Gallo decided that they wanted their label to support higher pricing, and their family name to be associated with a higher grade of product. They eventually became the largest producer of varietals in the world, as well.

The company's efforts to improve their brand's identity likely caused some confusion among certain consumers who had positioned Gallo in their minds as a good quality/good value, yet lower-priced brand. Until they reach their goal of becoming synonymous with fine wines as well as good-value wines, the Gallo team will search for a new equilibrium—the balance between what people expect from the Gallo name, what the Gallo family wants them to think of the Gallo brand, and what the Gallo wine is perceived to be when consumed.

An interesting positioning battle is shaping up within the airline industry involving the most profitable company, Southwest, and its more premium-priced rivals. United, for example, has converted some of its flights to "no-frill"/low-fare versions under the Shuttle By United sub-brand, designed to compete directly with Southwest. United has an advantage with a more extensive frequent-flier program and assigned seating. Southwest's advantage is that its turnaround time and efficient loading and unloading of passengers is the best around. Southwest also has Herb Kelleher, named 1994 CEO of the Year by *Fortune* magazine, while United's being managed as "the largest employee-owned company in the world."

However, Southwest's low price/high value brand identity could be jeopardized by an expensive dogfight that forces Southwest to change what has been a nearly flawless marketing strategy. It's even possible—though not probable given Kelleher's record—that Southwest could get caught up in a role reversal in which United comes off as the best value and Southwest as the second-class entry. More likely, the two companies will duke it out until one or the other finds the positioning to be too costly.

It's a tricky business, this positioning game.

How Positioning Rules Have Changed

In their recent book, *Marketing Myths That Are Killing Business*, Kevin Clancy and Robert Shulman contend that most marketers don't even understand or make good use of positionings, and that most major brands do not own a distinct positioning in the marketplace. In their words, "If most products and services are positioned at all, it's strictly in the minds of their marketing managers."[3] Clancy and Shulman believe that there are three reasons for this failure to position successfully: 1) Companies don't develop a clear positioning strategy to begin with, 2) they have not clearly articulated a positioning to potential buyers, and 3) there was never enough marketing support to sustain a proper positioning effort.

Behind these shortcomings are crucial misconceptions about positionings that can make it more difficult to create lasting brand identities. They fall into several categories (see Exhibit 4-2):

ACURA: A POSITIONING THAT THEY SAID COULDN'T BE DONE

A Japanese luxury car is an idea that's easy to accept today; back in the mid-1980s, it was anything but. Japanese brands like Honda, Toyota, and Nissan had captured large shares of the American car market, but always at the low end and mid-levels. In those days, the prestige side of the market was reserved solely for the surging German Mercedes and BMW makes, which had been feasting off of some of the poorer quality American-made models.

To say that the concept of a Japanese luxury car was met with skepticism would be grossly understating the case. The Honda corporation decided that it would be the pioneer. If the gamble paid off, North American Honda would get a crucial jump on its rivals. If it failed, the losses might set the corporation so far back financially that it would take years to recover.

The company's first decision may have been its most important positioning move: The new car line would *not* be called Honda, and it would carry very little association with the Honda brand name, other than under the hood where certain engine parts were labeled as manufactured by the parent company.

This was not an easy identity decision to make. The Honda name had come to mean the ultimate in automobile value in the United States, starting in 1975 when the innovative Civic had introduced the concept of a small car that was responsive and reliable. The Accord, Prelude, and CRX lines followed and reinforced the identity. The Accord, in particular, began picking up steam as Americans grew more frustrated with their own country's gas-guzzling, high-maintenance models. Consequently, the company rightly reasoned that Americans weren't likely to embrace a Honda that cost more than $20,000.

In deciding not to rely on its existing brand name, Honda accomplished two critical objectives: 1) resources of all types would be concentrated on creating this new brand, rather than having to compete internally for people and financial support with the well-established, extremely successful Honda brand; and 2) prospective buyers would not confuse the two brands in their minds, permitting Acura to build a more upscale identity without being burdened with the lower-price associations of Honda. It also prevented Honda from acquiring a reputation for higher-priced products that would have endangered its strong value story.

A new company called the Acura division of American Honda was created in 1985, manned by individuals who were to separate themselves wherever possible from Honda employees and manufacturing plants. The Acura line initially included a $20,000 Legend sedan and a $10,000 Integra sports coupe. (A few years later, a much more sleek Legend coupe and redesigned sedan were folded in.) American Honda also insisted that any dealers who were approved to carry the new line had to open up separate outlets that would sell Acuras only. To every extent possible, overlapping of the brands would be kept to a minimum. Eventually, of course, the word got out that the luxurious Legend and the sporty Integra were manufactured by the same people who made those long-lasting Hondas.

The brand's initial positioning prompt was a "precision-crafted automobile," a stance that matched the identity of finely tooled Japanese imports with the Acura brand name. Since that time, Toyota introduced its more expensive Lexus line, as did Nissan with Infiniti. Acura has more recently dialed its identity more upscale, using the theme line, "Some things are worth the price."

Today, the Acura line remains the largest-selling luxury foreign car brand in the country, more than 100,000 units ahead of Toyota's Lexus. Acura owes much of its large and growing franchise to its initial positioning as the first import to combine the reliability of Japanese imports with the precision performance of a new line of luxury automobiles.

EXHIBIT 4-2

Assumption	Reality
Brands are positioned within the marketplace	Brands are positioned within the mind of the prospect
Brands are positioned by the marketer	Brands are positioned by the prospect, with the help of positioning prompts from the marketer
Positioning is a decision, followed by an action taken by the marketer	Positioning is a continuous rethinking process usually (but not always) initiated by the marketer and consummated by the prospect
Brands are positioned against other brands in the category	Brands are positioned against other alternatives considered within the prospect's reality, usually (but not always) including other brands in the category
Once a brand positioning is set, it should remain unchanged	Positioning prompts must be adapted to changes in the marketplace
Only brands can be positioned	Categories are positioned by consumers just as often as are brands

Positioning assumptions and realities.

■ *The marketplace vs. the mindset*: We tend to nod in agreement when we hear that the battle for share takes place more in the consumer's mind than in the marketplace. But, we continue to talk about what's happening "out there" (in the physical marketplace) vs. what's going on "in there" (in the marketplace as seen in the mind of the prospect), probably because its easier to deal with the tangibles in the marketplace than with the vagaries within the human mind. Yet, brand teams that hope to be successful in the 1990s must spend some quality think time considering what goes on inside the individual prospect's own world, using the kind of ind*ivisual*izing perspective discussed in chapter 3.

■ *Who's in control here?* No marketers want to admit that they have less control over their brands' destinies than their customers have. Nevertheless, sellers rarely pull the strings of the buyers—it's more often the other way around. Apple thought the Newton was a terrific product as is; consumers thought Apple better think again before they sell it. Volkswagen thought the power of the Bug would extend into the Jetta and the Golf, but the product reliability wasn't there to make the case.

Even the most successful marketers are coaches in a game in which only customers play. A marketer can only guide customers toward how they might think of the brand in relation to other alternatives. It would have been a non sequitur to say that Wheaties was "positioned" as the cereal to eat because that's what sports heroes do. What really happened was that "The Breakfast of Champions" and "What the Big Boys Eat" campaigns sent out a message that resonated with people who were ready to accept it. Wheaties didn't position itself; it arranged for its brand to be positioned by its customers.

■ *It's not the act of positioning, it's the* _process_ *of positioning.* Positioning is not a unilateral marketer action, as in: "Let's position the brand this way." It's a continuous persuasion process, as in: "Let's encourage the customer to begin thinking of the brand this way."

True, sometimes a marketer gets lucky and sends out positioning prompts that are immediately adopted by prospects. For example, CompUSA has grown up in a few short years as the premier computer superstore, opening over 100 stores in just three years with total sales exceeding $2 billion. The chain brand offered itself up as the discount supermarket for computers and buyers bought it right off. In contrast, it took mega-brand Crest years to persuade its users to accept it as the toothpaste that fights cavities, and to build a leadership franchise based on that positioning. Guess which type of success story is more common.

■ *How big is the playing field for each brand?* What marketer has not spent months analyzing "the competition," defined most often as other brands in the category or, on rare occasions, as brands in a related category competing for a "share of stomach" or "share of the travel dollar," and so on? In the minds of prospects, the playing field is much less tightly defined and much less stable.

To the marketer, Kodak film might compete for share of market with Fuji. But at the time of purchase, the real competition may be Panasonic, if a family decides that a videocam can better capture a magic moment than a still camera. Of course, Fuji might not even be seriously considered if that consumer is unfamiliar with the Fuji brand (awareness building is one reason why all those Fuji blimps are flying over sporting events). Coppertone used to see other suntan lotions as their competition, but their most formidable foe today may be the American Cancer Society, which urges people to spend less time in the sun. The national TV networks used to compete mostly with themselves. Now their competitors are the other things people can do while watching a screen, including video games, computer on-line services, scores of cable alternatives and satellite receiving systems.

Depending on the category, the entire concept of "share of market" is sometimes more helpful as a general business measure than it is as a way to think about competitive positionings. Consumers are frequently in search of solutions to larger issues than one category can address. One reason for the success of such brands as Hunt's Ready Sauces and any number of Campbell's soups is that they offer cooks options of solutions, not just what a single product or even a single category can provide.

■ *Customer realities should be the source of all marketing strategies.* If it's irreverent to some marketers that customers, not they, are the architects of a positioning, then it may be downright heretical to suggest that what goes on in customers' lives should dictate marketing strategies as well. After all, the customers are not the ones who slave over the pricing or sales promotion or advertising strategy statements, or spend hours justifying them to management.

True enough, but the inspiration from each of those strategies should stem from the marketer's knowledge of what's happening in the life of the customer. It may be crystal clear to a marketer, for instance, that a sudden price decline will catch competitors napping, but what effect will such a move have on the way customers position the brand within their own lives? Budweiser lowered its list pricing in late 1993. That helped make

Bud more competitive on shelf, but has it helped or hurt its identity among Bud drinkers, an identity carefully crafted over decades to be synonymous with premium priced, as in premium quality, as in superior?

■ *Change is good—even for positionings.* Conventional marketing wisdom says that the positioning is the source of all strategies used in a brand's marketing mix and, therefore, it should be a constant, a bulwark of strength and steadiness for the rest of the marketing mix. Yet, in the tumultuous marketplace, other forces are prompting even the most tradition-bound brands to change their positioning tunes.

Heinz ketchup, for example, built an impressive franchise based on a single-product positioning—the thickest ketchup. That sole attribute, plus its vinegar-based taste, has set the gold standard in the category. But the category has stabilized, and has now fallen behind in dollar sales to salsas, leading Heinz to introduce a salsa-style ketchup a while back, and Campbell's to buy the Pace brand for more than 20 times the parent company's earnings. In addition, less expensive brands are taking historic share bites out of the leader's franchise, an indication that there are new customer realities that make thickness much less compelling than during the brand's halcyon days.

In essence, Heinz has been repositioned by customers despite the fact that its positioning prompts have remained remarkably consistent over the years (although its spending level has declined significantly).

■ *Categories can be positioned, too.* People carry attitudes about categories of products and services, just as they do for brands. If you did the research, you'd probably find that most Americans believe that soup is good for you, that facial tissues are an important part of a woman's life, that diamonds are a must at a wedding, that the business world would stop without copy machines, and that some things are worth the calories. Campbell's (soup), Kleenex (tissues), DeBeers (diamonds), Xerox (copying machines), and Hershey's (chocolate) have helped create successful positionings for their categories as well as their brands.

Pricing and Private Labels Force Positioning Changes

Price wars are as old as brands themselves. Brand managers at dozens of packaged goods companies have been tempted for decades to abandon long-term brand-building efforts in order to do battle with price brands. The airlines used to fire price cuts at one another primarily during the summer—now it's all year-round. Premium apparel labels must always contend with continuous deep discounting from knock-off brands. Retailers have screamed the word "SALE!" so often that it's all but meaningless.

Nowhere has the power of repositioning been more dramatically demonstrated than in the transformation of private labels from the perceived lower class of packaged goods to the most talked about products in the supermarket.

On Friday, April 2, 1993—forever more known as "Marlboro Friday"—Philip Morris chairman Michael Miles created an uproar that soon escalated into a financial riot. Miles announced that Philip Morris would be dropping the price of America's leading cigarette brand by as much as 20 percent, while also dramatically increasing advertising and sales promotion support. Wall Street interpreted his announcement as the sounding of retreat against private labels. Almost overnight, Philip Morris's stock lost $14.75 a share—an astonishing $13 billion in market value. Stock prices of other brand-dependent companies such as Campbell Soup, Colgate-Palmolive, and Heinz were hit hard as well.

Despite the concerns expressed throughout the business world, Procter & Gamble moved ahead a few weeks later and lowered the list price of its slumping Luvs disposable diaper brand by 16 percent, then later dropped the price of its premium Pampers brand by 5 percent, both of which turned out to be just the beginning of such moves by Procter and many others. (In stark contrast to the trend, the management of Coca-Cola notified their stockholders that their brand was as strong as ever and would not be discounted under any circumstances.)

The Philip Morris announcement was a signal that private labels had come a long way, and not only in the cigarette industry. The Private Label Manufacturers Association (PLMA) has estimated that more than 20 percent of current grocery store volume comes from lower-priced private labels, a 50 percent rise in just 10 years.

The key reasons given for this phenomenon: 1) store brands are significantly lower in price than most advertised brands and Americans are hooked on shopping for price; 2) private labels have vastly improved their relative value by increasing quality, while also holding below the retail price of their premium competition; and 3) while their per-unit gross margin is less than the premiums, they advertise infrequently, so net margins are higher.[4] In other words, private labels have significantly strengthened their positioning as individual value-added brands.

All of this has raised the question: What is a "real" brand? Just because a brand name is owned by the retailer doesn't make it inherently less valuable to the consumer. The President's Choice label out of the Loblaw chain in Canada has been tremendously successful because of its strong quality and reasonable pricing. Similar success stories are repeated in selected categories for the Safeway, Kroger, Winn-Dixie and other large chain brand lines. These labels are welcomed by store managers because they offer excellent margins, and they are helping to brand the chain itself by contributing to a positive identity.

A key element of any packaged brand's identity is its packaging design, and many private label brands are boldly simulating the design and color scheme of category leaders, such as Ultra, Downy, Tide, Pert Plus, and Crest. The largest brand builder of them all, Procter & Gamble, finally took some action to stop infringement on its brands' identities, despite the rancor it may cause among retailers that distribute its products. In September 1994, P&G sued the F&M drug store chain for brand name and label design infringement. As characterized by identity consultant John Lister of Lister Butler: "The cost of shutting down this competition is severe, but increasingly, brand marketers are starting to look at the P&G approach and not allow the slow but steady erosion of brand ownership."[5]

One factor that makes it tough on premium brands is the increasing quality of their lower-priced competitors. According to a Gallup/PLMA survey in 1992, when the private label revolution was just picking up steam, quality was the number one reason for buying store brands over nationally advertised brands (see Exhibit 4-3 for reasons for buying store brands).

The private label problem is often a premium brand problem. In some cases, it's what traditional brands have *not* done that is the root cause of their share erosions. Too many brands have failed to improve product quality in order to control costs of goods and services, and/or they have introduced flankers and line extensions that have flooded shelves with permutations whose value consumers have questioned.

Lynn Dornblaser, editor of *New Product News* magazine, has commented, "There appears to have been a definite increase in the recent past in the number of brand spin-offs as a percentage of the total new product introductions."[6] Marketing Intelligence Service tracked more than 21,000 SKU introductions through only the first two-thirds of 1994, propelled by huge gains in food and new beverages.

EXHIBIT 4-3

Factor	Very Important (%)
Quality	75
Price	67
Availability of store brands on shelves	36
Coupons	34
Habit	26
Packaging	20
Advertising	15

Reasons for buying store brands over nationally advertised brands.
Source: 1992 Gallup/PLMA Survey.

Other premium brands have escalated list (and therefore retail) prices year after year. David Beatty, president of Toronto's Weston Foods, has suggested that a brand is a "tax" that consumers pay for the knowledge that they are buying a brand they can trust. Considering it in that light, Marlboro raised the "taxes" on its super brand by nearly 10 percent annually for ten years, and the Kraft Cheese line raised prices like clockwork until, by 1992, it was charging 45 percent more than private labels.

Kellogg's has been criticized in the past for its policy to regularly increase list prices. The company's overall share fell four crucial share points in six years, from 41 percent in 1988 to 37 percent in 1994, representing about a $320 million loss in retail sales. Sales of lower-priced private labels doubled during the same time period. While Kellogg's has harvested handsome profits from its strategy, it's now working to rebuild its share via more advertising spending. Even Kellogg's management would admit that it is testing its customers' loyalty, although they seem certain that Kellogg's customers will not waver in their steadfastness to the Battle Creek brand.

Many, if not most, price hikes are driven by very legitimate desires to make a profit, but some marketers began counting on price increases to offset other costs, a strategy originally derived from the price-is-no-object mentality of the 1980s. In this particular decade, however, Americans are watching their budgets again, which has ushered in a whole new set of market dynamics positionings that are likely here to stay.

No brand manager likes to see share eroded by lower-priced competitors, but without the threat of the private labels, many brands might have gone on raising prices until they had irrevocably lost their customers' trust and their positionings of strong value. Private labels do indeed represent a continuing threat to the long-term stability of premium brands, but they have also turned out to be one heck of a wake-up call.

Yet, despite their advances, private labels are to date playing only a secondary role in most categories. According to C. Manly Molpus, president of the Grocery Manufacturers of America, 80 percent of the growth of store (also called "controlled") brands has been in 15 of the 240 product categories typically stocked in supermarkets. "Cut out those 15 and there is no such thing as controlled brand growth. Their sales are flat."[7] However, that situation could easily change if traditional brands fail to keep their prices in line, and to re-engineer their positioning prompts to meet the growing threat of store brands.

On the positive side, premium brands have shown an ability to rebound once they've revised their pricing policies. As evidence, the stock prices of many of those companies that market premium-priced brands have since rebounded as their price adjustments have had a positive effect on consumer attitudes and buying behavior. During the period of private-label battles between April 1993 and November 1994, Campbell's Soup lost and regained a significant part of its stock value, as did Hershey, Kellogg's, Heinz, and Pepsico.

Characteristics of Successful Positioning Campaigns

Positioning campaigns that work often share common characteristics that can serve as a guide for marketers as they seek to identify the most leveragable prompts given their selling circumstances. Here are some of the most important factors:

They are correctly and clearly targeted—The importance of smart targeting is obvious, but never more important than in the choosing of positioning prompts. No matter how brilliant the strategy, it can be wasted if it doesn't speak clearly, although not necessarily explicitly, to the right audience.

Some examples of explicit positioning theme lines: "Choosy Mothers Choose Jif," "Gillette—The Best a Man Can Get," and "Courtyard by Marriott—Designed by Business People for Business People." More implicit, but still focused about their intent: Acura's upscale "Some Things Are Worth the Price," and the "He Asked" campaign from Paine Webber, which positions the brokerage as more personalized and caring toward investors.

They promise relevant benefits—The clearer the connection between what is happening in a prospect's life and what is being offered by the marketed brand, the greater the odds that the prospect will invite the brand to be a part of his or her life. Relevance, the connection of brand offerings to consumers' lives, is how consumers prioritize the brands they decide to buy.

Carnival Cruises knows what the everyman's life is like, and that's why they can so convincingly invite ordinary folk to trade in their ordinary lives for a week or two of reasonably priced fantasy. Aetna Life & Casualty knows that health issues are weighing on the minds of most Americans, which is why they settled on a mature positioning prompt for a nation dealing with serious issues, "A Policy to Do More." Haggar slacks promises "Stuff you can wear," that is, comfortable, fashionless pants to those who could care less about fashion.

Their promises are backed up with persuasive support—In the vast majority of successful positioning cases, a compelling benefit is supported with persuasive reasons to believe. Often, these support points will be product features. Why should we believe that Johnson's Baby Shampoo is better for infants? Because of its "no tears" formula. Why should we believe that Gillette Clear Gel deodorant is better than Sure? Because it doesn't leave a chalky white residue.

Other support techniques may be less product-specific, but just as persuasive. When Dean Witter says "We measure success one investor at a time," they are providing a reason to believe their benefit of customized service, while also implying that the other brokerages are not as customized. Evian's campaign shows breathtaking photos of spectacular, snow-covered mountains with the simple line, "Our Factory," hoping to position their product as purer, more natural than the artificially concocted soft drinks and sports beverages against which they compete.

There are very few major brands that are asking consumers to position them a certain way without providing any visible support at all. Absolut vodka is a brand that is symbolic of a decade when consumers didn't seem to need as many reasons for anything, least of all what they bought. Using virtually no support for its positioning, Absolut simply made the bottle the star reminder of what to drink; a brand that persuaded people to buy it for no apparent reason, other than its inherent panache.

They serve as an integrated base with a compelling strategic per-

sonality—As one example of how positioning and personality can be blended seamlessly, the twin traits of genuineness and authenticity have suddenly reemerged as strategic anchors for some brands hoping to distance themselves once and for all from the superficial eighties. Chevrolet moved on from its "Heartbeat of America" approach to "Genuine Chevrolet" because its research indicated that genuineness presented the brand in a favorable light in terms of quality, trustworthiness, and honesty—in other words, the way that Chevrolet built its franchise during its salad days in the 1950s. "Genuine Jockey" is a campaign that sought to position that brand as higher in quality than its private label competition. Classico spaghetti sauce has proposed that consumers, "Taste the difference authencity makes." And, of course, Coke is attempting to retrieve its successful "It's the Real Thing" and "Coke Is It" heritage in a form called, "Always Coca-Cola."

Some brands have never really left their authentic positioning and personality. It's always been part of the Levi's brand and it's still on their labels. AT&T, which never entirely abandoned its genuineness positioning since the 1984 divestiture of the Baby Bells, has renovated the stance with its "True Voice" campaign. Pace Picante Sauce has built its franchise on the idea that any picante sauce made anywhere besides Texas (say, "New York Cit-y," for instance) is not really picante sauce.

There is a credible brand fit—Have you ever seen a television commercial that was beautifully produced, with a clear and compelling message, and yet was completely inappropriate to the product or service that sponsored the message? The only thing worse than a positioning prompt that cannot be supported by the brand is a proposed way to think about a brand that doesn't match the other signals the brand is sending out into the marketplace.

When Cadillac continued positioning itself as one of the world's great luxury cars in the 1980s, despite a spate of mechanical problems, the brand itself was harmed by the overpromise. In the case of Nissan's Infiniti introductory "rocks and trees" advertising, it wasn't so much a case of mismatch as no match. The advertising suggested a Zen-like experience and an unclear positioning. The campaign pulled curiosity-seekers into the showroom, but the the other marketing communications and the car itself created no real identity. The result was a dealer revolt, an eventual change in the ad agency, and new positioning prompts, this time much more product-focused.

In contrast, the marketing of Wrangler and Lee jeans by VF Corporation is a study in fit, and not just in the jeans. VF recognized several years ago that their two brands were appealing to polar opposites—rugged Westerners for Wrangler and aging baby boomers for Lee. They successfully matched their marketing efforts to fit these two disparate groups based on information that was the product of the largest research budget in the industry. VF's reward for doing their homework was double-digit growth for the flagship brands, and a combined company category share leadership over their archrival, Levi-Straus.

They are supported by sufficient marketing spending—With few exceptions, marketers just can't get there from here without committing to some sort of consistent marketing support program to communicate their positioning prompts. Occasionally, a few phenom brands crop up that make it big with relatively little help from a mega marketing budget, such as Corona Beer, and Cabbage Patch dolls. But perpetual brand leaders like Hertz, Marlboro, American Airlines, Tylenol, Campbell's, Budweiser, McDonald's, Ford, AT&T, and Gallo all lead their respective categories in one or more forms of consumer marketing support, not just in share of market.

True, some brands can afford to maintain larger budgets because they have the volume to support it, but they are staying on top by recognizing the need to support their positionings rather than be preempted by competition.

Those that fail to keep pace with competition often pay a cruel price. To cite just one example, the Zenith brand of electronics was once one of the most respected names in the field, one of many made in America. Now it's the only major American-owned electronics company. Last year, it spent just $1.8 million on advertising, compared to $24 million for RCA and $18 million for Philips. The company cut back because of financial

---

POSITIONING PITFALLS

Positioning work is not on the glamorous end of branding. It's strategic and a little on the theoretical side, so it's easy to spend too little think time on what may be the single most important decision a brand team can make. Here are some common pitfalls found on most positioning playing fields:

- *Acting like a seller instead of a buyer*—If we're truly customer-driven, then we don't try to tell the consumer how to drive the car. As we've discussed elsewhere, the marketer provides the prompts and the incentives, the customer does the actual positioning. Marketers' success is often a direct function of how well they listen, and how well they sincerely accept their role as second banana to the customer.

- *Thinking too small*—Too small, in this case, means concentrating positioning prompts on the most obvious "category." That may make sense if you are third or fourth in the share line and just hope to get closer to the top, but positioning prompts should be developed according to how the prospect looks at the options, and those may not include only the obvious competition. Department stores, for example, are now in the entertainment business. Entertainment businesses are often selling vacations. Fast-food chains are convenient ways to fight food boredom. Toymakers, among other things, are selling guilt avoidance to parents. Banks are seeking to be financial advisors instead of money barns. Phone companies want to be your link to the future.

- *Standing pat with half a hand*—You'll create the perfect positioning for your brand on the day you retire. Until then, challenge everything. In the 1990s, positionings are just as alive and evolving as brands themselves, so be ready and willing to adjust, assuming that changes in the marketplace require a significant shift in strategy. In the past, marketers have assumed that consistency is the most important attribute for any positioning plan, with flexibility of secondary importance. Depending on the category, it may well be the other way around in the more fluid 1990s.

■ *Falling in love with the prompt instead of the positioning—* Most common in the high-tech fields, this is the sin of creating something that the creators love before finding out if the prospect agrees. A new product technology, a new advertising campaign, an improved package, a sure-fire promotion, they all have the power to wow the marketing team, yet fall like deadweight in the mind of the prospect. There is no such thing as a winner until the consumer says so, and that includes in the positioning derby.

troubles and, in the process, created marketplace troubles as its TVs fell to the number number three slot.

Sufficient marketing support, by the way, does not have to mean big-time advertising budgets. Strong in-market results can also be accomplished with other communications approaches. In the public relations field alone, for example, major business gains have resulted for brands that used their PR prompts effectively. Oscar Mayer Wieners (30th anniversary of their theme song), Hershey's Kisses (launch of their Kisses with Almonds), Wisk laundry detergent (their Wisk Clean Clothes Drive for the homeless), Budget Rent-a-Car (35th Birthday Bash) are all brands that have successfully used public relations events to build their businesses.

Finding Positionings That Fit the Brand *and* the Customers

In 1972, after spending decades perfecting popcorn crossbreeds, Orville Redenbacher traveled from his popping corn fields in Valparaiso, Indiana, to Chicago to talk to an advertising agency.

There he explained who he was, gave the ad execs a sample of his product, and asked for help in coming up with a catchy new name. One week and $13,000 later, the ad agency had the answer: The new product should be called "Orville Redenbacher's Gourmet Popping Corn." As Orville likes to say, "It took those guys three weeks and $13,000 to come up with the same name my mother gave me." The moral of Orville's story: If you want to know how to sell your brand, use what fits the best.[8]

The brand team might think of the positioning development process as being in two parts: The first, as described in earlier chapters, involves looking at who your prospects and customers are as individuals, and who or what your brand is, and what you would like it to be. The second half of that preparation is the reviewing of how other brands have achieved successful positionings because they sent forth the right positioning prompts at the right time. What makes a positioning right or wrong? Any number of factors, the lead one being how credibly that positioning fits the brand that seeks it, and the customer it hopes to attract.

Positionings are not verifiable scientific hypotheses. There's a great deal of subjective interpretation and a high degree of risk involved in choosing to seek one positioning over another. That's why it makes sense to take a close look at alternative positioning types. They come in a variety of shapes and sizes, including:

■ *Feature-driven Prompts*—The second rule of selling (right after "Know Thy Customer") is to be clear about what's for sale. More marketers still rely on product/service features to differentiate their brands than any other single method. They do so in a huge variety of categories such as household cleaning products, over-the-counter drugs, high-tech hardware and software, banking, electronics, food, retailing, and automotive. In that last category alone, just watch football games on any given Sunday afternoon and you will witness a parade of 24-valve engines, leather upholstery, aerodynamically slick profiles, and movable minivan seats.

The advantage of feature positioning prompts is that the marketer never wanders too far from the core of what's for sale;

there's a strong likelihood that the positioning will be credible if the advertiser sticks to the facts. Unfortunately, a feature-oriented stance is often the most preemptible when the competition comes out with a faster this or a smoother that.

- *Problem/Solution Prompts*—There's a school of thought that *all* positionings are of the problem/solution type, since consumers often buy a product or use a service in order to solve a problem in their daily lives. Packaged goods brands are the most frequent users of problem/solution because their products tend to be designed to fill specific need niches. Rustoleum is the solution to rust prevention; Clorox to graying clothes; Grecian Formula 16 to graying pates; Pampers solves the problems of the very young and Attends for the more senior; Swanson Frozen Dinners for busy and hungry families; Doritos for busy and hungry snackers. What problem/solution positionings lack in imagination, they make up in directness and, very often, credibility.

- *Target-driven Positionings*—One of the most effective ways to seed a brand is to send out a positioning prompt that reflects well on potential buyers. The Nature Company has an on-line link with the environment and their promotional material makes it clear that they seek those who are sympatico. Levi's 501s equates "cool" to button flies, and all those who wear them. In a predominantly feature-driven category, Librex's "The Freedom of One" advertising for their computer hardware celebrates the creativity of the "liberated individual," unleashed by his or her machines' capabilities. Timberland shoes are worn by rugged individualists (in body or mind); no others need apply. These brands have achieved positionings based on who buys what they sell, not solely by what they sell.

- *Competition-driven Positionings*—By definition, a positioning deals with how a brand is viewed compared to its most obvious competitors, so the idea of a competition-driven positioning might seem redundant. Listerine and Scope have been battling at one another for years and have clearly defined their niches based on the shortcomings of the other. Scope has hammered at Listerine for creating "mediciny breath," while Listerine has claimed that Scope is less efficacious. Similar judge-me-by-my-rival approaches have cropped up between Taurus and

Accord, Sega and Nintendo, Hefty and Glad, and Brillo vs. SOS. Some of these positioning prompts draw their credibility as much from what their competitors *are not* as they do from what they *are*.

Competitive positionings that avoid comparative claims: The Energizer Bunny who keeps "going and going," inferring that Duracell doesn't; Duracell's "plastic family" returns the favor to Energizer; Top-Flite's "longest ball" positioning that claims superiority without always mentioning against what; and the Isuzu "Going Outside the Lines" positioning, which has its Rodeo traveling in amazing places that, the advertising implies, the competition wouldn't even attempt to scale.

■ *Emotional/Psychological Positionings*—We are still emotional animals, no matter how rational our digitized world may make us appear. How people feel about a brand is generally need- or desire-based, which means that emotional or psychological approaches often can be very effective as positioning prompts.

Michelin's advertising uses infants playing in the middle of tires, suggesting that your family's safety may depend on buying their brand (see Exhibit 4-4). Volvo has hinted that there's only one sure way to "Drive Safely," and that's by buying their Swedish imports. Volvo effectively locked down that positioning with subsequent advertising that features accident survivors. These people believe that they owe their lives to the sturdiness of Volvos, and now belong to one of the better named customer affinity groups—the Volvo Saved My Life Club.

■ *Benefit-driven Positionings*—"It pays to Discover." A nice positioning line for a successful credit card with a simple benefit—use it and get money back. Discover was among the first major cards to provide its users with a financial salve when they spent money they weren't carrying with them. Now, dozens of cards are offering benefits ranging from down payments on cars to credits on frequent-flier programs. Customers know they have to use a credit card anyway, so why not one that offers some nice payback along the way?

Another benefit-driven example is Kinko's, a growing 700-unit chain of copying and business services stores that is targeted toward small business. Their "Your branch office that never

EXHIBIT 4-4

ANNOUNCING A TIRE THAT MAY LAST AS LONG AS YOU OWN YOUR CAR.

*Our new all-season radial is backed by an 80,000 mile treadwear limited warranty. See dealer for details.

Extra rubber, extra steel, gives you extra protection against road hazards.

Revolutionary new design ensures even wear for even higher mileage.

Rest easy. With the smooth, quiet, comfortable ride we're famous for.

Once again Michelin raises the bar of excellence. With the highest mileage passenger tire we've ever made.

The XH4 maintains Michelin's renowned all-season performance from the first mile to the last.

More miles. More value. More Michelin.

MICHELIN
BECAUSE SO MUCH IS RIDING ON YOUR TIRES.

CONGRATULATIONS, IT'S A MICHELIN.
BACKED BY AN 80,000 MILE WARRANTY.*

Michelin uses babies in tires to emphasize their family safety positioning.

closes" campaign is an attempt to lure customers with the two benefits they seek most—a job done quickly (through a wide range of office services that can be provided on the spot) and 24-hour access.

■ *Aspirational Positionings*—These are positioning prompts that offer prospects a place they might like to go, or a person they might like to be, or a state of mind they might like to achieve. Collier's not only sells information with their encyclopedia CDs, they also sell fantasy and wonder. The controversial Joe Camel from the Camel brand has been criticized because it allegedly offers an identity of coolness that younger people could aspire to. And Calvin Klein? Well, let's just say that Calvin Klein is selling more than jeans.

During our recent recession, some believed that Americans were growing immune to aspirational-based positioning appeals, and were more inclined toward factual, product-oriented appeals. Certainly, difficult economic times will force more consumers to deal with the realities of life, but that can also persuade them that they could use more escapism rather than living with more reality. Given the rebounds of the travel and hospitality industries, diamonds from South Africa, and luxury cars, there's no reason to believe that consumers' desire to escape reality has been permanently dampened, even in more sobering times.

■ *Value Positionings*—Speaking of sobering, the last U.S. recession produced some profound changes in the way consumers looked at product and service options. As the word "value" lost its stigma as a euphemism for "cheap," it became one of the most legitimate positioning prompts for even the largest of marketers.

Led by McDonald's and Taco Bell, virtually all of the fast-food chains offered "value meals" as a lead item in their restaurant menus and advertising campaigns. Ditto for the car manufacturers who rolled out lower-priced models, price freezes, rebates, and reasonably priced lease programs during lean selling times. And those packaged goods brands that raised prices too fast were forced to back down when the consuming public threatened to stop consuming. Now, the airwaves are filled with announcements that premium brands are not as premium anymore.

Some of the Classics and Soon-to-Be Classics

Great writers read other great writers. Accomplished musicians spend much of their time listening to the techniques of their peers. Marketers who hope to discover the positioning that will take their brand over the top, can learn from some of the classics. A few brand positionings that have something to teach us all:

■ *Avis: "We're #2. We Try Harder" (Competition-based)*—It seems so obvious now, but it was no easy decision to publicly proclaim that your company was second, with the real danger that you would be seen as second-best. During the 1950s, while Hertz "put YOU in the driver's seat," Avis was winning more than its fair share of customers with a positioning (and equally engaging personality) that appealed to the service-sensitive public. They promised to please even more often than the leader, and people responded to that sincere desire to please. The brilliance of the strategy was that Avis was just another brand in the pack that trailed Hertz by a large margin. By proposing that prospects think of them as second in size but first in effort, they instantly placed themselves much higher in people's minds than they had occupied in the category share charts. Then they backed it up with the right kind of service. That tradition continues today.

■ *Pepsi's "Choice of a New Generation" (Aspirational)*—A bold and beautiful move by an underdog that took advantage of a sleeping dog. During the 1970s and 1980s, Pepsi used a series of advertising, packaging, and promotional moves to align itself with the young and the young at heart, implying that the oldsters should stick with that old standby, Coke. Mixing their strategic masterpiece with tactical side-by-side blind test comparisons called "The Pepsi Challenge," the brand actually pulled ahead of Coke in some markets, opening Americans' minds to the possibility that Coca-Cola was not necessarily the king of the colas. Coke eventually rebounded nicely, but no one in Atlanta will ever underestimate their arch rival again.

■ Rolling Stone's *Great Turnaround (Target-driven)*—*Rolling Stone* magazine was a product of the 1960s anti-establishment era in America. Many mainstream advertisers steered clear of the book because they assumed that its readership still considered San Francisco's Haight-Ashbury to be the center of the universe. Starting in 1985, the magazine began their "Perception/ Reality" print ad campaign, which deftly compared the popular reputation of the book's readership with reality, a reality that included articles of interest to baby boomers, and an audience who were suddenly in charge of everything they used to picket. *Rolling Stone* has now run more than 50 such ads and has seen its business mushroom, and its advertisers reposition the magazine in their own minds, right into the middle of the mainstream.

■ *The Maytag Repairman (Product/Reputation-based)*—This company positioning is the epitome of consistency and the persistence embodied in the Maytag repairman himself. Maytag has convinced a huge portion of American households that it makes the best appliances because repairs are few and far between. Using as their spokesman a repairman who never has anything to repair, the company has resisted the temptation to change its positioning prompts and its brand personality. The brand makes the right promise, and delivers on it.

■ *Arm & Hammer's Repositioning (Product-based)*—All but given up for dead, this baking soda found new life as a refrigerator deodorizer and ultimately produced an entire line of successful new products.

Arm & Hammer had little going for it but an old logo, old packaging, old-fashioned product, and some state-of-the-art thinking that created an important brand from the ashes. Today, the brand has become a brand family that has successfully entered the deodorant, toothpaste, and rug/furniture cleaning fields. Even more impressive, its baking soda base has spawned entire new wings of categories that have capitalized on the cleaning efficacy of the compound. Now, that's the power of positioning or, in this case, repositioning.

■ *Apple Computer (Product and Aspirational)*—Apple has experienced a well-documented roller coaster ride of positionings and business results since its founding less than 25 years ago. Its initial Macintosh positioning, with its "computer for the rest of us" theme, hit a bullseye with a small but influential segment of the burgeoning personal computer market, clearly setting it apart from IBM users and clone users. A few years later, Apple followed with "The Power to Be Your Best," an aspirational positioning theme line that promised each user the opportunity to reach his or her full potential.

Apple's operating system became the epitome of user-friendly and established a beachhead that held up for years until Microsoft's Windows made the icon technology available to the competition. Today, Apple is in the fight of its life and will likely end up as part of a larger company, or in a series of identity-changing alliances. It's a tribute to Apple's positioning and personality, by the way, that it is one of the best known brands in the world, even though its operating systems account for only about 10 percent of those in use.

■ *DeBeers (Emotion-based)*—This was not just a case of how to position a commodity product, it really involved changing an entire culture. Only in the past fifty years have diamonds become a favorite gift to show someone's love for another. Through a slow and meticulous public relations and advertising program begun in the 1930s, the DeBeers cartel reeducated the public about diamonds, recasting them from an exotic jewel for aristocrats to the symbol of love and commitment for the American common man.

DeBeers engineered one of the most masterful repositionings in the history of modern marketing, and at least one reason is that people came to believe that diamonds held the very same magical qualities that its marketing communications claimed. (The story is all the more remarkable when you consider that, for most of those decades of success, the country of origin was held in contempt by much of the world for human rights violations.)

■ *Intel's Inside (Product-based/Co-branding)*—Intel's microprocessors are buried deep in the internal workings of a computer, but thanks to smart alliances and clever co-branding with hardware manufacturers using their "Intel Inside" campaigns, they are now the leading brand of computer engine. Clearly, Intel has done a lot more right than simply repositioning its brand, but the marketing department can take credit for helping the company accelerate its growth in revenue and margins by branding their product as the reason why high-quality hardware does what it does best.

As we have discussed earlier, however, the Intel organization, driven by an engineer mentality, failed to see that with every brand victory comes a responsibility to stay close to the needs of the customer. By their own admission, it took Intel too long to realize that engineers can create brilliant products, but it's the customer who creates brilliant marketing successes. And, it's the customer who dismantles them when they fail to live up to expectations.

■ *Nyquil and Contac (Experience-based)*—An interesting positioning comparison between two successful brands. People with colds either stay at home or press on to work. Nyquil told the world it was "The nighttime sniffling, sneezing, coughing, aching, stuffy head, fever, so you can rest medicine," that is, for those who felt they just couldn't make it into work, or needed some sleep so that they could try again tomorrow. Contac, in contrast, offered their users a chance to go to work and feel better when they did, claiming that "Contac helps turn sick days into work days." Both brands let customers decide for themselves which kind of cold sufferers they want to be, then gave them good reasons to use their products.

■ *A Lifetime Strategy for Lifetime Network (Target-based)*—Lifetime cable took a good look at the demographics of the country's TV audiences and figured out real fast the power of the woman. They created a cable network that women could use as a haven from crime shows and incessant sports reports that are the usual haunts of their spouses and significant others. Lifetime carries such women-favored programming as *Sisters*, *L.A. Law* reruns, and a bevy of TV movies that deal with the subjects of most concern to women—abortion, spouse abuse, balancing home and office careers. Interspersed between programming are promotion slates that talk directly to women and show visual images of satisfied female faces.

On the surface, this appears to be just the first volley of narrowcasting positioning moves in the 500-channel wars to come.

But look more closely and you'll see a positioning prompt meant to permanently distinguish and lift Lifetime above future competition. Lifetime has preemptively established a place on the dial for the female point of view. That's a potent place to be, and a credible positioning in a soon-to-be-chaotic viewing environment.

■ *The Repositioning of Las Vegas (Experience-based)*—So you thought Vegas was a place? It's actually a brand, and a very deftly repositioned one at that. A few years ago, Las Vegas was hurting like most resorts as America's gamblers saw their recreation reserves dwindle during the recession. A few brilliant marketing decisions later, Las Vegas began to tout its plusses as a family entertainment resort town, quite a contrast to their previous identity as America's adults-only playground. Through a series of ads in feeder markets, and a controversial but highly successful "promo-special" on NBC starring Mirage's pirate-themed resort/casino, Las Vegas is attracting whole new segments of adults who now justify the trip as a family vacation (see Exhibit 4-5 for a summary of some of the best of the best positioning efforts).

Prompting a Power Positioning

Searching for a positioning with power requires both logical analysis and intuitive creativity, not to mention healthy portions of luck and serendipity. A brand's customers and prospects are likely to make purchase decisions based as much on emotion as on logic, because that's the way they live their lives. The marketing team may choose to do the same, but their search for the optimum positioning might best begin with a thorough review of what they know about their prospects and their brand, and a careful assessment of the alternatives.

Here are some suggested steps to identify possible positioning prompts for a brand:

Staking Out the Playing Field—The exercises proposed in earlier chapters were different ways of asking the management consultant's favorite question: What business are you really in? Sim-

EXHIBIT 4-5

Brand	Apparent Target	Major Benefit	Support	Positioning Line
Avis	Business travelers	Better service	More effort by Avis owner-employees	"We're #2. We try harder"
Pepsi	Non-loyal Coke drinkers	Taste/act young	Visual/ situational	"The Choice of a New Generation"
Rolling Stone Magazine	Advertisers	Reaches influential audience	Readership studies	*"Rolling Stone—* Myth/ Reality"
Apple Computer	Potential personal computer users	The ultimate in user-friendly	Icon-based operating procedures	"The computer for the rest of us"
Apple Computer	Personal/ Business Users	Enables user to reach full potential	Superior technology	"The power to be your best"
DeBeers	Men (purch.) Women (influencer)	Emotional gratification	Beauty, timelessness of product	"Diamonds are forever"
Intel (co-branded)	MIS mgrs./ End-users operation	Superior hardware	Micro-processor performance	"Intel Inside"

Classic positionings.

ilarly, understanding what benefits a brand offers its prospects is the first step in zeroing in on this critical positioning issue. If you sell computers, you may be in the information business, or the speed business, or the technology business. If you sell travel packages, you may be in the tourism business, or the recreation business, or the stress therapy business. The power of a positioning may very well depend on how accurately the brand's stewards can describe the mental playground in which their prospects expect to find their brand.

Confirming the Identity of Prospects and the Reality in Which They Live—It's critical to have a firm fix on the prospect because they are the ones who will be doing the positioning. The indi*visual*izing work suggested in chapter 3 starts paying off right here in the development of positioning prompts. The indi*visualization* of the prospect, plus whatever other profiling is available, enables the team to focus in on needs, desires, and benefits that become the building blocks of a successful positioning. Just as important, indi*visualization* draws a rendering of the individual prospect's life that can drive all positioning work, and be used as checkpoints for gauging success along the way.

Focusing on Relevant, Reality-based Customer Benefits—After completing the necessary research and reviewing the relevant examples from the positioning hall of fame, the marketing team should be able to succinctly describe a precise customer benefit that can be addressed in some way by the brand. The team members must be very clear in their own minds what customer benefits are being offered, and how they are based on real life needs and desires, regardless of how explicitly those benefits are displayed in marketing communications.

There are probably dozens of positioning formats being used by marketers and their agencies. One approach that seems to find favor among many successful marketing teams revolves around a "focus of sale" statement. The focus of sale is meant to be a distillation of all that has been learned about a brand, including what product/service benefits are likely to be the most compelling in persuading the chosen prospects to buy. If you are selling a line of furniture, the focus of sale might point toward long-lasting beauty for the home. If it's a brand of copier, the benefit focus may be long-lasting reliability. And, the focus of sale for a brand of expensive automobiles may be long-lasting luxury.

Constructing Credible Supports—Why is the benefit credible? What makes it relevant in an individual prospect's life? In what way is the benefit important to people's priorities? Why in the world should the prospect believe anything you say? These are the questions that a sound strategic support answers. As a marketer, you are offering something for sale that is theoretically helpful to the consumer, except that consumers do not fork over their trust as easily as in the past.

The support is what it sounds like, a reinforcement of the brand promise or benefit, a product-based or emotional or psychological reason why that benefit should be meaningful in the prospect's life. The same categories of information and attitude can be tapped for the support as are available for the benefit. In other words, the support may be explicit, implied, rational, emotional, ephemeral, animal, or mineral; the only common characteristic is that the positioning is better off with support included, however that might be communicated.

Also, keep in mind that product or service "news" can be a crucial part of a positioning's support. We tend to think of new flavors or new services as tactical enhancements to the brand, but they can also be integrated into the fundamental positioning. The rise of "business class" in airlines' offerings in the past ten years not only widened their product offering, it also expanded the pampering aspects of their service positionings. The addition of bleach to several detergents' formulations did the same thing in that it helped them reinforce their whitening performance positionings.

Envisioning the Personality—The personality must be just as strategic in the sense that it must appear to be a natural continuation of what the positioning represents, only from a tonal, emotional, more human perspective. As positioning options are considered, the team needs to be thinking ahead to the way in which their decisions may play out in terms of strategic personality.

Researching Worthy Alternatives—Researching positioning prompts can be difficult because the marketer must walk a fine line between testing a "pure," but sometimes bland positioning statement, and replicating the creativity that will ultimately be incorporated into finished marketing communications. The problem in the first instance is that a conservative rendering of the concept can fail to create enough interest among respondents to get useful feedback. In the other case, highly creative stimuli run the risk of skewing the results because one candidate is executed more dramatically than another (see Exhibit 4-6 for a re-cap of pros and cons of various positioning research methodol-ogies).

Keeping the Faith—Positioning work is often the focus of at-tention for a brief time, then set aside and forgotten. One way to avoid that mistake is to appoint a "keeper of the positioning" for the brand team, someone who becomes a walking reminder of what the brand is supposed to stand for in the life of the customer. This person can link up with a counterpart "keeper of the personality" (see chapter 5) and the two can work as a team

EXHIBIT 4-6

Design	Stimuli	Advantages	Disadvantages
Mall intercept interviewing	Rough ads	Projectable; good simulation of finished advert	Little opportunity for in-depth probing; may miss nuances
Focus groups	Rough ads/ storyboards	Can gauge tone of response and probe in-depth	Subject to usual group dynamics problems; storyboard not very close to finished ad
Broadscale surveying	Positioning statements with or without visual	Projectable; opportunity to test more alternatives	Little in-depth or tone probing; statements not representative of in-market stimuli
One-on-one interviewing	One or more of the stimuli listed above	Best in-depth opportunity	Expensive; not always projectable
One or more of the designs listed above	Finished marketing communications	Best combination of project-able and in-depth	Most expensive and time-consuming

Positioning research alternatives.

to shine a spotlight on the key components of the total brand identity.

That can be accomplished in any number of ways, such as a series of quotes from customers that are tacked to every available wallspace in the marketing department and in its agencies. Videotape excerpts of customer interviews can be made available for viewing at key times in the marketing planning process, or whenever the brand team needs reminding of its ideal positioning. Or, periodic focus groups or one-on-one interviews can be set up to verify or refine the desired positioning.

The way in which consumers and business-to-business prospects position and reposition a brand in their own realities sets the strategic course of that brand forever. Marketers cannot strictly control how positionings are created or evolve, but they can have the single greatest influence on them by sending the most powerful possible signals into the marketplace.

However that's accomplished, the superior brand stewards continuously refine their positioning prompts to give their brands the strongest advantage versus competition, and the strongest strategic base on which to build a compelling brand personality.

5

Humanizing the Identity

New York—Pan Am Corp.'s name and trademark blue globe, one of the world's most recognized brands, was auctioned for $1.325 million yesterday to a Maryland investment group. Rather than use the fabled name to start a new airline, Eclipse Holdings Inc. of Rockville, Md., hopes to charge other airlines to use Pan Am's logo. . . . "Maybe we'll even have Pan Am T-shirts," said David Lockwood, president of Eclipse.

—*Gannett News Service*
December 2, 1993

T-shirts. The fate of a classic brand. An airline with a legendary past and personality that exemplified America's global reach. A brand disassembled during the ferocious fighting of the airline industry, but with an identity that will linger long after the name is sold and re-sold. A fading memory, and the symbol of what can happen when a brand loses its power in the marketplace, only to die ignominiously in bankruptcy court.

What died that day was the Pan Am brand, but what will be missed is Pan Am's personality. The airline that once ruled the Western skies had a pride and confidence you could see in its airplanes and its people. It was a brand people depended on to

150

carry the mail and to carry their loved ones. And it seemed right, somehow, that there should be an enormous building squarely in the middle of Manhattan that bore its name. Its profits and losses, logo and advertising slogans, even its brand positioning, have been long forgotten. But those who still remember Pan Am remember the personality it bore.

The Strategic Personality: The Human Side of the Identity

The personality of a likable person disarms your defenses. You learn new information about that person differently than you might otherwise. You're more willing to overlook flaws and more likely to search for strengths. They say that "love is blind" because when two people are extremely attracted to one another there is a personality match (among other things) that overwhelms all the senses, sometimes including common sense.

In matters of branding, a personality helps to humanize an otherwise inanimate object or service so that a prospect's defenses are lowered. An attractive personality can presell the prospect before the purchase, reinforce the purchase decision, and help forge an emotional link that binds the buyer to the brand for years to come.

A distinguishing personality can offer the single most important reason why one brand will be chosen over another, particularly as the product and service features of competing brands grow more similar. The personality gives the consumer something to relate to that can be more vivid than the perceived positioning, more alive than the physical attributes of the product, more complete than whatever is conveyed by the brand name alone. It can be the difference that tips the consumer toward trial, or the one factor that subconsciously binds the user to the brand and prevents switching to a competitor.

The personality is, in some ways, much more real than the other aspects of a brand because it is the outstretched hand that touches the customer as an individual. That's why it's typically described as what a brand would be if it were a human being.

The personality is the rendering of the brand in reference points that we also use to describe one another. Because true brands have a life of their own as they play a role in our lives, it's a brand's personality that defines the outline of that life. When a consumer thinks of a brand as located in a certain place in their constellation of choices, the brand has been seeded, but it may not have been linked emotionally to its prospects. The element that makes the brand come alive, that bestows it with human features that make it more accessible and more touchable, is the brand personality.

How a brand's personality is perceived depends as much on who the receiver is as what kind of signals are being sent from the brand. The personality cultivated for Wrigley's gum, for instance, epitomizes wholesomeness. The twins who periodically represent Doublemint could not be more virginal. The smokers who need a break from nicotine are as prodigal children. For believers in the old values, Wrigley's is what America used to be like (and, God willing) will be like once again. Wrigley has branded its brand with a distinctive, clear personality.

A brand's personality is closely associated with its "image." Consultant and researcher Alexander Biel believes that image types can be divided into three types: the image of the "provider" of the product and service (either a brand or a company), the image of the user, and the image of the product and service itself.[1] Each brand capitalizes upon one or more of these components.

Provider-driven images tend to be services because there is a greater need to build confidence in the provider when there is less of a tangible product to sell. Brands that lean most heavily on the provider image include insurance companies, such as Travelers we'll-shelter-you umbrella, or the long-running "You're in Good Hands with Allstate" campaign. These brands are positioned as the trustworthy provider, and their brand personalities reflect that same paternal attitude. The provider's reassurances also play a major role in the personalities of General Motors' Mr. Goodwrench brand and the Midas brand. In both cases, mechanics symbolize the trusting personality the brands are hoping to communicate, particularly to the increasing number of female car owners who fear being ripped off by repairmen who prey on the mechanically challenged (see Exhibit 5-1 for an example of Midas's advertising).

Personalities that focus on the image of a service user are often attempting to link the brand with the existing or aspired-to personality of that user. Club Med, for example, initially built its business by creating a positioning and personality that looked tantalizing to young singles. While its advertising touted Club Med properties as great getaways ("The Antidote to Civiliza-

EXHIBIT 5-1

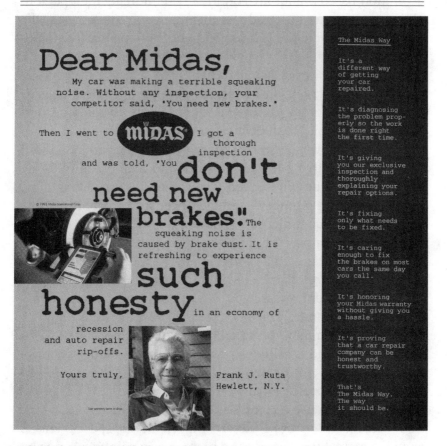

Midas advertising uses customer testimonials to reinforce its trustworthy personality.

Reprinted with permission of Midas International Corporation.

tion"), the party atmosphere at the resorts themselves created an "underground" personality that also communicated that Club Meds were the place to go to meet the perfect stranger.

More recently, the company has sought to change its identity to more of a family vacation place offering opportunities to learn about the world around you and have fun at the same time. This is both a positioning and personality change for Club Med in order to expand its appeal, and to steer clear of the "party place" reputation that's less appealing in a time calling for social responsibility and safe sex.

Chanel, Jenny Craig, Weight Watchers, The Gap, and other aspiration-based brands are continually reinforcing their personalities as much as the products themselves. In these cases, the user-driven personality is believed to be more persuasive to potential users because few consumers are completely content with who they are, or what they look like.

Product/service-oriented personalities often include a considerably less glamorous group of brands. Clorox, Lysol, Tide, and Kraft, for example, base their personalities on the product and the product delivery. Some of these personalities are enhanced with characters that add more texture and memorability to the brand, such as the Jolly Green Giant, the Pillsbury Doughboy, the Liquid Plumr plumbers, and the Cheer spokesnebbish. These appeals tend to be utilitarian in nature in the belief that a brand personality is supposed to focus on the product.

Appliance brands, also counted among the less exciting personality types, are often believed to have commodity-like identities. Yet, in recent research by Whirlpool Corporation, the major appliance brands Whirlpool and KitchenAid were found to have definite feminine personalities. The Whirlpool brand was seen as gentle and sensitive, as personified by a modern family-oriented woman (see Exhibit 5-2), while KitchenAid was viewed as a competent professional woman.

Some brands use a combination of personality components. The Oldsmobile Aurora advertising (with its special effects showing carmaking in space and highways in paintings) appears to be focusing on the product, but the brand is also sending clear signals about the kind of person who should be driving it. KFC

EXHIBIT 5-2

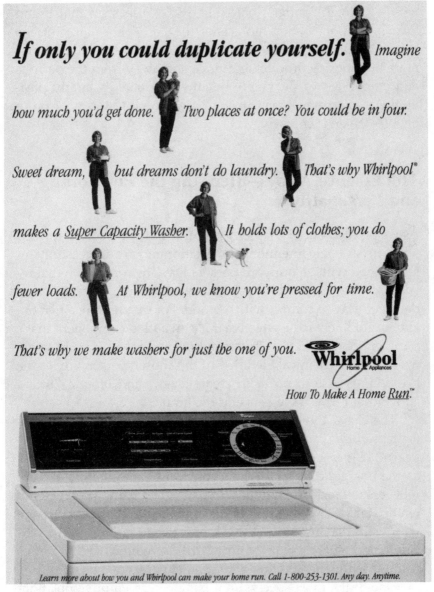

Whirlpool's print advertising reflects its personality as a gentle, sensitive brand for family-oriented women.

This ad is supplied with permission from Whirlpool Corporation.

dabbled with using more user-oriented advertising (that is, the townspeople of Lake Edna), but ultimately returned to the womb with a Colonel Sanders look-alike who, at least in that brand team's opinion, better represents the core personality of the brand. McDonald's value programs in recent years have shifted more attention to product and price and away from the patrons and employees of the chain, but the McDonald's family positioning would never permit the brand to stray too far from a people-driven identity.

The Essence Alloy—Blending the Positioning and Personality

As we pointed out in chapter 1, a brand's identity core is formed when its strategic intentions (its positioning) are successfully intermingled with an outward personality. The concoction that results can be the single most important reason why prospects decide to stay in contact with a brand. For that reason, a personality is not likely to be effective if it's an added component that's hung on a brand like a Christmas tree ornament. Instead, there needs to be a chemical blending of the chosen personality to the positioning base in order to create a new and unique "brand alloy" that forms the essence of the brand.

The closer the brand personality can be related to the strategic premise of a brand, the more consistent the brand will appear to its prospects. For example, Nuprin has been positioned as the analgesic to take when you want the toughest of pain relievers to tackle the toughest of pains. The brand used veteran tennis star Jimmy Connors to make it clear that anyone his age who's still playing competitive tennis needs serious pain medicine. The "Nuke It with Nuprin" theme reinforces the brand's result-oriented positioning and parallel personality.

One of the most successful mixings of preemptive positioning and personality came together for Motel 6. The self-proclaimed "largest chain of company-operated economy motels in the U.S.," was founded in 1962. After enjoying some early success, the chain's occupancy rates began slipping rapidly during the 1980s. The Richards Group ad agency was hired and convinced management to make modest changes to increase its appeal, including phones in every room and free movies. In 1986, the chain began their famous down-home network radio campaign, using as its spokesman Tom Bodett, a folksy former National Public Radio commentator. Motel 6 sent out positioning prompts that helped redefine itself as the ultimate in lower-priced value, and Bodett's own personality meshed beautifully with the positioning.

Motel 6's radio advertising is extremely consistent from spot to spot, always starting with the sounds of a fiddle and Bodett's "Hi, I'm Tom Bodett for Motel 6," and always closing with "We'll leave the light on for you." They're now attempting to translate their brand's personality into TV with extremely low-key, blank-screen ads that reflect the smart sparseness of the chain as a whole. Importantly, their spending support of the brand has also been consistent, starting in the $8 million range in 1985 and growing to an estimated $15 million in 1994.

The result has been one of the most successful repositionings and personality creations in the history of the hospitality industry. Motel 6 has grown to more than 760 motels in all 48 contiguous states in the United States, the perfect example of what can be accomplished with a seamless melding of strong positioning, personality, and execution. That's how formidable identities are built.

The Link to the Prospect

Most people know how to interact with other people, but they are less sure about how to interact with things. A brand's personality can also be the facilitator of communication between consumer and brand, the link through which a relationship evolves. If a brand is positioned in someone's mind as the least-fattening snack, a prospect may decide to buy it for purely dietary reasons. If that same brand also has a personality that conveys a party-like atmosphere, then it has increased its chances of further maintaining a relationship with its user because people are more likely to stay with a diet brand that's both nonfattening *and* fun, even if "fun" isn't a major part of how the brand is positioned.

Diet soft drinks make good use of this personality approach by showing slim drinkers (positioning prompt), who seek good taste (positioning prompt), and who are power partiers that know how to have a good time (personality prompt). Of course, the party-goer prompts can also be part of the positioning if the brand team believes it should be a more fundamental part of the selling messages.

Positioning prompts alone may not be enough to create trial and repurchase of a brand. The Chrysler brands struggled for years in the 1960s and 1970s when their car designs and their accompanying brand personalities paled in comparison to their more aggressive GM and Ford competition. Over the years, some Chrysler models and brands have created some personality excitement in the marketplace, such as the Dodge Duster in the 1960s, the Dodge Charger in the 1970s, the Dodge/Plymouth minivans in the 1980s, and the Dodge Ram trucks and Plymouth Neon in the 1990s. Another personality triumph saved the corporation from collapse in the 1980s, only this time the personality cult grew up around its chairman and savior, Lee Iacocca. Iacocca's own forceful personality helped add much needed charisma to the company's dependable, but yeoman-like Chrysler "K" cars.

Some important personality points can also be scored by using what might appear to be positioning prompts. The Downy fabric softener bottle has tumbled into soft towels for decades as a reminder of what Downy does, but also of what Downy *is*—a friendly brand associated with making your family feel warm and cuddly. Joy dishwashing liquid cleans dishes so they are "a nice reflection on you," meaning, as a "close friend" that understands how important it is for you to look good to your family and guests. Folgers Crystals was shown being served at all the best restaurants, not just to prove that it was of restaurant quality, but also to prove that you were safe to "be seen with it" (serve it), no matter who might be drinking your coffee. These brands proved that something as functional as a product demo may be very effective in communicating a brand's emotion-based personality.

How Important Is It to Have a Personality?

The frenetic world we live in forces us to organize what we see or risk information overload. Far too many sights, sounds, images, and ideas bombard us daily for us to take them all in. Jack Trout and Al Ries cited that observation more than twenty years ago as the reason why consumers are forced to organize brands in their minds. Today, it's an even more formidable problem for individuals to arrange commercial clutter and brand proliferation into some understandable order. Brand personalities help them do that efficiently.

We think of a friend or a relative or a colleague as belonging in a certain "place" in our lives that represents how we have positioned that person relative to where we and others are. Each person we have met has a distinct personality that further aids us in classifying him or her, and in rank ordering how important we will allow them to be in our lives. These personalities provide the connectedness that suggests how we should feel toward them emotionally.

Without personalities, the important people in our lives might be no different than the bus driver we never meet but on whose bus we ride every morning. They would have a role, but they would not be approachable and, therefore, essentially would be unknowable. As long as brands are without a personality in our eyes, it's more difficult for them to establish a relationship with us.

Brand personalities may also represent a brand's best shot at differentiation. In categories where brand positionings are similar, personalities give brands a fighting chance to carve out a niche in the consumer's mind.

In the insanely competitive beverage industry, for instance, Dr. Pepper/Seven-Up Companies is in the brand personality business. Creating differentiating personalities is how they market. For close to 30 years, the Seven-Up brand has merchandised its brilliant "Uncola" identity as a personality nonconformer. Most recently, the brand has made good use of its counter-personality and built strong share levels as Americans increasingly look beyond colas for refreshment. With its theme line, "When you want the taste of un, there's only one," Seven-Up uses its "cool spots" characters to reinforce its iconoclastic brand personality, and to send a competitive positioning prompt. A similar approach was used for their Dr. Pepper brand, most memorably with the "He's a Pepper, You're a Pepper. . ." campaign a few years back. These personalities are helping to keep Seven-Up and Dr. Pepper alive and well on the soft drink battlefield.

A brand's personality is the emotional part of what has been called the "brand experience," the entire set of actions and feelings that surround experience with brands. The minidramas about "Tony and Sharon," the neighbor-couple in the Taster's Choice advertising, are also surrounding the brand with a romantic cachet that it simply couldn't have conjured up with positioning prompts alone. Another brand storytelling series was launched in September 1994 involving "Grammercy Press," a small publishing house that undergoes a transformation with the technological help of MCI. In both the Taster's Choice and MCI cases, the viewer gets a solid feel for the context in which the brand operates. Seeing the brand's environment played out through the story characters' lives helps create a bridge between brand and prospect.

The U.S. Postal Service conveys emotions like enthusiasm and dedication through its "We'll Deliver for You" campaign. Pillsbury communicates its homespun goodness through the one-second giggle of the Doughboy. Even the dialogue-free Corona beer commercials send clear emotional messages about the beer and the kind of people who are supposed to be attracted to its laid-back personality.

A brand's personality can be the strongest single emotional hook that snags the interest of a prospect and sustains the regular usage of a convert, something that positionings alone can rarely accomplish.

Establishing a brand relationship sometimes involves relating the brand personality to the personality of the user. Brut aftershave is not just masculine, it's a way to feel more masculine than you already are, and to feel that way every morning. Starter and Russell brands of athletic wear have built large businesses by inducing customers to wear their favorite pro or college team's logos on clothing that connects wearers with the personalities of the teams they love. Every major magazine from *Scientific American* to The *New Yorker* has a specific brand personality that it attempts to project onto potential readers. You may read your *Scientific American* partly because you're proud that you can understand the technical articles, and partly because you want others to know that you understand technical articles. Likewise, you may flaunt your *New Yorker* because it says something about your sophistication.

Is it mandatory for a brand to have a highly visible or dominant personality? Absolutely not. If you scan a list of the top 100 brands in this country you will see that there are brands in virtually all categories that have very few discernible personality traits, or their personalities are so subtle that they are known only to their core users. Tetley Tea is the third largest tea brand in the United States, but how many consumers could describe its brand personality? Northwest Airlines is one of the largest and most successful carriers in the world, but its personality seems less clear than United's or Amercan's.

A strong, identifiable personality is not an imperative, but it can make it easier for customers and prospects alike to understand what the marketer has to offer. Even more important, a brand with a clear and distinctive personality presents the would-be buyer with something he or she can relate to as an individual, and that's getting to be a prerequisite for success in our increasingly individual-driven marketplace.

Personifying the Brand

One of the more typical questions to ask focus group respondents these days is: "Who would this brand be if it were human?" There's a reason why that question has become a research cliche; it can yield some valuable consumer truths because it encourages consumers literally to think about a brand on their own terms.

During the last decade, Visa has consistently gained share (now at about 46 percent) and expanded its card base from 93 million in 1985 to well over 150 million as of this writing. In 1994, Visa elected to stay with its "Everywhere you want to be" campaign, and who can blame them after hanging up numbers like those?

Nevertheless, the Visa brand does run some risk that their bon vivant personality may not be ideally suited to the more practical 1990s. The brand's campaign contrasts markedly with MasterCard's more down-to-earth "Smart Money" program launched in 1993. MasterCard has seen strong share gains in recent years, much of them due to their successful co-branding efforts, but their personality renovation probably also deserves some credit.

Reportedly in response to MasterCard's restaging, Visa has begun to weave more executions into their commercial pools that show less glamorous card usage situations. Exhibit 5-3 hypothesizes about the brand personifications of the Visa credit card, based on its "We're everywhere you want to be" imagery, and MasterCard, based on its "Smart Money" campaign. Exhibit 5-4 shows one of the ads in MasterCard's campaign.

Another common way to dimensionalize the personality of a brand is by combining human and nonhuman imagery. What, researchers have asked, would this or that brand be if it were a car? an animal? a celebrity? or a movie? These items carry personalities of their own, placed there by us humans, who have a

EXHIBIT 5-3

Visa	MasterCard
Higher income, impulsive purchaser, adventurous, enjoys life's luxuries, confident, lots of friends, takes care to look attractive, world traveler	Middle income, a careful planner of purchases, cautiously optimistic about economy, family-oriented, interested in substance over style

Projected brand personifications.

It's Not A Personality. *It's A Tool.*

A credit card has nothing to do with what kind of person

you are. What it has to do with is how easy it is for you to

deal with things. So if you want a machete to hack through

the jungle of daily life, get a MasterCard. No card is

more accepted on   the planet. You can use it to get

cash all over   the world. And our monthly

statement   is a really smart way to keep track

of all your spending. But hey, it still won't make you any

more witty or charming than you already are. *MasterCard.*

It's more than a credit card. It's smart money. MasterCard

© 1994 MasterCard International Incorporated

A MasterCard print ad that demonstrates its brand's personality by
denying the importance of personality.
© 1995 MasterCard Intl, Inc. Used with permission.

curious habit of anthropomorphizing at the drop of a hat. Using the Visa and MasterCard examples once again, Exhibit 5-5 suggests how those two brands project human and nonhuman profiles which can be useful in developing marketing strategies.

Person-to-Brand Relationships

One measure of a brand-customer relationship is pride. This is the "badge" or "necktie" value of a brand, related to the phenomenon once called "conspicuous consumption," the purchase of a product or service primarily so that its associations would reflect positively on the user. Cadillac cars and Omega watches used to epitomize this attitude everywhere in America, and still do in certain regions. In other parts of the country, Mercedes cars, Rolex watches, Bally shoes, Armani clothing, and just about anything that comes in Tiffany's little blue box may have more of an impact on the ego scale.

These brands, and the personalities associated with them, communicate that their users have the money and the discriminating taste to buy products and services that others are supposed to lust after. The badge value of a brand is about aligning one's self with an enviable brand personality, just as someone

EXHIBIT 5-5

Category	Visa	MasterCard
Cars	BMW, Lexus, Cadillac	Taurus, Honda, Ford Explorer
Celebrities	Sharon Stone, Cindy Crawford	Tom Hanks, Walter Matthau
Animals	Jaguar, thoroughbred horse, Persian cat	Fox, work horse, golden retriever
Architecture	Tudor, Georgian	Cape Cod, California ranch
Travel Destinations	London, Paris, Aspen	Yosemite, Washington, D.C., Orlando

Projected brand associations.

might hope to do by attending a party with an attractive or witty companion.

Even brands using mass communications send relationship signals to us; we respond by trying or rejecting the product or service. If we buy it, we are opening the door to a possible relationship. If the brand's strategic personality does its job, it doesn't just sit there, it empowers us, or relieves us, or uplifts us, or sympathizes with us. Depending on the category and the power of the brand's personality, it can provide us with certain feedback.

Researcher Max Blackston of Research International has been one of several to investigate the concept of brand relationships. He has written: "Like a relationship with another person, everything we need to know about the brand relationship is going on inside the consumer's head. Thus, the real question we need to ask is, 'What do the consumers think that the brand thinks of them?' "[2] An intriguing thought that takes the concept of a "living brand" and turns it around on the marketer.

Some forms of brand relationship exist everywhere you look and they are often laden with emotion. Our cars, for instance, are much more than just transportation, they're one end of a two-way relationship that's been called "America's love affair with the automobile." The particular kind of "love" we have for our car is greatly influenced by the personality of the brand. A Ford Aerostar has a completely different personality than a Jeep Cherokee, yet both primarily are used to carry families around suburbia. A key personality difference in the two brands is the latent four-wheel drive "animal" inside the Cherokee suburban persona that can be unleashed any time the family wants to climb a 30-degree slope on vacation in the mountains. The allure of the Cherokee personality attracted Chevy to the category with its Blazer series, and prompted Ford to create the most successful 4x4 of them all, the Explorer.

Brand Charisma: God-Given or Man-Made?

A few people have charisma, most don't. FDR had it. So did John Kennedy and Ronald Reagan. Not so Jimmy Carter or George

COMPARING THE PERSONALITY OF THREE LONG-DISTANCE BRANDS

Who would have guessed that a once commodity-like category such as long-distance telephone service would have spawned one of the wildest brand shootouts this side of Visa and American Express? They are definitely a study in personality contrasts, these three long lines brands called AT&T, MCI, and Sprint.

AT&T, of course, put long distance on the marketing map with its classic "Reach Out and Touch Someone" campaign, imbuing a poignancy to those moments when two people have an intimate, but physically distant relationship. That was meant to be a category sale, and it worked: long-distance usage rose sharply. It also gave an entrepreneur named William G. McGowan an idea that eventually became MCI, a major alternative source of long-distance service for those who were willing to leave the security of AT&T in order to save money on their long-distance bills. In other words, many American consumers bought into the AT&T brand's premise, but began wondering aloud if they had to buy into its pricing as well.

MCI spent 20 years slowly growing its business segments, then rallied their consumer side in 1991 when the company introduced "Friends & Family," a bold discounting promotion that became the first real sub-brand in the category. They followed with "Friends of the Firm" in 1992, the small-business version of the same promotion, and "Best Friends," rolled out in December 1993.

What MCI has achieved in recent years is much more than a successful positioning; they have created a long-term brand personality based on their major rival's potential Achilles heel, namely, that AT&T is a big company that could come off as caring very little for the little guy. While AT&T has been shackled with the 500-pound gorilla persona, MCI has talked "friends." In short, MCI engineered a full reversal from the days when it was AT&T that had stood for person-to-person emotion. Now, it is MCI that is "reaching out" and helping their customers to touch someone.

Another important part of MCI's winning personality is reflected in the energy and commitment of their employees. As many as 50 commercials a year have been created to support MCI's promotions, often using employees to underline the customer-service orientation of the company. The employees put a face on the company, something AT&T has had a more difficult time establishing.

Eventually, AT&T countered MCI with their "i" Plan, which sought to customize service to fit the needs of the individual customer. The "i" Plan suffered from vagueness and too much complexity as a promotional concept, according to PreTesting Company, which tested the "i" Plan ads among 400 consumers. A new marketing head and new ad agency were hired and the company moved on to another series of campaigns in the hope of regaining momentum. During this trying period, the lack of continuity and uneven attempts at rehumanizing the AT&T personality clearly hurt its ability to defend against share attacks by MCI.

Meanwhile, back in Kansas City, Sprint was hoping to benefit from the leaders' battles, while also taking advantage of the category growth stimulated by the war. Sprint took the high ground with the help of the classy Candice Bergen. She has brought a strong balance of humor and attitude to the fray, helping Sprint carve out a personality that's right for the times. It hasn't hurt a bit that Bergen has become a major hit in the title role of "Murphy Brown," a 1990s version of liberation and smarts who gets in just enough controversy to attract the right kind of publicity.

Sprint has also scored some points with the reintroduction of a voice-activated calling card system that provides some technological distinctiveness to the brand. It's "dropping pin" mnemonic has been emblematic of its original positioning as a technologically superior alternative to the other carriers.

As of this writing, AT&T has made some strong strides with its "True Savings" programs, and its Consumer Communications Division won the Baldrige Award for superior business practices. Estimates place the company's share of the $75 billion industry at over 60 percent, but that's a loss of six share points in recent years, compared to a four-point gain for MCI, reportedly at over 20 percent and gaining, with Sprint at 10 percent.

With all the shooting going on, whichever company expects to gain share had best keep a likable personality on the front lines.

Bush. Charisma is that certain something that induces supporters to close their eyes and follow by faith alone. It's what makes the same phrase uttered by two different individuals come out boring in one instance and heroic in the other. When someone with charisma walks into a room, all eyes, ears, and hearts turn in that direction. You can't see it, touch it, or smell it, but when its in the air, there's no mistaking it.

Professor Norman Smothers of California State University at Hayward has closely observed brands in the marketplace to determine if they, like people, can have charisma. Exploring such brands as Marlboro, Absolut vodka, and Nike, Smothers has made a convincing case that certain brands have extended their allure even beyond conventional personality, and have created a pervasive "brand charisma." Dr. Smothers has come to four conclusions about charisma:

- Certain brands definitely have charisma;
- Brand charisma is anchored with compelling metaphors (e.g., Nike = high status and athletic achievement);
- For charisma to be created, the very meaning of a product must be transformed (for example, a cigarette = entry into "Marlboro Country");
- Brand charisma can create extreme loyalty and motivation (e.g., Air Jordan shoes command extraordinary prices).[3]

Once established, charisma can make a significant difference in a brand's worth. Brands like Hallmark, The Gap, and Sony enjoy greater price elasticity, more enduring brand loyalty, and generate incremental unpaid publicity, all of which can contribute significantly to sales and profitability.

However, creating charisma from scratch is extremely difficult. Bartles & Jaymes wine coolers enjoyed a few years of charisma using two seemingly uncharismatic spokesmen. The original "Joe Isuzu," the apochryphal liar, brought major doses of charisma to an unknown Japanese car line. On the other hand, the Subaru car and truck brand has been trying to create charisma for years without much success.

Snapple Natural Beverages is an example of an extraordinary business triumph due in part to brand charisma. Introduced in 1980 by a health foods company in Queens, New York, the brand began to catch on as the alternative to traditional soft drinks when it targeted young adults with radio advertising, especially on the controversial, but very popular Howard Stern show. The Stern connection was a turning point that helped launch the off-beat personality of the brand.

Snapple's television advertising has been even more effective. The campaign takes cameras to the homes and workplaces of Snapple fans to see if their letters that describe their passion for Snapple are really true. The advertising has some marvelous twists and turns, such as sending former New York City mayor Ed Koch out to jawbone a fan from the Midwest who had written that "Snapple is the only good thing to come out of New York."

The company has enjoyed a meteoric rise, with revenues at $24 million in 1989 and $516 million in 1993. In late 1994, the company was purchased by Quaker for $1.7 billion, despite recent earnings declines. It will be interesting to see if the Snapple brand can maintain its distinctive personality and charisma under the auspices of its new owner, which also markets the highly successful Gatorade brand.

Charisma is a sort of hyper-personality. Brands with charisma have a magnified focus to their personalities that pulls in and holds users. The QVC on-air shopping experience is an example of a brand that has charisma, and its real power of attraction is probably best understood by those who have become hooked by its mesmerizing sales pitches. The Apple PowerBook also developed a certain charisma almost as soon as it was introduced. With its advanced design and Apple parentage, the product took off out of the gate and has continued to sell well in a burgeoning new category. Apple felt confident enough about the charisma of its sub-brand in 1994 that it ran outdoor posters with no visual and only one word: "PowerBook."

The obvious "it" brands, the ones that overpower their categories and attract broad audience attention, often have trouble controlling their own potency. Snapple was forced to prune some of its 59 flavors because demand outstripped capacity. A similar problem occured with SnackWell's cookies. At its peak, Domino's had so many orders that it could not meet its self-imposed 30-minute delivery hurdle, in a few cases causing tragic accidents that wreaked havoc on the chain's brand identity.

The Permanence of Personality

While a positioning may evolve, a brand's strategic personality often must remain steady in order to present a consistent persona to the consuming public, just as our personalities as human beings tend to remain the same once fully formed. In his book, *Romancing the Brand*, David Martin, the celebrated founder of the Martin Agency in Richmond, Virginia, says: "Great brands are built over a long period of time with advertising that is faithful to product personality. . . . Brand personality is permanent. Lose it and lose the franchise."[4]

Wendy's, Lexus, Quaker cereals, CBS News, Bloomingdale's, Visa credit cards, Safeway, Alaska Airlines, Alamo Rent a Car, *Time* magazine, Vicks Nyquil, Hidden Valley Ranch salad dressings—all have established personalities that have not changed for years and are not likely to change any time soon.

Campbell's, on the other hand, evolved their positioning. Moving from their "Soup is good food" strategy to "Never underestimate the power of soup," Campbell's became more aggressive in their statement of soup's nutritional value, and they began to change the tone of their personality from nurturing to more active and contemporary. The brand has been able to accomplish that with no loss in continuity because it had laid such a strong foundation of nutrition that a tonal change did not cause disruption in the identity that had been solidified decades ago.

Häagen-Dazs ice cream brand was created to epitomize indulgence. The high-fat brand flourished in the "anything goes" moods of the 1980s, and captured the lead of the superpremium category, which has since come to represent $300 million in retail sales. But when the more reserved, socially conscious themes of the 1990s came to town, Häagen-Dazs found itself hotly pursued by the growing Ben & Jerry's brand.

In response, Häagen-Dazs maintained its indulgent positioning and personality prompts, but applied them to lower-fat products such as frozen yogurt and sorbets. Importantly, the brand's worldwide advertising continued to emphasize "intense" flavors, punctuated with a theme line, "Dedicated to Pleasure." In short, they stayed with what got them to the top, but with a 1990s product twist.

Maintaining continuity in a strategic personality offers a brand a number of critical advantages: First, a stable personality provides a brand with a visible "center" toward which present and future customers can be drawn. Put another way, how can a brand or a person expect to be liked if what is supposed to be likable keeps changing? That is the dilemma of the automobile companies that must update models to help them stay fresh in the public's eyes, but without losing the magic of the brand personality that made them successful in the first place. (Entertainers face the same challenge throughout their careers. The personality that made them famous must evolve without losing its initial appeal.)

Similarly, a stable brand personality is better able to sustain brand loyalty even when product and service evolutions must be made. If I have known and liked my bank, or a particular clothing store chain, or my favorite brand of yogurt, then I have probably grown comfortable with their brand personalities in addition to appreciating their product or service performance. If, over the course of years, my bank changes its branch location, or my store drastically changes its decor, or my favorite brand of yogurt is discontinued by my favorite supermarket, part of what kept me loyal to those brands has been replaced. I am a prospect "in play"; that is, I am vulnerable to competitive poaching *unless* I am so attracted to the brand's personality and decide to transfer that loyalty to another branch, another store location that has not been redecorated, or another style of yogurt that is stocked at my store.

Finally, to maintain a consistent personality is to feed focus to a company's own brand ambassadors. People who are given a distinct brand persona to help grow and keep alive, are on a mission, not just on a job. Saturn's workers traveled to Spring Hill, Tennessee, to help create a new brand identity, in the form of a new car with a unique personality. From all reports, the personality of the Saturn brand is still pulling in car shoppers, even though the product itself is in need of updating.

Where Do Brand Personalities Come From?

You could argue that brand personalities should be the product of careful analysis and logical thought since the personality is the strategic extension of the brand's positioning. The fact is that brand personalities are, almost by definition, more emotion- than logic-driven because they reflect the feelings people have about brands, and the way those brands transmit feelings back to them.

Personalities can emerge from all corners of a brand work area. The Apple Macintosh "computer for the rest of us" personality—and positioning—was as much an end-product of the original Steven Jobs work team as the hardware itself. So was the original Mustang personality that was born within a similar skunk works setting at Ford, run by Ford Division's young president, Lee Iacocca in 1963. Federal Express started as an idea in Fred Smith's college term paper and ended up as a multibillion dollar business, but its brand personality was largely established in its early years through its very funny introductory advertising.

In more mundane packaged goods categories, brand personalities may emanate from the product performance itself. The Lysol brand personality has something to do with obsessive hygiene, a perfect choice for a line of household cleaning products.

Huggies are known for their dryness protection, but also for their sensitivity to the anxieties of new mothers. Listerine and Scope both draw their personalities from their product form, and from their mutual feistiness in battling their rival.

Personalities can also be derived from the people who sponsor the message. United Airlines recast their personality when employees bought out the airline in 1994. Within 24 hours of the buyout, huge four-color posters of smiling owner/employees were seen in airports from San Francisco to New York, reading: "Welcome to OUR friendly skies." The United changeover instantly projected a new kind of brand personality, more human and more empathetic with customers because the companies' owners were no longer distant managers, but ordinary folk like the customers themselves.

A brand's users can also be a source of personality. American Express's "Membership Has Its Privileges" print campaign, gorgeously shot by Annie Leibovitz, was an example of a brand personality being defined by its users through the artistry of a brilliant photographer. The Gap, The Limited, Banana Republic, Sharper Image, and Gymboree are retail brands that frequently use their patrons as human projectors of their brand personalities.

Brand Personality from Brand Spokesperson

In borrowing someone else's name to serve as the brand flag, the theory is that the personality traits of a spokesperson will spill over onto the brand. Back in 1992, however, Research Systems Corporation revealed that it had studied more than 5,000 commercials and concluded that celebrities neither help nor hurt a message. If a brand has something relevant and exciting to say, a celebrity may help spotlight that advantage. But, if a brand is not able to distinguish its message from its competition, a celebrity won't help the cause.[5]

Another study by Wagner A. Kamakura and Jagdish Agrawal, two marketing researchers from the University of Pittsburgh and California State University at Hayward, respectively, concluded that the use of celebrity endorsements can improve the stock performance of the host company, at least to some degree. Their research surveyed a 12-year span of advertising including companies and endorsers such as Bristol-Myers Squibb (using Joe Montana), Gillette (Marvin Hagler), and American Express (Paul Newman).

Brand personalities can also emerge from the founders of the brands, such as Jenny Craig, who personifies her diet center brand, or Ben & Jerry, Jimmy Dean, and Paul Newman, each of whom overtly or subtly personify their brands and their brands' personalities. Yet, having a famous founder does not necessarily guarantee success. Witness Phyllis George's Chicken by George, Sinatra's spaghetti sauce, Tommy Lasorda's spaghetti sauce, and Lee Iacocca's Villa Nicola olive oil, all of which failed to live up to expectations.

Unfortunately, Murphy's law can often apply to the use of personalities. No matter how well the use of a personality is planned out, the unforeseen can crop up. Sponsors who hired Michael Jackson, Burt Reynolds, Madonna, and O.J. Simpson have had to scramble to disassociate themselves from those stars when their personal lives suddenly turned controversial.

Nevertheless, some of the better known attempts at using celebrities or other spokespersons have worked out very well, adding significant credibility to the personality of the sponsoring brand. For example:

■ *Dean Witter*—A real man brought back in character form to talk about the founding principles of the company. The brand's television campaign uses film that's been made to look as if it was shot in the 1930s (see Exhibit 5-6). It's an effective way to talk about the guiding vision of a firm, particularly when the vision is in sync with the 1990s emphasis on individuality ("We Measure Success One Investor at a Time").

■ *Nike*—Nike seems to be able to rotate lead spokespersons and not lose much continuity. First there was Bo Jackson when that remarkable athlete's abilities gave rise to the "Bo Knows" campaign. When Jackson's hip problems caused a decline on the field, Michael Jordan's "Air Jordan" carried the ball. When Jor-

EXHIBIT 5-6

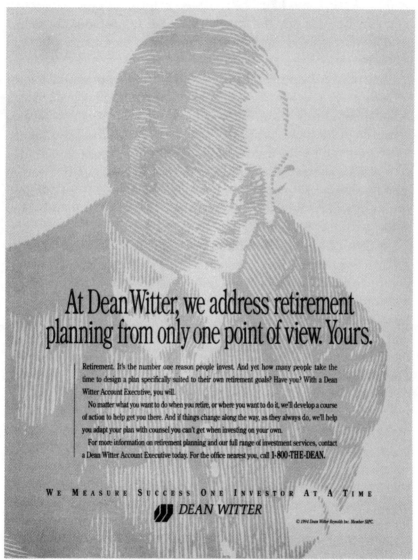

The Dean Witter brokerage uses its founder in character form to solidify its brand identity.

Used with permission. © 1995 Dean Witter Reynolds, Inc.

dan retired (at least from basketball, at least for now), Charles Barkley was showcased, this time as a sort of antihero. Barkley will soon retire and likely be replaced in the spotlight by baseball phenom Ken Griffey, Jr. Nike's "Just Do It" personality seems flexible enough to draw on any number of superstars. As long as they're superhuman, that is.

Starting in late 1993, Nike added a provocative new "star" to its lineup, a spokesman unlike anyone who had ever held a Nike shoe. On-the-edge actor Dennis Hopper portrays several semipsychotic types who take sports dementia to new levels. Observers can't quite agree about whether Hopper is a good idea or a quirky aberration. Who knows, maybe he'll come to represent the insane side of sports freaks everywhere. Then the only question will be how long will fans want to stare at their insane side.

■ *Depend*—A tough product to sell because it reminds its prospects of their own mortality. June Allyson is an inspired choice as a spokesperson. She is as contemporary as you can get for someone in her golden years. There's a definite feeling from this brand's personality of "I'm OK, you're OK," a reassurance and calm that Allyson brings to the product messages, and to the product users who suffer terrible anxiety about their incontinence.

■ *Wesson Oil*—There are not many categories more pedestrian than cooking oil, but Wesson has discovered that excitement isn't nearly as important as sincerity. Florence Henderson became Wesson's spokesperson in 1976 and the former *Brady Bunch* mom has provided the kind of continuity and credibility that Wesson has needed to outdistance the better-known Crisco brand. Year after year, Henderson has helped Wesson maintain its lead in the category despite the brand being significantly outspent by its Procter & Gamble competitor.

■ *Weight Watchers*—For years, the weight management marketers have used celebrity endorsers who miraculously kept the pounds off. Now Weight Watchers has found a heavyweight who may be one of the biggest winners of them all. Kathleen Sullivan, former ABC and CBS newsperson, has shared her personal struggles with America, including her loss of job and spouse, as a real-life calorie craver who will always fight the battle of the bulge. Business has shot up since Sullivan's confessions have been aired, a case of a celebrity testimonial that people buy into because they can relate to the star as a human being, not just as an icon.

■ *Sprint*—Candice Bergen, *Advertising Age* magazine's 1993 spokesperson of the year, deserves every penny she gets. Bergen personifies the smart, sophisticated, slightly sarcastic attitude that has helped Sprint dig a well-protected bunker in which to duck below the murderous cross fire between MCI and AT&T. Bergen may be an important reason why Sprint has maintained enough positive awareness to hang onto the number 3 position in what might otherwise be a two-company race.

■ *Orville Redenbacher's*—When representatives from Hunt-Wesson and Ketchum Advertising first met Orville Redenbacher, they realized that their best move was to turn on the camera and get out of the way. Within 18 months of the airing of Orville's first national commercial in 1976, the brand took over leadership of the category and hasn't been seriously challenged since. Over the years, Orville has been the essence of credibility (yes, he really *did* spend 40 years in the Indiana fields perfecting popping corn hybrids). He has talked convincingly with midwestern honesty about the subject he knows more about than anyone else. If ever there was a natural spokesperson for a brand, Orville Redenbacher is the man.

■ *Wendy's*—The silver medal for credibility might go to Dave Thomas, who founded the Wendy's chain and named it after his daughter. For the past few years, Thomas has also given the Wendy's brand an irresistible personality. He's not slick or sensational, and he may not even be strategic. Yet lovable Dave, with his sheepish grin and innocent looks, has come to represent the average Joe in search of a good fast meal at a decent price, and a founder with a deep interest in quality control. People just plain like Dave, and that's half the battle in a category filled with so many claims and images that even the hamburger has gotten too complicated. Said adman Jim McKennan, who helped create the "Dave" campaign, "Dave is the brand. . . . He's the key to Fort Knox and the guards are on vacation."[6]

Exactly What *Is* the Personality of "The World's Best Brand"?

Coca-Cola was named by *Fortune* magazine in 1993 as "The World's Best Brand," and named in 1994 by *Financial World* magazine as "the world's most valuable brand." The market value of the Coca-Cola company as a whole was $4 billion in 1980 and today stands at more than $50 billion, largely due to a still-dominant U.S. presence, strong international expansion, domestic branding coups like Diet Coke, and *despite* domestic setbacks like New Coke. After absorbing body blows from arch rival Pepsi in the 1980s, Coke still sits atop the U.S. soft drink market.

In September of 1991, Coke officials shocked the advertising and marketing world when they announced that Michael Ovitz's Creative Artists Agency (CAA), known up until then primarily as a leading talent agency, had been hired as a creative consultant to supplement the work by Coke's primary ad agency, McCann-Erickson Worldwide.

Eighteen months later, Coke introduced CAA's initial campaign to the public—26 commercials, which reportedly cost over $10 million to produce. Those ads, and several more by McCann-Erickson, began running with McCann's theme line, "Always Coca-Cola." *New York Times* columnist Stuart Elliott described the campaign as "one of the most contentious in advertising. It has been castigated for a perceived lack of focus and brand-building characteristics, yet also praised for shaking up the tired traditions of Coca-Cola and soft-drink advertising."[7]

The CAA experiment had even greater implications for the Coca-Cola Company no matter who created its commercials. The brand has embarked on what might be called a "self-select" approach to brand personality in which the personality commercial that appeals most to you is the one you "select" (that is, choose to align yourself with) to represent the Coke you know.

This novel approach may very well work because it brilliantly takes what Pepsi left behind (and what they "forced" on Coke), namely the past, and idealizes it so attractively that it pulls us *backwards* in a nostalgic and yet aspirational way. The charming animation of the polar bears, the reprise of the curvy 1940s Coke bottle, the classic red-disk logo (what Coke's Sergio Zyman calls "a 360-degree trademark" aimed at all ages[8]), the simple jingle—all of these elements make us want to return to an enchanting world that existed before most of us were born.

Coca-Cola Classic has roughly a 27 percent share of the major soft drink business, compared to 22 percent for regular Pepsi. During the 1993–94 running of the "Always" campaign, Coke Classic sales rose sharply.[9] Yet Coke could be vulnerable to attack from Pepsi and the emerging noncolas if its brand identity becomes diffused.

It may be several more years before we understand the full impact of the "Always Coca-Cola" campaign and its rainbow approach to advertising execution. So far, though, what began to look like an identity risk may yet turn out to be an identity coup.

■ *Quaker Oatmeal*—There are some interesting similarities and revealing differences between Orville Redenbacher, Dave Thomas, and Wilford Brimley, the Quaker spokesman, whose career was renewed by a grandfatherly role in the hit movie *Cocoon*. All three project the same homespun identities that fit their brands, and their personalities go down easy compared to more strident pitch men. Orville Redenbacher is a dyed-in-the-wool Indiana corn breeder, and Dave Thomas knows fast food. Wilford Brimley, however, is an actor who is seen in different vehicles that could run counter to his Quaker persona (for example, his role as the law firm security chief in the movie *The Firm*).

It's the Little Things: Personality Points of Focus

Think about some of the brands over the years that have carried memorable personalities: Star-Kist tuna (Charlie the Tuna), Charmin bathroom tissue (Mr. Whipple), Old Spice (the roving sailor), Jolly Green Giant (that big green guy), Bartles & Jaymes (the odd couple), Levi's Dockers (lounging boomers), Betty Crocker (the perennial cook-mom), Prudential (the Rock of Gibraltar), The Traveler's (the umbrella). What keeps these brand personalities vivid in our memories is a point of focus, a particular person, place, or thing that opens a gateway for other associations that solidify the full brand identity.

Some of these memorable elements are prominent parts of a brand's communications, such as United Airlines' "Rhapsody in Blue" theme that is constantly being reorchestrated to keep it fresh. Or, the "Tony the Tiger" animated character that stars in every execution of the Kellogg's Frosted Flakes commercials. Others may be more subtle, such as the Hush Puppies mascot, which is a gentle reminder that there are few shoes on this earth as comfortable as Hush Puppies, just as there are few things more comfortable looking than a droopy-eyed basset hound (see Exhibit 5-7 for a summary of personality points of focus).

The personality, like most other brand components, is best communicated and made memorable by centering it on a single point of focus or on a cluster of closely related elements. If that focus is both positive and top-of-mind, the brand has a better chance of being invited into the customer's life.

The Likely Importance of Likability

A brand's personality can strongly influence whether the brand identity is accepted and appreciated by its potential constituencies. A brand's positioning establishes its credibility, but its likability is a direct function of its personality. A brand's personality can make it more attractive, or it can become a key reason for its downfall because of consumer indifference or dislike.

EXHIBIT 5-7

Brand	Personality	Past or Present Personality Points of Focus
Bartles & Jaymes	Funky, but high quality	Memorable spokespersons that gave a new kind of drink a likable personality
Levi's Jeans	Strong, durable, cool for all ages	Strong, living heritage and evocative advertising
Campbell's Soups	Like Mom: watches out for me, makes sure I eat right	Consistency of product and imagery. From "M-m-m, good," to the "Power" of soup
Dewar's Scotch	Contemporary achiever	Profiles of exceptional people who are also Dewar's drinkers
Hallmark Cards	Sensitive, empathetic, thoughtful	Consistently high-quality line of products with broad variety; warm and human advertising
UPS	Efficient, dependable, good value	Brown trucks, brown courier uniforms; shipping gifts at Christmas
Ben & Jerry's Ice Cream	Societally conscious, superior quality	Company's social philosophy as seen in packaging and publicity

Selected powerful brand personalities.

Every brand steward wants his or her brand to be thought of as a friend in need. Friends, human or brand, are more likely to be accepted if they are already liked.

How well a product performs has a definite effect on how well it is liked, and how well it is liked has a similar effect on how well it is perceived to perform. American beers can be very similar to one another in taste and appearance, which is why they relentlessly create the most likeable, unique personalities possible. Airlines are no different. Any executive road warrior will tell you that most airlines offer different color schemes and different departure sites, but the rest of their services are often a similar blend of government-regulated sameness. They, too, do whatever they can to create a likable personality that might give them an edge over nearly identical competitors.

Likability was once considered one of those brand attributes that was a little too superficial to lose sleep over. How important could it be to be likable when there are much more substantive ways to judge a brand and its communications, such as awareness, persuasiveness, product performance, or customer service? *Very* important, according to research that discovered that performance and service are frequently judged through the lens of likability.

In 1985, the Ogilvy Center conducted a study of 73 prime-time commercials for 57 products in 11 categories. The research measured the sales effectiveness of the commercials based on the persuasion procedure developed by the research firm Mapes & Ross. The researchers found that the people who liked a particular commercial were twice as likely to be persuaded by that commercial compared to those who "somewhat" liked the commercial, or felt neutral toward it.[10]

Four years later, the Advertising Research Foundation conducted its Copy Research Validity Study to determine which advertising copy research measures were most accurate in predicting sales results. Five food and health and beauty aids brands with shares of market ranging from 7 percent to 35 percent were evaluated, using in-market test methods. More than 12,000 interviews were conducted. The test commercials positively affected sales by +8 percent to +41 percent. Numerous factors were measured: recall, persuasion, attitude ratings, awareness, and liking. Of those, liking was the most accurate predictor of positive sales results.[11]

The U.S. Army is a brand that has made a remarkable comeback in likability. In the 1960s and 1970s, the reputation of all of this country's armed services suffered from the aftermath of the divisive Vietnam War. Gradually, the army regained a reputation as a viable career alternative for young people to choose when coming out of high school. With the help of a strategically focused, well-executed marketing program themed "Be All That You Can Be," the army shifted its perceived personality from that of a hard-nosed drill sergeant to a career counselor who helped young men and women achieve their full potential.

The loyal relationship between consumer and brand can sometimes be built entirely upon likability. The Disney brand may be the most skillful purveyor of likability through its entertainment parks and film releases. This is a brand that was born and bred to be childlike in its wonder and enthusiasm, and it has rarely wandered off the mark.

Another convert to the likability approach, MetLife, has spent tens of millions of dollars using Charles Schulz's "Peanuts" gang to warm up their insurance brand and make it more likable. Jell-o brand pudding has effectively used Bill Cosby as their symbol of likability, playing off of his enormous popularity among Americans of all ages. And, of course, pet food marketers have used cuddly kittens, talking dogs, dancing cats, and other "pet-o-nalities" to add likability to their sales pitches.

Likability and awareness were integral to the initial success of the Plymouth/Dodge Neon subcompact introduced in 1993. Using $80 million worth of outdoor, print, and television advertising with only a single "Hi" as it's headline, Neon was specifically not created with a pushy personality for fear of turning off skeptical Generation X'ers who supposedly are interested in simple propositions, like their parents who drove the Volkswagen bug thirty years before. Even the Japanese automakers are impressed with this brand; they're using it as a role model for future efforts in the subcompact segment.

Seven Steps toward a Strategic Personality

While it's difficult to create a brand personality using a purely rational process, there are some steps that can be taken to home in on promising directions. Developing a strategic personality should start with a review of all quantitative data and other research that might shed some light on the needs, desires, and attitudes of the audiences who will judge the brand personality.

The brand team can then review the agreed-to positioning and envision what general personality parameters best fit the

WOULD YOU INTRODUCE YOUR BRAND TO YOUR SISTER?

Do you really *like* your brand? Does your brand have a personality you are proud of? Would you want to be seen at a restaurant with your brand? Determining how likable your brand is may reveal some potential strengths or subtle flaws that could be contributing to your sales performance. Give your brand a straw-poll likability test by asking each member of the marketing team to walk through this brief drill:

- Make a list of the three people you like most in this world, and three people you could do without.
- Assign each of the six people a rating from 1 to 10, with 1 being your favorite and 10 your least favorite.
- Now, using the same rating system, rate your brand in terms of likability, as well as all competitors. List as many reasons as possible why you gave the ratings you did.
- When you've completed the exercise, share your ratings and your rationale with other members of the brand team.

For obvious reasons, your team should be the group that is most favorably disposed toward your brand. If the brand was rated by them as very likable, then something could be learned about future personality building by exploring their reasoning, and perhaps incorporating it into future quantitative research for validation. If the brand did not fare well, then some quick action may be needed. At the very least, some serious personality research among customers and prospects might be called for.

brand's strategic stance. For example, if the product is a motor oil like Castrol that's positioned to protect high-performance engines, the personality traits associated with a mild-mannered businessman are probably not going to work as well as a brand personality that's more compatible with fast cars. If the brand is Gerber baby food, a personality that is cute and cuddly might appear to fit the positioning, but might not be persuasive to mothers who take a more rational, no-nonsense attitude toward feeding their infants nutritious food. Exhibit 5-8 compares the apparent positionings and personalities of selected brands.

Above all, brand team members who are involved in the personality development process must let go of their quantitative

EXHIBIT 5-8

Brand	Apparent Positioning	Personality Traits	Comment
Isuzu Rodeo	The vehicle for the adventurous spirit	A wild man in a gray flannel suit	Good match, with little risk of over-promise, yet still competitive
Wrigley's Gum	Enjoyment for smokers who aren't able to get smoking satisfaction	Straightforward, problem solver	A novel approach that fits the times
J. C. Penney	Penney's has changed	High energy with quality tone	Tough to reconcile with Penney's heritage, but could update identity
Tums	Tums has more calcium	Serious-minded, for people with a problem	Effectively addresses women's calcium concerns
Paine Webber	PW provides its clients with advice they can use	Real-world, low key, convincing	Personality is a credible extension of the positioning

Projected brand personality/positioning matchings.

safety straps and rely on that most intangible of intangibles, intuition. Intuitive reasoning is more suited to musings about a brand personality than to the more methodical approaches that are often required to construct positioning prompts. Intuition is a much-maligned aspect of marketing planning that began falling into disfavor as the economy's woes worsened in the early 1990s and the stakes in the marketing game rose. Yet intuitive management skills are still considered to be absolutely vital to any CEO's repertoire, and the same can be said for marketing execs in search of the perfect brand personality.

In their book, *Creativity in Business*, Michael Ray and Rochelle Myers list what they see as a series of truths about the use of intuition in business, all of which also apply to the process of establishing a brand personality:

- "Intuition is a gift that must be developed," meaning that it is a skill that anyone can nurture.
- "Intuition complements reason," meaning that it is the combination of facts, interpretation and intuition that leads to the best business decisions.
- "Intuition is unemotional," meaning that it does not spring from emotional reactions, but from calculated thinking processes.
- "Intuition demands action," meaning that intuition leads to ideas that demand to be acted on immediately.
- "Intuition is mistake free," meaning that the only mistake you can make is failing to act upon your intuition.[12]

Just as important as using intuitive thinking is allowing those who are best qualified to develop a brand personality to work on their own. Though marketing is a team process, somewhere along the way the team has got to give way to individual think time and concept development. Committee decision making can be useful in building esprit de corps, but it can be a counterproductive way to create something as intuitive-driven as brand personalities.

The right brand personality may very well emerge from a new advertising campaign, or a public relations event, or some novel direct marketing ideas, any of which is often best crafted alone or by creative partners.

Whichever creative team, or marketing strategist, or intuitive manager comes up with a viable personality for the brand, the rest of the team may eventually play a role in evaluating and contributing to its development. Here are some suggestions to keep in mind when that opportunity arises:

1. *Weigh the alternatives with a single customer in mind.* Strong personalities, whether human or brand, are most effective when they touch each person as an individual. When Sega and Nintendo and LucasArts devise their video and computer games, for example, they are expecting the prospect to envision himself playing the games to higher and higher levels. Part of the personality of these brands is their connection to the individual user. Part of their success as designers depends on projecting and anticipating how individuals will experience their games.

2. *Envision the personality as extending seamlessly from the positioning.* The positioning is the base of the personality and the personality is an extension of the positioning. It's the power of synergy and synthesis, the strategic center of the brand identity interwoven with the brand's countenance. The stronger the tie between the positioning and personality, the better the chance that consumers will be hit with the full impact of both.

Marlboro is a single, unified identity. It's impossible to tell where the positioning ends and the personality begins. Grey Poupon is what its commercials appear to be—superior and proud of it. Kodak's "True Colors" campaign positioned the company's film as the ultimate in quality color reproduction. To humanize it, Kodak used a symbol of extraordinary clarity, the crystalline tones of a boy tenor, combined with the breathtaking crispness of stunning color photography. The effect was a merging of media and message that convincingly validated Kodak's brand identity as *the* expert in this particular field.

3. *Focus the personality on a core emotion.* Personalities are inextricably tied to human emotion. In the famous DeBeers diamond marketing program described in chapter 4, you could argue that the core brand emotion is love. But the giving of a

diamond by one person to another might also involve forgiveness, friendship, fulfillment, desire, pride, or simple impetuousness. Each of these emotions could be used to help shape the brand's personality, but they could also confuse the issue if they were all considered the central emotion of the personality. In the case of DeBeers, the personality appears to involve the emotions that surround an eternal bond. Otherwise described as: "Diamonds Are Forever."

4. *Make likability a high priority.* Likability is a key plank in the bridge that should be built between customer and brand. It's one of the most important lures any brand can offer. The Evereedy bunny is as likable as he is durable. Jimmy Dean is a genuinely likable sort who wouldn't steer anybody wrong, so why not buy the guy's sausage? The French-accented parrot who implores us to buy Whiskas cat food so *he* doesn't have to become cat food is—above all else—just plain likable. It's a powerful personality that succeeds in using a bird to persuade humans to buy food for a cat.

5. *Find room in the brand personality for confidence.* Confidence in a brand is important because, without it, a prospect is not likely to believe the brand's claims. No matter what you may think about the car, the Lexus advertising oozes confidence. From its "The Relentless Pursuit of Perfection" theme line to the way it caresses each feature of the automobile, the Lexus campaigns have played a significant role in the success of the brand because they have established a personality that confidently reassures once and future buyers that Lexus is among the best available.

There used to be a similar feeling of confidence in the IBM personality when everything it touched spoke of trustworthiness. The product people, the sales force, the advertising, the collateral material—all communicated that "we know what we're doing" without ever having to say the words. One of the company's more recent business-to-business campaigns ("There's Never Been a Better Time to Do Business with IBM") is attempting to regain that self-assuredness, and improving sales and profit reports are adding some momentum to their efforts. However, as hard as IBMers are working to climb back to the top of the mountain, it may be some time before America will believe that the new IBM can achieve its former juggernaut status, and the confident personality that went with it.

6. *Invest in your investment (a recurring theme).* Building a brand identity, and the personality that is a critical part of it, is like investing in the care and feeding of a child. An infant will be completely helpless and dependent on you for the first year or so, then mobility will stretch those bonds, followed by the first stage of serious personality development known, in a masterpiece of understatement, as the "terrible twos." From there, the child will grow in maturity until independence is achieved.

A brand requires the same nurturing investments in time, talent, energy, and money. As brand equity expert David Aaker has said: "One way [to be more efficient in marketing] is just to do things right the first time around. It starts with getting the identity right. If you have a brand identity that works, you're just monumentally efficient."[13]

Scan the LNA-BAR competitive media spending books and compare the share of voice of leading brands with their shares of market. You'll notice that the winners keep winning by investing and reinvesting in prudent marketing spending. Just in the past two years, brands such as Rold Gold pretzels, the Ethan Allen furniture chain, Prodigy on-line service, Campbell's Soup, Haggar slacks, Norwegian Cruise Line, Pond's skin-care line, and Snapple beverages have all attributed their major sales gains at least partly to increased marketing support.

Conversely, Bayer aspirin, a staple for decades in millions of households, has hit hard times because its stewards failed to defend their brand's identity when it came under attack from private labels and nonaspirin pain relievers. The newly introduced nonaspirin, Bayer Select, was given a budget of over $100 million, while the main brand's funding was cut by 17 percent in 1993 and 1994. The predictable happened: a significant share decline for a highly profitable brand.

A similar fate awaited Dial Corporation's Lunch Bucket line of single-serve meals. Once the darling of the convenience food aisle in the late 1980s with annual retail sales at about $50 million, Lunch Bucket eventually attracted low-priced competition.

A few years later, the brand was competing on price alone and its advertising support fell from a high of around $15 million to less than a fifth of that level. Sales today are estimated to be at about what the advertising budget was during the brand's heyday. There were certainly other complicating factors in this story, but withdrawing most of the brand's consumer support in favor of short-term profits was definitely a contributing cause of Lunch Bucket's descent.

Creativity and smarts will start you down the road toward a stronger brand, but success almost invariably comes with a price tag, particularly if the only way for your prospects to be aware that you've made the right personality moves is to *let them know* that you've made the right personality moves.

7. *Establish a "keeper of the personality" to work with the "keeper of the positioning."* There's no substitute for personal accountability when it comes to brand building. Make it clear that at least one individual from the brand team is responsible for the creation and sustenance of the strategic personality. Have that individual work hand in hand with the group's positioning guru, making sure that they both understand the importance of their roles, and that they will be held accountable for all things good and bad that fall into their areas of expertise. It's the safest way to erect an alarm system that will keep your strategic and personality framing intact, and in good maintenance.

Identifying the right personality for a brand is a tremendous challenge for the marketing team because it is the least concrete issue the team will tackle. Deciding on a brand personality objective requires that team members commit to serious discussion, intensive information reviews, and a willingness to let educated intuition guide their decisions.

There may be no tougher job in marketing than creating an effective brand personality, and nothing easier than letting it slip away. "Lose it," David Martin said, "and lose the franchise."

PART TWO

Identity Building in the Real World

6

Managing Identity Contacts in the Real World

Earl Holding is worth $800 million. He earned his money using his own style of hands-on management; he sometimes waits on tables in his Little America hotels and mans the cash register at his Sun Valley ski resort. He's a private man who goes public incognito when he wants to find out how his customers like to be treated and how well his operations are treating them. Earl's not the only one in his family who works for a living. His wife, Carol, has been seen cleaning hotel rooms at Sun Valley, and his kids regularly work the shelves at the resort's gift shops. These are people who have more entertaining things they could be doing, and plenty of money to do them with.

Earl Holding and his family are experts at brand building. They know that their businesses are only as healthy as the way they appear at the customer's level. They also know that the best way to find out how strong the relationship is between a brand and its customers is by seeing firsthand how the brand comes in contact with its customers.

Smart marketers walk on the street where their customers

live, anticipating and capitalizing on opportunities when a brand comes in contact with prospective buyers. It's here that a brand sends out hundreds of "contacts" that touch consumers, contacts that can be managed into a cohesive program of powerful sales stimulants or be allowed to scatter into a disorganized array of diffused messages.

The Rise of Street-Smart Practicality

We have seen the pendulum swing back from the spendthrift 1980s into our current decade, which began its run with recessionary stagnation, layoffs, and homelessness. Since the latest recession, Americans have used a different pair of eyeglasses to peer at what lies ahead. We are more realistic about what we can achieve materially in our lifetimes, and about what our children will not achieve after we're gone. Our fundamental confidence in the American economy has once again been restored, but this time it's tinged with a wariness about depending too heavily on the permanence of employment. We are reasonably sure that the whole economic scaffolding will not come crumbling down upon us, yet our trust has been hobbled with a skepticism that may stay with us for generations to come.

More and more of us are drawn toward a street-smart practicality, a hybrid of the pragmatism of New England and the skepticism of Missouri. We are weary of being burned, then salved, then burned again by the cyclical nature of things economic. Prosperity is a relative term that reminds us that we are all descendants of the Great Depression. We may continue to watch TV for escape from the real world, but it's not as easy as it once was because the real world is less escapable. There are more than a few reasons why "Rosanne," the prime-time show that looks at life near the bottom of the income scale, is followed by 18 million households every week.[1]

Americans seem prouder than ever of their newly honed talent to find a good value, irrespective of their incomes. It's what the *New York Times* has called "nouveau cheap," our inclination to spend less, save more, and shop doggedly for a better price.

It's converted most retailers into value shopkeepers, even when their goods sell at the high end. Recession or no, there's still a market for the *Tightwad Gazette*, a monthly newsletter out of Leeds, Maine, and the *Living Cheap News* from San Jose, California. Even Donald Trump was reportedly sighted inside a Kmart. (As far as the observer could tell, he was not lost.)

Understanding consumers' new street-smart mentality may make all the difference in a marketplace where brands that are out of touch with the street are out of luck. If you listen closely, you can hear those questions consumers are asking themselves more frequently than ever, questions like: "Do I really need this?", "Where can I get this cheaper?", "If I wait a bit longer, will they discount it?", and "Is the price negotiable?"

This renewed pragmatism is as common among marketers as among their prospects. Ad agency professionals are decrying the lack of boldness and risk taking in an industry that used to be famous for living on the edge. Marketing departments are more conservative than their predecessors, relying less on completely new products and more on "brand families," those clusters of products huddled for safety's sake under a single brand umbrella.

In previous decades, the odds for success in new products were not much better than they are today, but somehow a 1-in-10 chance seemed more doable, and it appeared more likely that a company could recover should it stumble. Today, even with the economy robust once again, capital spending is tighter, payout time frames are shorter, and management's "wait-and-see" attitude can turn overnight into "let's make some money or move on."

Welcome to Retail

Accountability is enjoying a renaissance. Businesspeople have always been expected to perform to exacting standards, or make way for those who can. Now, accountability is even more important because every marketing move seems riskier. We have all been led to the inevitable conclusion that marketing must sell.

What a concept. Marketing doesn't just build unaided aware-ness, or shift attitudes, or increase memorability. It doesn't just make a brand more likable, or less objectionable, or simply create credibility, or bolster persuasiveness, or rally enthusiasm, or ex-cite employees, or even make the board of directors feel better. Marketing must sell the goods just as surely as does the sales force. That's why all first-day orientations for rookie marketeers should begin with the introductory salute, "Welcome to retail," whether the business is retail or not.

If you own or manage a retail outlet, it takes less than 24 hours to find out if a new tactic has worked. If the receipts total is not where it should be after the first day or two of a special promotion, you start looking for reasons why, and you don't stop until you've made whatever course corrections are neces-sary. This mentality—the feeling that tangible results must be delivered early and often or immediate changes must be made— has never been more prevalent in American business than it is today, especially in those publicly traded corporations that are followed by the hawk eyes of financial analysts. It's very difficult to stay on a particular course strategically unless a program moves the needle early on. If you are in marketing in the 1990s, you are in the retail business, and building a better brand iden-tity is a critical part of enabling any retailer to succeed.

"Image" and "Tactical" Are Both Identity Builders

One consequence of this increased accountability is renewed de-bate about the sales effectiveness of "image" versus "tactical" marketing strategies. The issue for brand marketers is whether they should build their brands from the top down, that is, by establishing an overall identity that casts a halo effect over in-dividual products and services, or from the bottom up, using tactical messages that eventually establish an identity as an end product.

In the past, "image" communications have often involved

emotion-based selling approaches that seek to create particular attitudes toward a brand. "Tactical" communications are usually focused on product/service features, and price and/or promotions. Typical marketing programs might include combinations of each, for example:

- image-only communications, occasionally supplemented with promotions or other programs to stimulate short-term sales (used commonly by the soft drink and beer brands);
- image-driven communications, with tactical efforts flowing from the image support (as seen from AT&T and Apple computer); or
- tactical-driven programs that seek to stimulate sales in the short term and result in a tactical-type image for the brand (the analgesics). (See Exhibit 6-1 for graphic representations of these approaches.)

Despite the trend toward more tactical programs, there are many in the marketing communications field, this author included, who argue that emotions will always play a major role in any purchase that involves human beings. If so, then communicating brand identities will always be an exercise in fusing the emotional with the practical.

EXHIBIT 6-1

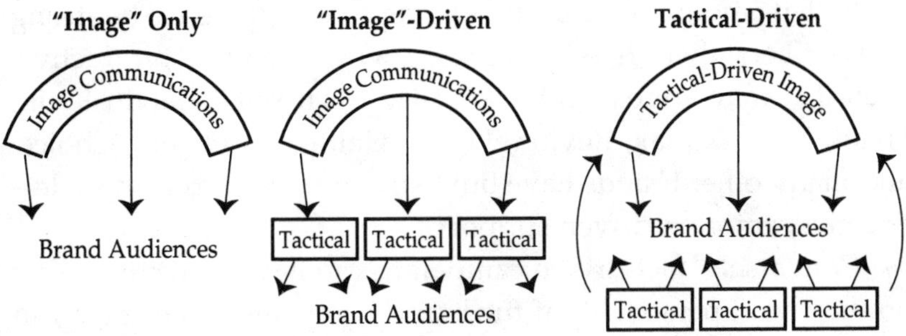

Types of "image"/tactical campaigns.

We are using the term "image" because that is the word used most often to refer to non-tactical marketing communications. An alternative term would be "identity campaigns."

Nevertheless, in light of the new practicalities, there appear to be fewer purely image-based communications programs in the marketplace, although it's difficult to find statistical evidence to verify that observation. Image communications are common in certain categories such as fragrances, beauty aids, beverages, apparel, indulgent food, and so on. More often, though, marketers are calling on a combination of image and tactical appeals to sustain their brand identities longer-term, while also making short-term quotas.

American Airlines, for one, has run image television advertising that carries the theme "Something Special in the Air," portraying emotional situations such as business travelers who have to get to important family reunions or airline employees who have to make sure that their job is done right for the sake of American's customers. Using retail newspaper ads, however, the same brand might send out far more impressions in the form of rate and destination ads, also using the "Something Special" theme.

Southwest Airlines, in contrast, uses a more value-oriented, tactical theme, "Just Plane Smart," and applies it across all media and for virtually all selling occasions. Southwest may be the closest to where the future of brand marketing is headed, in that it uses tactical advertising interchangeably with "image" support, rather than the more common view that image theme lines must drape over tactical communications.

Still, if emotion-driven advertising can be proven to be strong sales drivers, then there's no reason why it can't be productive, even if it may appear to be so-called "soft sell." Calvin Klein, Hyatt, Nike, Kodak, Revlon, Levi's, Hallmark, Taster's Choice, and many other brands have built strong franchises using sales-effective, emotion-driven support.

Conversely, fact-driven campaigns can have a positive effect on the brand personality if the brand competes in a category in which factual advertising is rare. Years ago, for instance, Budweiser proved that you could hammer away about the ingredients in beer and make progress in a basically emotion-oriented category.

Co-Branding Your Troubles Away

It's the latest rage . . . all the name brands are doing it. Desperately seeking ways to cut expenses and extend their identities, brands are partnering with compatible products and services wherever and whenever it's feasible. Just to name a few: Pillsbury joined with Nabisco to create Oreo Bars Baking Mix and Frosting. Not to be outdone, Betty Crocker mated with Mars and begat M&M's Cookie Bars baking mix. Betty didn't stop there; she scooped up the citrus brand king and created Betty Crocker Super Moist Cake Mix with Sunkist Lemons. Delicious Cookies picked up the award for the most co-brands in a supporting role by kneading in Land o' Lakes butter, Skippy peanut butter, Welch's juices, Chiquita bananas, Butterfingers, Raisinettes, and Heath Toffee Bars.

The co-branding phenomenon is not restricted to the baking category. Several hotel chains now prominently advertise that they provide AT&T-brand phone service. MasterCard has co-branded with a passel of top companies, including Chemical Bank and Shell Oil, TWA and GTE, General Electric and Ford, and Visa and Apple Computer. The master of retail co-branding is American Express, which has been running co-op advertising for years to remind consumers that their favorite restaurants, hotels, and airlines are strong supporters of Amex.

While the logistical and financial advantages of co-branding are clear, a question looms about whether such tactical moves are helping or hurting the brand identities involved. In most cases, the co-brand partners are compatible thematically and in terms of product and service quality, so they are likely protecting their identities in that sense.

Before joining the co-branding party, brand stewards should be certain that their potential partner is not only compatible with their host brand, but is also not likely to overshadow or in other ways dilute their brand's identity. A case in point has been hailed as the single most successful co-branding effort in the history of technology marketing—"Intel Inside." As we discussed in chapter 4, Intel talked its major hardware partners into participating in a co-op program that placed "Intel Inside" flags on advertising and packaging, resulting in a skyrocketing of the brand's awareness and prestige. However, IBM pulled out of the program in late 1994, and Compaq has been openly critical, questioning whether Intel is better served than the hardware that carries its chips. Intel's Pentium problems have only complicated the brand's co-branding efforts.

And, in what may be the ultimate co-branding move, Mercedes has announced plans to introduce a Swatch Watch-style automobile in 1997. Mercedes is not commenting on what a Swatch Mercedes will look like, except to say that it will likely be too heavy to carry on your wrist.

No two brands have exactly the same impact on the consumer; one partner in every co-branding partnership will receive more attention than its counterpart. If that risk is accurately assessed and accepted by the junior partner, and it's still a net gain for its brand identity, then the partnership is a sound one. Co-branding creates new excitement for the brands involved; the question that should always be raised before signing on the dotted line is whether the partnership creates the kind of excitement that builds brand identity or the kind that diffuses it.

Brand Building through Identity Contacts

Professors Don Schultz, Stanley Tanenbaum, and Robert Lauterborn discuss in their book, *Integrated Marketing Communications*, a term called customer or brand "contacts." They define the term as "any information-bearing experience that a customer or prospect has with the brand, the product category, or the market that relates to the marketer's product or service."[2] Applying that thought to brand identity, what might be called "identity contacts" would be whenever a brand touches prospects in such a way that it communicates its identity.

It's the marketing team's job to prioritize identity contacts, and to judge how they might contribute to the brand identity, and in what way they are relevant to the realities of the consumer's everyday life. In Exhibit 6-2, we take a look at a spread of

EXHIBIT 6-2

Brand	Example Brand Identity Contact	Contribution to Brand Identity
Acura Car Dealers	Follow-up phone call after car servicing	Reminder that dealer cares about customer service; method to check up on efficiency/courtesy of service department; opportunity to remind customer of upcoming sales
Bank of America	ATMs	Frequent customer interaction; reminder of convenience benefits; logo registration; promotion announcements
McDonald's	Ronald McDonald Houses for the families of seriously ill children	In addition to its humanitarian value, RM Houses remind parents of McDonald's commitment to the American family
MCI	Electronic billboard tabulating how much MCI customers have saved.	Brand name registration in compelling way; reminder of savings positioning; revisable numbers send signal that MCI is on top of what's happening in prices
Reebok Shoes	Close-up of Reebok logo on shoes of player in NBA championship	Brand associated with the best athletes in their sport; reinforcement of superior quality of product, and prestige of being worn by winners

Brand identity contact contributions.

contacts for a number of brands and identify what each contributes to the host brand.

Brands are whatever they are perceived to be at their point of contact with a prospective user. Brands are often in contact with their customers and prospects in hundreds of ways and through hundreds of channels, many of which are potentially huge sources of growth for a franchise if they are managed correctly.

For example, if a detergent brand wants to emphasize its new cleaning capabilities, a brand team can do more than just change a copy strategy and run new advertising; they can determine how all or most of the brand identity contacts can be manipulated to increase emphasis on cleaning efficacy. Can the salesmen wear lapel pins that remind retailers of the new product efficacy? Can the case boxes be reprinted to add bursts about the reformulization? Can the brand's coupons carry a new cleaning message? Are there opportunities to sponsor events where "clean" is on the minds of participants, such as rodeos (where "how to clean your jeans" signs might have impact) or football games (where down-and-dirty linemen could be used as spokesmen in some collectible posters). Is there a PR story that could be generated about the cleaning of today's new fabrics and how important it is to have the "right kind of clean"? Could the brand sponsor neighborhood "cleanups" to rid the streets of litter and remind citizens of the cleaning efficacy of the brand? Or, could the brand publicly support environmental initiatives?

Marketing communications contacts may be particularly important because they can set a tone for subsequent contacts. The nostalgic introductory advertising for the Mazda Miata helped stage the brand as a stylish throwback to the era of racy sportsters, a theme carried throughout the brand's contact program. MCI's rate campaign establishes the commitment of their staff before you make your first call, and when you do make that call, the employee at the other end of the line is liable to act just as those in the commercial did because he or she has also seen the advertising and knows what kind of performance that management expects.

Making the Grassroots Grow

So-called grassroots marketing is a form of brand contact that has really hit its stride in the last few years. Sponsorships of everything from local baseball teams to off-center musical events have been sought by marketers looking to carry their brands into the consumer's backyard. Jose Cuervo tequila, for instance, set an objective of bolstering its 54 percent share and building the category by sponsoring zany events that might attract new users to the fold. Among their many efforts, they have been the backers of the Octuba Fest, featuring 100 tuba-playing brand builders serenading Grand Central Station travelers, who also get to make their own music with free kazoos.

Wave Promotions, Inc., of Washington, D.C., specializes in what has come to be called "ambush marketing." In the summer of 1993, 25 fully costumed "pirates" stormed the beaches of New Jersey to hand out free bags of snack food. They used the same unorthodox sampling techniques in supermarkets, in ski resorts, and on public sidewalks, all on behalf of such major brands as Smartfood, MTV, and Coca-Cola. Ambush events are completely unannounced, and usually bring with them large amounts of excitement, bewilderment, and an occasional complaint, such as when two Wave samplers were arrested by security guards at a "Who" rock concert.

The most prolific event marketer is probably Marlboro, which has bought into a variety of alternative media since the removal of tobacco advertising from television. Marlboro has sponsored so many events and sports teams over the last 20 years that their signage has practically become part of the landscape. Most recently, the Marlboro Adventure Team became the most elaborate and expensive promotional event in history. The program prompted millions of Americans to trade "miles" for sporting gear, and reportedly generated as much as $675 million in new revenue for the brand during 1993 alone. As legal constraints from legislators and protests from public health activists continue, unorthodox marketing approaches are becoming a staple for Marlboro and other tobacco brands.

Planned and Unplanned Word of Mouth

Word-of-mouth advertising, a common by-product of grassroots marketing, is well worth the effort it takes to generate. Word of mouth is still considered the most potent marketing communication of all because it's dispensed by the most credible sources of all—ordinary citizens who don't carry the built-in bias of com-

The Many Identity Contacts of a Major Electronics Brand

How many ways can one brand touch people? In the case of a major electronics company, a brand makes contact with people in hundreds of ways. Brands come in contact with wholesalers, warehouse workers, delivery truck drivers, repair people, salespersons, shoppers, passersby and untold others, each of whom could become a user, a prospect, or a purchase influencer.

EXHIBIT 6-3
Brand Identity Contact Review (Abridged)

Large Electronics Brand

Brand Identity Contact	Brand Identity Targets	Contact Impression Opportunity	Estimated Frequency*
Case label (in-store)	Retail warehouse people, salespeople, consumers	Name recognition in clutter of competitive products	Warehouse/ salespeople— 100 + /day; consumers— 5 + per visit
Product label (in-store)	Salespeople, consumers	Name recognition plus association with quality products on display	Salespeople— 500 + /day; consumers— 20 + per visit
Product label (in-use)	Current user, prospective user	Positive purchase reinforcement; enticement for future purchase	1–5 per use
Advertising	Consumers, retail buyers	Brand name awareness; positive brand imagery; positive brand attribute registration	Variable based on reach/ frequency of media plan

Large Electronics Brand			
Brand Identity Contact	**Brand Identity Targets**	**Contact Impression Opportunity**	**Estimated Frequency***
Product brochures	Consumers	Claim registration	3–4 per consumer per brochure
Instruction manuals	Consumers	Reinforce purchase decision; ensure proper product operation (i.e., customer satisfaction)	10+ per customer
Retail delivery truck signage	Retailers, consumers	Reinforce strong relationship with corporation; add to brand recognition	10+/day for driver; 1,000+ per day for consumers

*Estimates are for comparison purposes only and would have to be verified by appropriate research and field observation.

mercial sponsors. When your brand is lucky enough to be the beneficiary of word of mouth, your identity problems may be over, and your capacity problems may just be beginning.

Some of the better-known beneficiaries of word-of-mouth phenomena: Cabbage Patch dolls nearly destroyed millions of parent-daughter relationships when their unbelievably hot products ran into short supply in the 1980s. Dakin Inc., the manufacturer of the 40-something Ginny dolls, has seen astronomical sales increases recently, partly fueled by doll collectors all over the world who turned out by the thousands to celebrate the doll's birthday several years ago. Mattel, keeper of the doll queen, has carefully orchestrated Barbie affinity groups, which has helped that brand to reach more than $1 billion in annual sales.

Henry Weinhard's and Coors are brands that both owe much of their early success to being 1960s cult beers with strong word of mouth outside their traditional marketing areas. Similarly, Corona beer became known in the 1980s as the cool brand to buy among young adults. The brand did virtually no advertising during the first few years of its brief, but storied rise in popularity.

While it's difficult to intentionally create positive word-of-mouth advertising, it can be done if you've got the right product, the right strategy, and the right set of circumstances. Chrysler's LH line (Dodge Intrepid, Chrysler Concorde, and Eagle Vision) is one example of a brand set that benefited from positive word of mouth. The company's dealers in 25 sales zones offered an LH model for the weekend to local opinion leaders. Based on research conducted after the test, Chrysler estimated that the cars got 32,000 personal exposures in just three months. More than 98 percent of the survey respondents said they would recommend the cars to a friend, and 90 percent said that their opinions regarding Chrysler had improved as a result of the experience.[3]

An even more impressive word-of-mouth event was staged in 1993 when 100,000 Harley-Davidson owners converged on Milwaukee for a celebration of their righteous Harleyness. Observers were there from General Motors who borrowed a page from the Harley book and held a "homecoming" of their own the following year in Spring Hill, Tennessee, for up to 44,000 Saturn owners. Both of these events not only solidified relationships with current brand owners, they provided tremendous new word-of-mouth momentum for the brand identities of Harley-Davidson and Saturn.

However, identities built through word of mouth are also running some risks. Brands whose fame spreads quickly and spontaneously can reach new heights much faster than through more methodical marketing plans. At the same time, some of the word-of-mouth successes can be fleeting, as some of the marketers of the brands just mentioned can attest. Once strong word of mouth is achieved, it needs to be converted into a sustainable brand identity, a conversion that may be at least as difficult as achieving the word of mouth itself.

WORD-OF-MOUTH WONDERS: SNACKWELL'S AND STARBUCKS

SnackWell's Devil's Food fat-free cookies took off like a choc-olate rocket when consumers discovered that they actually tasted as good as the real thing. The brand was launched with an indulgence strategy and a strong marketing push at introduction, but support soon slid into overdrive. Despite the slowing of marketing spending, Nabisco had such a hard time keeping the product in stock that supermarkets created customer waiting lists for the brand, and the company was forced to run ads apologizing for the delays in meeting con-sumer demand.

That didn't go far enough for the retail trade, who wanted product faster than Nabisco could deliver it. In fact, the company had to bring out a diversionary entry in the line—Double Fudge Cookie Cakes—in an effort to take the pressure off the devil's food product, which was only able to be manufactured at a measured clip without major new capital investment.

SnackWell's word of mouth was fed by nearly unbeliev-able stories of consumers hoarding the product when they could find it, or going to extraordinary lengths to find it in the first place. One woman reportedly followed a route truck back to a distribution center to track down where the cookies could be found. The brand has since incorporated the "we'll follow you anywhere" phenomenon into their ad campaign, which portrays fictional shoppers who will stop at nothing to get their hands on Snackwell's.

How well does word of mouth work? The SnackWell's line is now worth more than $200 million in retail sales.

Starbucks, on the other hand, is a case of orchestrated word of mouth. The explosively successful coffeehouse chain out of Seattle (named after the coffee-loving first mate in Her-man Melville's *Moby Dick*), routinely takes steps to increase the buzz about its store openings.

Starbucks accelerates trial through what Vice President for Marketing George Reynolds has called "proactive public relations."[4] That includes serving the brews at all the "in" places in each locale when they hit town, plus dispensing it via mobile backpack urns that accompany executives when they make PR stops. This contact momentum is multiplied by catalogs, packaging, coupons, direct mail, and point-of-purchase displays. Public relations efforts yielded stories in *Fortune*'s "100 Fastest Growing Companies" issue and in *Newsweek*, plus scores of other national publications.

All of this has led to a good news/bad news scenario as competition begins to gallop in and Starbucks (as of this writing) refuses to enter the retail supermarket scene with its own brand. Marketing a grocery brand of beans might not be the right move for Starbucks. After all, as one financial analyst has said, "They don't market. They've established a major presence all through word of mouth."[5]

The Employee as Identity Contact

Jan Carlzon, CEO of Scandinavian Airlines (SAS), in 1987 wrote an influential book called *Moments of Truth*, in which he recounted some of the lessons he learned as he rose through the ranks of the travel industry. Carlzon came to believe that the most crucial moments for a service company are in those brief seconds when its customers come in direct contact with its employees:

> Last year, each of our 10 million customers came in contact with approximately five SAS employees, and this contact lasted an average of 15 seconds each time. Thus, SAS is "created" in the minds of our customers 50 million times a year, 15 seconds at a time. These 50 million "moments of truth" are the moments that ultimately determine whether SAS will succeed or fail.[6]

It's only been in the past decade or so that employers in general, and marketing companies in particular, have discovered how important it is to foster superior training and internal communications to keep employees active and interested in what's happening to their brands. There is solid evidence that employees are not only happier in a company with sharp internal communications, they also become better brand ambassadors.

For example, based on a variety of research studies conducted at such companies as General Electric, Hewlett-Packard, General Motors, and others, here are some of the most important findings about employee communications, related in this case to creating the best possible brand identity.

- *The most effective internal communications are face-to-face.* Researchers have verified that when managers successfully communicate on a one-to-one basis with their team members, the employees are happier and better informed. That's an opportunity to talk about the brand, and about how each employee can support selling efforts.
- *Not surprisingly, the best employee communications programs are two-way, with as much company listening as there is information down-loading.* Internal communications is no different than personal relations—the more interactively involved the employee feels, the more likely that he or she will be to support what the company is trying to achieve, including a strong brand identity program.
- *More employees than in the past are interested in how their company's products and services are doing in the marketplace.* They realize that their jobs may depend on the competitiveness of their company, and they are ready and eager to do whatever they can to help build their company's brands.
- *Companies that are most adept at communicating with their employees use a carefully devised blend of old and new media to keep their people up to date.* Traditional print is mixed with the immediacy of satellite communications and the persuasiveness of well-produced videos to present a multimedia array of information to employees. The advent of more interactive media will also present exciting new opportunities to keep employees informed and involved in their company and its brands.

There are too many forces working against the success of a brand for a company to take the view that only a select few of its employees should be involved in strengthening the brand identity. As high-tech marketing consultant Regis McKenna has said: "Marketing today is not a function; it is a way of doing business. Marketing is not a new ad campaign or this month's promotion. Marketing has to be all-pervasive, part of everyone's job description, from the receptionists to the board of directors."[7]

A critical part of that job description is the fostering and proselytizing of the brand identity.

Managing Identity Contacts Using "Convergent Communications"

The first organized attempts at coordinating marketing messages among a mix of marketing media were called "integrated communications." These efforts were touted by the largest advertising agencies during the 1970s as they began to gobble up specialty sales promotion, direct marketing, public relations, and consulting firms. Young & Rubicam called their version "The Whole Egg," Ogilvy & Mather countered with "Ogilvy Orchestration." Integrated marketing never really caught fire because advertisers viewed it as a ploy by agencies to capture more revenue. Plus, marketers were already very happy with the relatively simple process of buying mass media, and few had the patience to deal with the logistical problems of tying together all those diverse communications programs.

Yet, there were some integrated marketing success stories. General Electric's long-running "We Bring Good Things to Life" campaign was a good example of a traditional integrated effort, driven less by strategic customer needs than by the need to pull GE's 100-plus product lines and ten unrelated ad campaigns under one umbrella that was strategically compatible with the brand's identity as an all-American, trustworthy brand. The corporate program started with primetime network TV, then moved into print and radio, all reinforced with public relations, merchandising, and yellow pages directory programs.

In an updated example, Crystal Pepsi was introduced several years ago using a "mass integrated" approach with a wide range of media and promotional programs to sell in and through the brand. In addition to major introductory advertising aimed at their teen/young-adult targets, the brand gave away "savings cards" good for discounts at a variety of stores, sampled the product in malls, ran a "Back-to-Cool" sweepstakes, and sponsored the 63-city "Mindblender" tour of video-carnival shows. These efforts may have created general awareness of the new product, but there is a question about whether they made the disparate elements work together synergistically to speak to consumer benefits.

And therein is the possible flaw in these types of programs: their reason for being can be based more on marketers' tactical needs for coordinated efforts than on a strategic priority to address consumers' needs with focused benefits.

Renamed as "integrated marketing communications" (IMC), integrated campaigns have made a comeback in the 1990s, and have been expanded to include using supermarket scan data, consumer usage research, and database management to weave together advertising and sales promotion efforts into a single fabric of marketing programs. This time around, integrated marketing will stick because marketing companies are interested in increasing spending efficiencies.

A variation on the integrated marketing approach that seeks to combine the best of the older and new integrated programs is called "convergent communications." While integrated marketing efforts can focus on marketers' logistical challenges (for example, ensuring that the direct marketing vehicle and the awareness advertising carry the same look and theme line), convergent communications concentrate on how a brand's overall identity is presented to individual consumers *within the framework of their particular needs*. In that way, it can be more intentionally strategic than conventional integrated approaches that may still tend to be more tactically driven (see Exhibit 6-4 for graphic explanation of differences between integrated and convergent communications).

As an example, low-fare leader Southwest Airlines has suc-

EXHIBIT 6-4

Traditional Integrated Programs		Convergent Communications
Marketer's need to synchronize various programs	← Reason for Being →	To create programs that address consumers' needs with maximum impact
Common strategy, look, and theme	← Approach →	Common elements, but modified according to medium's capability to communicate benefit
Consistent advertising promotion, PR, direct marketing, interactive, etc.	← Communications Created →	Consistent advertising, promotion, PR, direct marketing, interactive, etc.
Well-coordinated marketing communications program	← End Result →	Well-coordinated program with maximum benefit communication

Integrated vs. convergent communications.

cessfully registered both its "Just Plane Smart" theme and the strategic value message underlying it.

When Southwest inaugurates a service, the brand often starts off with public relations events. Five weeks prior to the start of their Baltimore service a few years ago, Southwest Chairman Herb Kelleher held a press conference and gave Maryland Governor Donald Schaefer a flotation device, what Kelleher called a "lifesaver" from exorbitant airfares for the people of Baltimore. To emphasize their low $49 fares, the company hired former Baltimore Oriole great Boog Powell to give hitting lessons to 49 school kids. TV commercials sporting the "Just Plane Smart" theme congratulated the people of Baltimore for being smart enough to allow Southwest to service the city. In short, all of the brand identity contacts focused on the low-fare positioning and the $49 fare itself. The communications messages "converged" on the one strategic benefit that was of greatest importance in the minds of the brand's individual prospects, namely, saving money.

The National Potato Board has also used convergent communications to help boost the at-home consumption of America's favorite vegetable. Alternative side dish brands have become a growing part of Americans' menu planning, due in part to the $125 million in advertising rice and pasta brands spend each year, compared to less than five percent of that amount by the potato industry. Strategically, the board's five-year program is focusing on consumers' desires to eat the right foods that also appeal to their taste buds. Potatoes are thus being advertised as "the only starch that's also a fresh vegetable."

The potato program is a full convergent communications campaign employing elements from advertising (a broad print ad campaign), public relations (food article placement, food industry publicity), retail trade (produce manager promotions), direct marketing (establishment of "Good Mom" clubs), and interactive marketing (produce department recipe kiosks). All of these identity contact points are being focused on consumers' need to prepare food for their families that's good tasting and good for them. The Potato Board is already seeing significant new support from the retail trade and the resurgence of potatoes in the American menu.

A convergent campaign, of course, can involve much more than just marketing communications. It might also include: product/service development that is focused on meeting certain consumer needs; a pricing approach that responds to consumers' search for good value, but without sacrificing the non-pricing issues that surround the positioning; or a promotion plan that provides purchase incentives that are thematically in line with other brand moves. The point is that all of the elements of the marketing mix are harnessed into a single-minded program that starts and ends with consumer needs.

The 1990s are turning out to be a decade in which the more practical, pragmatic programs—from word of mouth campaigns to convergent communications programs—will have the best success in building brand identities. In the following chapters, we will examine more closely how some great brands have incorporated these approaches into their successful branding efforts.

7

Cases I

A Shoe, a Mouse,
Brands around the House

The strongest brand identities are the easiest to recognize and the toughest to emulate. They command a presence in their respective categories and far beyond them. The most enduring, while not invincible, are like fine athletes in their prime—impossibly talented, obsessive about building success on successes, supremely confident regardless of the odds. They are very, very tough to unseat.

Six Studies in Brand Identity

This chapter and the next will tell the story of five brands and one company of brands, each of which has demonstrated something important about identity building. Stewards of four of the brands are masters at achieving their business goals. One is a company full of vigorous brands coping with turbulent change. The sixth case is a brand with all the potential of the others, but its rotating cast of stewards and its inconsistent marketing approach have prevented it from reaching its full potential.

The cases in this chapter:

■ The Walt Disney Company—Founded by a graphic artist with a flair for the commercial whose successor has merchandised his creative estate into one of the largest entertainment companies in the world. The Disney empire has experienced some significant problems in recent years, but this brand still has more positive associations attached to it than any other in the country, if not the world.

■ Nike, Inc.—A dominant sports and fashion brand that, as late as 1989, was a runner-up in the running shoe category. Now, it's close to redefining how sports athletes of all kinds will be merchandised across the globe, but not without an arena-full of controversy. This is the story of how a maturing identity was reenergized and taken to the edge of the envelope.

■ The Procter & Gamble Company—For decades, Cincinnati was packaged goods brand central. More recently, the hostile forces we have discussed throughout this book have had a more profound effect on this company than on any other, up to and including Philip Morris. Procter has now been forced by a turbulent marketplace to seek the repositioning of its brands as lower-priced, higher-value entries.

And, our cases in the next chapter:

■ Southwestern Bell Yellow Pages (aka "Swbyp's")—Competing in one of the most mundane categories, the Swbyp's profile is about the re-branding of an information staple that was too often out of sight, out of mind. Now Swbyp's is a big new brand, reborn within the five middle America states where Southwestern Bell does business. This is an identity that was given a full makeover, from positioning to personality.

■ Saturn Corporation—Sponsor of one of the most successful car introductions in recent memory, and all the more remarkable considering it was created from scratch under the auspices of Detroit's then most troubled automaker. Saturn is an all-American brand identity that was built from the ground up in less than five years, and despite outrageous odds.

■ Burger King—A case of a brand identity unrealized, BK has suffered grievously from the effects of discontinuity and re-active marketing. And yet Burger King is also a modern marketing miracle because it remains one of America's largest retail food companies that is still in search of an identity. Based on what's currently cooking on their grill, the search may be near its end.

Why These Six?

The brands chosen are particularly interesting in terms of identity management. All six (when you consider P&G's brands as a group) have been successful despite notable shortcomings. They each have an identity heritage to work with even in the case of Saturn, which is a relatively new brand.

Rarely has it been easy for the managers involved with these brands to accomplish their goals. Fortunately, as brand stewards, they invested heavily in the business-building programs, both in terms of marketing spending, as well as with their own energies, their careers, their personal lives. They risked defeat, as many committed business people do, but they did so in order to create and build brands, not simply to make some quick earnings and move on.

The brands in the next two chapters are involved in many different businesses: entertainment products and services, athletic apparel, packaged food, household goods, personal care products, telephone directories, automobiles, and fast food. Their customers are interested in distraction and fun, physical performance, cleaning and personal hygiene, information, transportation, and a fast, cheap meal. Their heritages range from three companies with roots that are more than half a century old (Southwestern Bell, Procter & Gamble, and Disney), to maturing companies that must cope with middle-age crises (Nike and Burger King), to an upstart that has lived a lifetime in half a decade (Saturn).

But the common denominators among the strongest brand identities are even more important:

■ Each is clearly and distinctively positioned, even when the brand's business is multifaceted in nature. Nike *is* performance, so much so that even when consumers buy their apparel for style reasons, it's associated more with performance than fashion. Saturn is "a different kind of car company," and will always be that unless it's swallowed up by General Motors. Swbyp's is a resource where people get what they want out of life. It can never again be just the yellow pages. Disney is family entertainment, with an overlay of fun and fantasy that is impossible to clone. And, Procter brands were among the first to practice the art of positioning in their respective categories.

■ Each has a unique personality that contributes significantly to the brand's power in the marketplace. Disney's magic is undeniable. Saturn draws its personality from the people who build the cars and from those who buy them. Nike is personified by both the all-world athlete and ordinary citizens seeking to beat their personal bests. Swbyp's is a place to shop like no other. P&G regularly uses product performance to create brand personality.

■ They tend to sell much more than what the product or service delivers. P&G fathered that approach among packaged goods. Nike is selling shoes *and* an attitude. Swbyp's is selling information to help you out in life, not just a book with yellow pages. Saturn is selling a company, a group of employees, not just a car. Disney is selling escapism in a dozen different forms.

■ All are highly successful when it comes to managing brands toward better business results. Nike and Disney dominate their categories. Swbyp's is a large, growing concern in a declining category. Saturn, while not making the money GM had hoped, has created a brand equity far in excess of its bottom line contributions. Procter & Gamble continues to lead in many categories. And, Burger King, despite its inconsistencies, is the strong number-two fast-food name in a huge and highly competitive category.

There is one additional trait that the successful marketers discussed in this chapter have in common: an unshakable faith in the power of their brands and the brand identities they have helped mold. Not a blind trust, but a deep, pragmatic certitude that they can make their brands into something more important than just the products or services they represent.

THE DISNEY SAGA: STRENGTHENING A STRONG IDENTITY

In the 1994 Total Research EquiTrend survey mentioned in previous chapters, Disney (specifically Disney World and Disneyland) was ranked as the premier brand in the nation. Jim Alleborn, Total Research's vice president for marketing, has said: "Disney is just one of the brands that seems to do everything right. It's wholesome, high-tech, nurturing, kid-friendly, escapism, sentimentalism all wrapped up in one brand."[1]

As we will see, the Disney brand is far from perfect, but its brand stewards have done many more things right than they have done wrong, a tradition that started with the main man himself.

A Mouse Named Mickey, a Man Named Walt

Walt and his brother, Roy, came to California to start an animated film company after World War I, but it soon failed. They tried again with a film studio in 1923. Five years later, it gave birth to a legacy in the form of a silent cartoon called *Plane Crazy*, starring an indefatigable mouse that gradually became a fixture in theaters across America.

"Plain crazy" was also how some people referred to the Disney brothers a few years later when they tried to sell their idea for the country's first animated full-length feature. In 1937, they proved their critics wrong for the first of many times when they hit it big with *Snow White and the Seven Dwarfs*, followed eventually by other animated triumphs, *Fantasia, Pinocchio, Dumbo* and *Bambi*.

Of all the risks Walt and Roy Disney would eventually take in their long careers, the *Snow White* enterprise was proportionately their biggest gamble. Few people believed that Americans would pay what little money they had to watch a feature-length animated picture in the middle of the Depression. That first big success also became the symbolic beginning of one of the most powerful and enduring brand identities in the world. The Disney name would forevermore be associated with the hope, the inevitable triumph of good over evil, the "magic" that audiences saw come to life in *Snow White*.

The Disneys' film production business continued to thrive, and they eventually jumped into TV in a big way with *The Mickey Mouse Club* in 1955. That show became an emotional meeting place for an entire generation of Boomers who were in grade school at the time. Every weekday afternoon the country's adolescents fell in permanent love with Cubbie, Lonnie, and Annette. Sunday nights were owned by various Disney shows for 29 straight years as they invited America to stop time and enjoy innocent excursions away from the increasingly troublesome news of the real world. The Disney television success story continues into the present with 1994's number-one rated network show, "Home Improvement."

Even more significant than the Disneys' ventures into films and TV were the creation of worlds of their own, starting with Disneyland in Anaheim, California, in 1955. A decade after the completion of the "happiest place on earth," Walt Disney died. Brother Roy lived until 1971, the same year Disney World opened in Orlando, Florida. The futuristic EPCOT Center, described by its designers as "a permanent World's Fair of imagination, discovery, education, and exploration that will never be completed," followed in 1982.[2]

The Back Alley behind Main Street, U.S.A.

As with any of the classic Disney tales, the success of their corporate ventures was not all sweetness and light. There were persistent stories about Walt's obsession with how his employees should look and act, and the increasingly conservative (some say reactionary) political leanings of the brothers that flourished during the McCarthy era. But what threatened the Disney empire most significantly came to roost after Walt's death in the form of corporate infighting that almost swept away the brand.

When Walt Disney died in 1966, the company was both profitable and stable. Roy took over the chairmanship until his death in 1971. In subsequent years, the company produced few hits. Inflation and the theme parks increased corporate sales to $2 billion by 1984, but the stock price languished and earnings were fading fast.

During the early 1980s, the corporation's president and CEO was Ronald Miller, a veteran of the company and, just as important, Walt's son-in-law. Wall Street began to think that Miller was in over his head and that his more cautionary nature was allowing the company to flounder. In early 1984, financier Saul Steinberg began buying up undervalued stock, with a stated plan to sell the studio and most of the valuable undeveloped acreage around Disney World in central Florida. It was commonly believed at the time that Steinberg was just running up the stock price in order to snag huge profits, the so-called greenmail technique that had gained favor among corporate pirates in the 1980s.

At that point, board member Sid Bass used his considerable stock leverage to reinstate Roy O. Disney (cofounder Roy's son, and Walt's nephew) and bring his huge share block back on the board. After successfully rebuffing the Steinberg hostile takeover bid, Bass and Disney went looking for a new CEO and found him in the creative former head of Paramount Pictures, Michael Eisner. They added COO Frank Wells from Warner Bros., and Roy Disney was made head of the animation division. The stock was selling at $55 when Eisner's team took over in 1984; it hit $120 within two years and split four-to-one.

Proselytizing the Disney Brand

With fiscal 1994 revenue of $8.5 billion and income at $1.7 billion, the Walt Disney Company is one of the most valuable and influential entertainment organizations in the world. They make their money in theme parks, films, television production and distribution, consumer products and, soon, in "programming content" for whatever the information superhighway turns out to be. Their business comes down to protecting and capitalizing on the value of the Disney brand identity, although a number of their ventures have spun off into non-Disney related areas (for example, Touchstone Pictures).

The Walt Disney Company knows how to use its brand identity to leverage a winner when it gets one. In the late 1980s, the company began producing a series of hugely successful animated features, in the tradition of *Snow White* and *Bambi*. Some of the Disney original films and rereleases have sold an astonishing number of videotapes: *Pinocchio,* 13.4 million tapes in 1993 alone; *Beauty and the Beast,* 22 million in 1992. *Aladdin* has made over $50 million and counting. The mega-hit of 1994, *The Lion King,* may end up as the biggest money-making film in history. And, a rerelease of *Snow White* in late 1994 sold 17 million tapes in three weeks, worth roughly $300 million.

All of this is much more than good business, it's the blossoming of a brand that is like no other. Eisner and his people are not just seeking ways to make money in the short term, they are finding ways to profitably seed and reseed the Disney brand identity so that it will grow and multiply (in the form of brand equity.)

The Magical Disney Brand Identity

Early on, Walt Disney knew he was onto something that was important to people when he watched a large part of the population fall for a high-pitched mouse, a goofy dog, and an obstreperous duck. Disney and his successors entranced their countrymen with stories that dealt in the basic stuff of life—struggles for freedom (Cinderella, Snow White), escape from oppression (all those evil witches and bad guys), loyalty (Old Yeller, Jimminy Crickett), and love, always love.

One example of how the brand's heritage is subtly reproduced: The Mickey Mouse character was drawn as a series of

EuroDisney & Tokyo Disneyland: What Went Right, What Went Wrong

It's a little hard to believe that they are both Disney ventures, let alone that the successful one has *less* Disney involvement than the version that is struggling to survive. Tokyo Disneyland is a huge success. Opened in 1974, the park has recently averaged 16 million visitors a year, spending $85 apiece. On many counts, it's more successful than any other Disney park. Unhappily, the park is not owned by the Walt Disney Company, but by Japanese interests through The Oriental Land Company. Disney management had their doubts about jumping with both feet in the first major offshore Disney park, so they took only a 5–10 percent royalty stake in the rides and concessions. Among other things, Eisner and company underestimated the rabid devotion the Japanese have for all things American.

The success of Tokyo Disneyland, plus the improving European economic market, gave the company reason to believe that a park near Paris might provide much of the opportunistic revenue lost from the only partial relationship with Japanese venture. But results from the two parks have been as different as the locales themselves. EuroDisney suffered a $905 million loss in the fiscal year ending September 1993, and caused the parent Walt Disney Company to take a $350 million charge on their normally sparkling books. The financial situation got so bad in 1993–94 that it looked like the venture was going to go belly-up. An eleventh hour restructuring of bank loans and an infusion of funds from other investors saved the day in 1994.

A major cause of the EuroDisney dilemma was that things were simply too expensive, even for the pricey Paris region, at a time when Europe was suffering from recession. The price of everything—from hotel rooms to merchandise to admission tickets—was considered too steep. The hotels had an average occupancy rate of only 55 percent, partly because the park is so close to Paris that visitors prefer to stay there.

While Eisner and his team may have made some poor business decisions, both parks are a testament to the Disney brand and what strength it has worldwide. From the moment both parks opened, Asians and Europeans raced to take part in happy escapes to fantasy. The ventures proved that the Disney brand is eminently exportable through the universally loved Disney characters, and in the form of a permanent Disney facility in a foreign land.

circles, which was the genesis of Disney's use of round imagery. As extensions of that grand plan, Disneyland is built around Sleeping Beauty's castle, EPCOT revolves around a lake, and Disney/MGM Studios surround a reproduction of Grauman's Chinese Theatre. As John Hench, one of the original Disney designers, once explained: "Walt's thing was reassurance ... the message is, 'You're going to be O.K.' "[3]

The Disney brand is clearly positioned as the symbol of happiness and well-being in whatever venue it appears. The brand's personality is most often revealed in the eclectic group of characters that inhabit the Disney landscape: Mickey and Donald, Pinocchio and Snow White, Roger Rabbit and Annette Funicello, Tinkerbell and Dumbo, the stormy elegance of *Fantasia* and the laughable silliness of *Honey, I Shrunk the Kids*. The brand specializes in likable, lovable, everybody-has-a-good-time characters, a toon town full of luminaries real and animated who, in a swirling blend of fantasy and wizardry, have been fused into a single brand personality of unparalleled potency.

To ride herd on the brand, their Brand Image Group conducts telephone surveys and other research to ensure that the identity is being maintained throughout the Disney empire. Adjustments are made immediately if the Disney identity is found to be askew. In Disney parks, employees are painstakingly trained as "cast members" who are uniformly instructed on how to be relentlessly cheerful, training techniques that have been studied and copied by service organizations all over the world.

Periodically, the same policy has also been criticized as creating synthetic experiences. Yet, other Disney brand watchers, obviously including the company's management, believe it's an important element of the brand's success. As one believer wrote in a letter to the editor of the *Los Angeles Times*: "The Disney Look works. It is one reason Disneyland has changed the image of amusement parks from that of dirty places operated by surly personnel to that of a clean place staffed by courteous, well-groomed employees."[4] So there.

In 1992, Disney expanded its brand contacts to include an Anaheim-based NHL hockey franchise, the Mighty Ducks, named after their successful movie by the same name. The entire Mighty Ducks experience has revealed another major reason why the Disney brand identity is so strong, namely, the way in which the company mobilizes all of its forces to achieve a goal. Sort of the George Patton approach to brand building.

As the Mighty Ducks franchise began to take shape, Disney's consumer products division pumped out huge quantities of Mighty Ducks hats, shirts, sweats, and everything else imaginable, all sporting the campy, horror movie–style Ducks logo, which became one of the most sought-after accessory emblems in team sports after only one season. More than 200 Disney retail outlets sell Ducks memorabilia. Disneyland's Imagineering Group created the pregame and intermission entertainment for the Ducks home contests. The Disney Development Corporation designed the Ducks offices. Disney employees are often required to sell tickets to games. Disneyland itself sponsors and conducts a Mighty Ducks sweepstakes. Disneyland package tours include Ducks tickets. And, of course, the movies help sell the team. The commercially successful *The Mighty Ducks* was followed in 1994 with a sequel, *D2—The Mighty Ducks*.

In true Disney fashion, the team itself finished with a surprisingly strong rookie season record that boasted 33 wins, and they're already considered to be a future force in the league. Just another Disney success in the making.

And Then There Was One: The Disney Team Shows Its Fragility

As strong as it is, the Disney brand has been subjected to some serious threats in recent years. In July 1993, the company issued 100-year bonds in an extraordinary show of confidence in its long-term potential. Less than six months later, Moody's Investors Services lowered its long-term securities ratings because of problems with EuroDisney.

The company's most serious crisis since 1984 came as a result of a series of devastating events. Michael Eisner's close friend and COO, Frank Wells, was killed in a helicopter crash in April of 1994. A few months later, Eisner endured quadruple bypass heart surgery, prompting concern about his succession plans. Then, just before Labor Day, Jeffrey Katzenberg, the brilliant head of Walt Disney Studios, left the organization at the end of a brief but bloody power struggle. The dark days continued when Gary Kalkin, the 44-year-old marketing head of Disney's Buena Vista Pictures, died of complications from AIDS in January 1995. Suddenly, the original team that had rebuilt the company into a giant in the industry was cut down to one, less-than-robust CEO.

The remaining team members are struggling to learn something that Walt accomplished decades before: how to refit the Disney organization and its brand identity to provide for new thinking, but without losing the essence of what the Disney name means to adults and children all over the world.

Plus, Disney wants to extend its leadership in television, movies, and other entertainment productions. Yet some of this once and future empire is at risk if the brand cannot be stabilized with new leadership below Eisner until he retires and energized with continued vision long after he's left the company.

What Can We Learn from Disney?

In the mid-1980s, during the damaging boardroom skirmishes that killed off many companies in that merge-and-purge era, financial analysts openly admitted that they would be "saddened" to see the Disney enterprise fall victim to the arbitrager's axe. Saddened? Wall Street hard bodies? Those battle-scarred veterans of financial bloodlettings understood that Disney was in the business of happiness, and even they did not want to see happiness raided and redistributed. The Disney brand was and is loved and nurtured as much as any business entity can be. While other fine companies were absorbed or otherwise fell by the wayside, those who embraced what Walt Disney created kept a brand identity alive until it could be reconstituted.

There is no real magic when it comes to the financials of the entertainment business. Disney has been wildly successful in the movies when their theme parks have needed renovating. More recently, their parks have done well (except in Paris) while their non-animated films have suffered major losses at the box office. Such forgettables as *The Air Up There*, *Blame It on the Bellboy*, and *Money for Nothing* have failed outright, and even *The Three Musketeers* and *Sister Act 2: Back in the Habit* fell short of expectations. Still, everyone in Hollywood and the real world expects Disney to straighten out their problems and get back to the business of building an irreplaceable brand identity that has been tarnished slightly by film flops and organizational turmoil.

Disney management acts in a way that could be a template for identity building:

■ They understand the power of their brand. They know what the Disney name can mean because they are living what Walt learned early in his career. Disney is positioned as a family entertainment brand, with special emphasis on children. It's been said that they practice a variation of the Jesuit credo: Give me a child early in life, and he'll be our customer for life.

■ Management works within the parameters of their brand's identity. They are realistic about its limitations. Disney people cannot change the world, but they're expert at creating a temporary retreat from it. They know when their brand is being stretched too far, when it's becoming rusty or dusty, when it's becoming inbred and needs fresh light.

■ They monitor all the parts, and know how all the parts fit the whole. Cross-selling and synergistic brand building are part of the Disney way of life, and have a major effect on the Disney brand identity. Their parks, their hotels and resorts, their movies, their merchandising, their hockey team, all share in common an integrated approach to marketing and identity maintenance.

■ They are evangelistic about their very own good-time religion. From the introductions at the new employees' orientations to the way guests are welcomed at the parks, every family, every moviegoer, every Mighty Ducks fan is invigorated by an irrepressible faith that Disney is good, and so, let's just relax and enjoy ourselves. Disney people are unabashedly obsessive; if they have a fault, it tends toward being so focused that they fail to see factors outside their line of vision. Like any zealots worth their salt, they seem unconcerned with criticism if what they are doing builds their brand, and builds equity for their stakeholders.

■ They control and manipulate brand contacts with ruthless attention to detail. Litter detracts from the Disney brand, so their parks don't have any. There is only one Mickey Mouse, so when one Mickey Mouse character is walking around the park greeting little people, no other Mickey actor is permitted to be in the park. Why? Because the Disney brand would not tolerate the Santa Claus problem ("But Mommy, if we just saw Santa in the store . . . who's *he?*"). If they cannot use the Disney brand the way it should be used in a sports team or a cruise line or on a T-shirt, then they buy the enterprise outright to ensure complete control.

When your brand's in the magic business, you have to be vigilant in protecting its identity. It's the job of Michael Eisner and his successors to keep the Disney brand identity alive. The world is not likely to let them fail.

THE NIKE LEGEND: A PSYCHE-DRIVEN IDENTITY

In 1958, Phil Knight, a middle-distance runner at the University of Oregon, had something besides track in common with his coach, Bill Bowerman. Neither of them thought much of the track shoes made in America. Bowerman tried to sell some designs to shoe companies, but got nowhere fast, so in 1964 he and Knight created their own company, called Blue Ribbon Sports. It cost each of the partners an initial investment of $300. In 1972, they changed their corporate name to Nike, after the Greek goddess of victory. They asked graduate student Carolyn Davidson to design their "swoosh" logo, for which she was paid $35.

From the beginning, Nike has been a company driven by self-imposed performance standards, run by iconoclasts preoccupied with determining their own fate. You can read about it in the introduction to the Nike 1993 annual report:

> Take a moment to consider a world record. It is a paradox. Un-approachable yet inevitable. The key to its attainment is strength, not just of muscle but of conviction, a belief in your own mastery of circumstances. This is the nature of power. It is our inspiration.[5]

Power is their inspiration, and the source of that power emanates from a remarkable brand identity.

The Power of the Swoosh

Nike sales hover around the $4 billion mark, with annual earnings in the $400 million range, a decent return on Knight's and Bowerman's $300 investment. The Beaverton, Oregon-based company does business in 50 categories of footwear and apparel in more than 100 countries. As with many category leaders, one of the keys to Nike's growth has been the company's commitment to innovation, beginning with its founding by two guys in search of a better track shoe. In 1975, Bill Bowerman invented the famous "waffle" sole that reshaped the look of running shoes for a generation. In 1985 came the "Air Jordan" shoe, a name inspired by the leaps of Michael Jordan, followed by a series of other "Air" models (the inflatable Air Pressures and Air Raid), and other types of footwear such as the Aqua Sock water shoes.

Professional superstars are the company's most visible brand contact vehicles. Nike brand stewards continually search for just the right kind of athlete, someone who will not only represent himself well, but will represent the Nike brand as his own. When

Nike people land who they want, they are likely to be a major factor in "managing" that athlete's career.

A few examples: In 1991, Nike ordered "its" athletes to withdraw from a portion of the NBA's licensing agreement for goods bearing their likenesses. In 1993, Nike beat out the league for the rights to Michael Jordan T-shirts. At the time, NBA Deputy Commissioner Russ Granik said, "In marketing, Nike is far more powerful than the league."[6]

Nike Sports Management, a division that offers total management contracts, including endorsements, career guidance, and marketing advice, has enabled early signers like Notre Dame quarterback Rick Mirer the leverage to just say "no" when negotiating with sports teams, because Nike's power gave him enough financial independence ($16 million for five years) to wait for the right offer. Basketball star Alonzo Mourning once sat out until the fourth game of the season before signing with the Charlotte (N.C.) Hornets because, he said, "The Hornets knew I really didn't have to take anything. . . . I work for Nike."[7]

The Nike Identity: Performance with an Attitude

Phil Knight, the company's cofounder and CEO for most of Nike's life, continues to be the keeper of its identity. Knight has analyzed and reanalyzed what makes Nike tick, and what will keep it on top. As he told the *Harvard Business Review* in a 1992 interview:

> Understanding the consumer is just part of good marketing. You also have to understand the brand. That whole experience forced us to define what the Nike brand really meant, and it taught us the importance of focus. . . . A brand is something that has a clear-cut identity among consumers, which a company creates by sending out a clear, consistent message over a period of years until it achieves a critical mass of marketing.[8]

Nike's positioning is a brand promise: To provide its customers with whatever it takes for them to perform to the best of their individual athletic abilities—both physical and mental. As part

of the bargain, they also get all the personal fulfillment and exhilaration that comes with accomplishing personal goals. Nike
creates shoes and other sports apparel for those who want to
achieve their personal best, and if those people pass someone on
the left as they're doing it, so much the better.

Nike is represented mostly by professional athletes who personify its tenets, but the company sells shoes and apparel to millions of individuals who want to achieve the same kind of personal triumphs that they watch on television, only in their own,
less public way. "Just Do It," a phrase created in 1987 by adman
Dan Wieden, is their individual call to action.

In achieving the Nike positioning, just as significant as its
emphasis on performance has been its avoidance of what is referred to in Beaverton as "the f-word," meaning "fashion." During the 1980s when the athletic shoe category was anybody's
race, the aspirants fell into two camps: brands that bet that fashion was what everyone was looking for as long as the shoe's
performance was satisfactory, and the Nike camp that focused
on performance, and equated fashion with physical and marketing wimpiness.

What made this rivalry interesting was that *both* points of
view were right. Professional athletes and weekend joggers alike
care about what their shoes look like; looks are always important. But the right positioning door to enter the category was the
performance door because, once performance was established,
fashion could be integrated into the shoe designs and the brand
personality. What some companies discovered to their dismay
was that it did not often work the other way around. This was
the positioning insight that helped propel Nike to a point where
performance did not fight fashion, rather, performance became
fashionable.

Some of the Best Advertising Ever

In the marketing world, and the rest of the world, Nike advertising is sprinting toward legendary status. The brand's television advertising is where the Nike brand sends out its primary

branding messages, and for years it's been among the top ten of the most popular campaigns in the United States. (Popularity doesn't necessarily mean the advertising works, but in this case, it does). Nike's print work, particularly their women's campaign, is also considered to be some of the best around.

The Nike ad agency is Wieden & Kennedy, a Portland group that opened their doors with a portion of the Nike account in the early 1980s. The Nike/W&K partnership has turned out to be one of the most fertile in recent advertising history. Some of their best known Nike advertising is a litany of hall of fame–quality ads.

One memorable campaign turned Bo Jackson into a media star, particularly a couplet of spots that celebrated his once Supermanesque talents. The first commercial began by talking seriously about Bo's abilities as seen through the eyes of extraordinary athletes from several sports (Michael Jordan: "Bo knows basketball"). But the back half of the sixty-second commercial places tongue in cheek, with John McEnroe questioning Bo the tennis player; Wayne Gretzky deciding "Ahh . . . no" when it comes to Bo playing hockey; and Bo Diddly listening to Jackson's pitiful guitar playing, then proclaiming, "Bo . . . you don't know diddly." The second spot, which ran later that year, starts out in a similar way, but ends with Jackson having learned how to play a mean guitar (and in only six months), and the great Bo Diddly becoming just another convert to the great Bo Jackson.

What do these and other celebrity athlete spots have to do with Nike's brand identity? Just this: Nike athletes are achievers in the extreme. They do not compromise. When Bo Jackson literally climbed the centerfield wall in Comiskey Park to spear a fly ball, or Michael Jordan blissfully disregarded Newton's law of gravitation, or Charles Barkley carried an extra quarter ton of opposition in a slow-moving brawl toward the basket—at those moments those men believed that performance was all that mattered. Not coincidentally, so does the shoe company that hired them.

The Nike women's print advertising is not as spectacular as that for the male side of the house, but the impact may have been as great, dollar for dollar. Originally called "Dialogue" and introduced in 1990, the women's campaigns forge an emotional bond with their audience, dealing sensitively with women's compulsion to overcome psychological obstacles such as the fear of aging, to understand the strengths and shortcomings of their bodies, and to exercise the freedom of their rediscovered physicality. While Nike's celebrity athlete advertising has spotlighted spectacular performance, the women's campaigns have explored how the individual female athlete reaches deep inside to overcome a thousand years of foolish misconceptions about what women cannot do. A satisfying reminder that Nike was, after all, the *goddess* of victory.

Ultimately, the Nike advertising returns to the solitary striver, intense to the point of exhaustion, alone in a pack where there's no one to help but the real you. They are the athlete's advocate, seeking to be at the soul of sport. Where did it come from, this penetrating understanding of the individual as athlete? From Phil Knight and Bill Bowerman, who knew what it was like to slip into a "runner's high"? From the years of talking to men and women with uncanny skills? From two admen called Wieden and Kennedy, who instinctively sensed what champions feel? Or, was it from the shoes themselves that, when the swoosh is applied, are imbued with a taste for victory?

Is the Nike Brand *Too* Powerful?

Brandweek magazine once observed, "Nike no longer markets product. It markets Nike, and expects sales will follow."[9] Nike has built a great brand, but not a universally liked one. There have been allegations of payoffs to amateur athletes, reported garnering of endorsements from collegiate coaches, hard-to-the-wall negotiations with sports leagues, and controversial control of professional athletes and their careers. Despite it all, and because of it all, Phil Knight was named in 1993 as "The Most Powerful Man in Sports" by the *Sporting News*.

Even the advertising that has meant so much to Nike's success has wandered into some odd surroundings from time to time, such as the last two years when the brand ran a series of

THE REVOLUTION AND "JUST DO IT"

In 1986, Nike was a distant second to Reebok. Chiat Day, creators of the famous Apple "1984" commercial two years before, was Nike's primary advertising agency, and a small Portland agency called Wieden & Kennedy (W&K) was used as a secondary source of ideas and work. When the decision was made to move the business entirely to Wieden, W&K staffers Janet Champ and Susan Hoffman saw this as an opportunity to seat Nike as the fountainhead for America's newfound obsession with fitness. They came up with the thought that Nike offered a "revolution" in fitness for those with the courage to seek it out.

W&K obtained the rights from Capitol Records to use the original sound track of the song "Revolution" from the earlier Beatles album. When the commercial first aired in 1987, the company was told to cease and desist by Apple Records, the Beatles's London recording company that claimed to have all rights to the song. The ensuing legal battle could not have been more beneficial to Nike. The brouhaha created more word of mouth than their ad budget ever could have generated. The result was an explosive re-start for the Nike brand. Nike gained momentum that enabled the brand to capture the category lead and never look back.

In 1988, the brand made another landmark move. It was in that year that Nike began using the endline, "Just Do It," a marvelously ambiguous statement of empowerment. "Just Do It" urges action, and also implies that any goal, sports-related or not, is achievable if individuals just get off their tail ends and give it a serious shot. According to its author, Dan Wieden, "('Just Do It') comes out of the idea that sports is action and decision and not philosophy. At some point, you need to act, and not get caught up in uncertainty. And I think people respond to that, particularly in this complex society. There's a sense of freedom in that action."

"Just Do It" has since become a national rallying cry and a personal motivator for individuals of all ages and backgrounds when they're having a difficult time overcoming inertia in their lives.

nearly incoherent ads using a psychotic-looking Dennis Hopper as a crazed referee/fan. Those who love the campaign think it is the personification of ultimate fanness. To the other half of the planet, the spots are a bizarre attempt at stretching the meaning of the Nike brand somewhere beyond the pale. As usual, the Nike people know what the campaign's all about and that seems to be good enough for them.

The most disturbing controversy surrounding the brand has centered on the selling of the Nike shoes to inner-city youths. Legislators, social workers, prominent clergy, and others have criticized the culture that Nike is accused of exploiting, a culture that sees some young people steal and even commit violence in order to wear the latest Nike hightops. In chapter 4, we speculated about the positioning ramifications of the "Just Do It" theme line. Nike critics have interpreted it to mean "Just do whatever you have to do" to wear the best. Retorted Dan Wieden in the *New York Times Magazine:* "For someone to say 'Just Do It' means 'exercise' to the white middle class, while blacks in the ghetto would interpret it as a call to commit crime or do drugs . . . that's a racist perception."[10] Perhaps, but it's a perception that refuses to fade.

The Nike brand has hatched a generation of rabid brand builders, marketers who believe that they are making marketing history, and they're not about to let a little criticism stand in their way. Nike advertising manager Rob DeFlorio once commented, "The people who represent this brand are tough, irreverent types, willing to be out there, take a chance, willing to be loved, hated or respected in the name of the brand."[11]

Nike's Unpredictable Future

The people of Nike have built a solid-gold brand that should be leverageable for generations to come, although that's not quite a certainty given some sobering business facts. Company sales approached $4 billion in revenue in 1993, then fell to well below that level in 1994 because of sliding basketball and sneaker sales. Nike's earnings shrank 22 percent during the same period, triggering a stock price decline of more than 40 percent. Nike's problems are being reflected in its main line product quality ratings as well, according to The 1994 EquiTrend Survey. The survey ranked Nike 38th, compared to 28th just a year earlier, and 25th in 1990.

Market watchers say that some of the young people who drove the company's phenomenal growth are tiring of the look and the hype associated with Nike's high-profile footwear. The very elements that attracted such loyal followers in the past—endorsements from celebrity athletes—have become less valuable assets as younger Americans search for what they now regard as more credible symbols of striving, such as hiking boots and other outdoors-oriented shoes.

On the competitive front, Reebok has once again shown its old strength as a resurgent brand, with a CEO in Paul Fireman whose determination to catch and pass Nike may exceed even Phil Knight's drive to preside over a globally dominant brand.

Internally, like many successful start-ups that hit it big, Nike's biggest fear is what bigness breeds. Nike managers are struggling to maintain the original Nike culture, in the wake of meteoric growth, followed by softening market trends. The Nike name is now incredibly powerful and yet very vulnerable. If soul-searching and priority reordering lies ahead, Nike will be in good company; similar troubles plagued Sears, IBM, and General Motors, among others. Nike hipness will not necessarily protect it from such a fate.

Phil Knight and his management team face some tough decisions about how to continue to build the Nike brand equity without destroying the culture that gave it growth. Nike can still build share in the running shoe category, but each share point will be harder than the last to capture, given the stubbornness of the competition and the already strong levels the brand enjoys. There's lots of room to grow in the apparel industry, but even the elasticity of the Nike name has its limits and finding those limits may be a painful and costly process.

There is great hope within the Nike organization (shared by many on Wall Street) that European and Asian market expansion will fuel strong new growth. That's not a certainty, however, given the differences between those retail trade environments and that in the United States, and the fluctuating currency markets that can have serious cost-of-goods implications to a global apparel company. The even bigger question is whether the Nike personality can stretch and adapt to the changing mores of global markets.

What Can We Learn from Nike?

Nike has demonstrated that nothing is as powerful as the power of the individual. The people at Nike understand that the determination it takes to achieve anything is, by definition, a personal struggle. Teams win or lose games; individuals succeed or fail. The Nike performance positioning and individualistic personality translates into: whatever it takes for an individual to achieve what that individual has set as the goal. That's a strong place for any brand to be, particularly in this age of renewed individualism.

We have also observed that the power of some brands can border on being excessive, and that excess can kill what an identity builds. Most of the negative allegations about Nike's power abuses are unproven, but they serve to remind us that there's a fine line between seeking dominance as a brand to rise above competition and clutter, and seeking so much control that you invite reprisals from the marketplace.

The Nike people never stop thinking about what their brand is, has been, and can be. They maintain an irreverent hipness with the same kind of fervor that sustains the Disney magic and the driving competitiveness of Microsoft. Nike's campus in Beaverton is populated with zealots who care about their world because they invented it, and because they are certain that its precepts are right for the world at large. "Just Do It" is the brand's *demand* that human beings reject what they don't like. In short, to do what Nike itself has done.

Finally, Nike has proven again that success in brand building requires unbridled passion for the essence of the brand. Like Disney, Nike people have been accused of an unhealthy obsession with their brand. To paraphrase Barry Goldwater, extremism in defense of brands is not a vice, or so some brand builders believe.

In the fall of 1977, Blue Ribbon Sports ran a series of print ads in the back of *Runner's World* magazine. The ads were signed with the tagline: "THERE IS NO FINISH LINE." That's as good a summary as you will find of Phil Knight's philosophy, and the identity of the brand he built.

PROCTER'S PLAN:
THE SHIFTING OF BRAND IDENTITIES

Feeling the Squeeze

On April 12, 1837, William Procter and James Gamble cranked up their soap and candle operation in Cincinnati. More than 150 years later, Mr. Procter and Mr. Gamble's somewhat larger firm was to face one of its most serious challenges since its inception.

P&G is a $30 billion giant among giants, operating in 54 countries. Its list of brands reads like the prototypical shopping list: Tide, Pampers, Head & Shoulders, Bounce, Crest, Vicks, Ivory, Charmin, Downy, Noxzema, Pert, Cover Girl, Cheer, Duncan Hines, Folgers, and so on. This is the company that essentially invented the brand management concept in the 1950s, and has successfully marketed leading brands on almost every aisle of the supermarket. They have always needed the retail trade, but the trade has needed them almost as much, at least until the uprising by private labels as we entered the 1990s.

Procter & Gamble had built its franchises on the basis of premium brand identities that usually included excellent products, backed by unparalleled marketing and product research, innovative new products and line extensions, premium pricing (versus private label, but often at competitive levels with other premium brands), and large advertising budgets.

In order to maintain strong trade relations and keep retail pricing as low as possible, the company also paid untold millions to supermarket chains around the country in the form of "allowances"—cash or credit allocations for merchandising, advertising or display assistance, or simply for the right to stock their brands on a chain's shelves.

The retail trade in the United States began to exercise its leverage, as distributors to consumers, just as its counterparts in Canada and Europe had done years earlier. Brands like Procter's were faced with the higher trade costs of competing, and the need to raise list prices in order to maintain margins. At the same time, retailers became much more aggressive in marketing their own lower-priced labels, which put additional price pressures on premium brands. Meanwhile, the consumer began to search for low-priced quality, and suddenly Procter and dozens of other packaged goods manufacturers were caught in a squeeze like none they had ever experienced before.

How Procter Responded and Why

The company at first fought the valiant fight with its usual array of advertising, consumer promotions, and couponing, laced with what it hoped would be sufficient trade support, all funded with premium pricing. But, the trade grew stronger by the month and consumers grew more impatient with premium brands that raised prices, or kept them at levels that seemed less justifiable than in the past.

P&G research indicated that the company was often not delivering the value consumers were demanding. In fact, a typical American family who bought Procter brands instead of private label would pay an average of $725 more per year. More and more of P&G's stalwart brands were reeling from significant share losses, including Comet, Spic & Span, and Pampers.

CEO Ed Artzt implemented a corporate-wide reevaluation process, involving many months of internal discussions led by outside consultants. When the analyses and soul-searching were over, the company began one of the most intensive reengineering jobs any major U.S. corporation had yet attempted. The plan called for a series of fundamental transformations in the way that Procter conducted business, including:

■ Organizational restructuring that reduced mid-level staffing and made each individual and group more responsible for results;

■ Changing production procedures to increase efficiencies (for example, reducing the time it takes to change a production line from two days to two hours);

■ Pruning back the marginal brands, such as Citrus Hill orange juice, Solo laundry detergent, and White Cloud toilet tissue;

■ Restaging older brands into new categories; for example, expanding Mr. Clean from the hard surface arena to glass cleaners, and Spic & Span from floor cleaner into bathroom cleaner;

■ Laying off approximately 13,000 of the company's 102,000 workers worldwide to reduce costs, an unprecedented move in P&G's history;

■ Closing 20 percent of the company's 147 factories around the world; and very importantly,

■ Implementing an Everyday Low Pricing (EDLP) or "value pricing" policy in 1991, which was then expanded in 1993–94. This policy reduces prices, cuts back in couponing, and significantly increases advertising in order to maintain consumer demand. Under EDLP, retailers received fewer financial incentives, but theoretically made more money in the increased sales velocity of the Procter brands.

EDLP seeks to stabilize the "up and down" pricing of the past, which was based on periodic trade deals, and to narrow the gap between P&G's premium brands and lower-priced competition. According to CEO Artzt, the company begins losing market share when its brands are more than 30 percent higher than private label. Procter waited until some of its gaps had grown to more than 35 percent.

Once the price cutbacks began in earnest in the spring of 1993, the company reduced the price on its diaper line alone 3 times in 12 months. The rollback litany included 5 percent, 7 percent, and 5 percent cuts for Pampers and Luvs; 9 percent, 9 percent, and 15 percent for Tide, Cheer, and Era; 6 percent for Downy, and similar cuts along the way for Pringles, Ivory, and Safeguard. Coupled with these price rollbacks were reductions in trade support expenditures. Advertising budgets have frequently been maintained or increased, especially in the most competitive categories, and couponing is often reduced or eliminated.

The Results

An estimated three-fourths of P&G's brands are now involved in some form of EDLP. Because pricing and value impression is so critical in packaged goods categories, the moves by Procter will undoubtedly have a strong impact on the identities of the individual brands involved. They're already having an impact on sales.

For the fiscal year ending June of 1994, P&G achieved a record $2.2 billion in earnings, compared to a $656 million loss the previous year, which was negatively affected by restructuring charge-offs. In its final quarter of that fiscal year, the company made $406 million, compared to a $1.2 billion loss the previous year that did *not* include restructuring effects. At the same time, P&G announced that 22 of the 32 categories in which their brands compete as leaders were showing signs of strong recovery.

The jury is still out on whether P&G's value-pricing strategy will have long-term staying power. Retailers have come to count on incentives to guarantee part of their own margins, and EDLP limits their flexibility in strategically buying product at lower list prices and maintaining retail levels in order to maximize their own margins. Nevertheless, more and more retailers are reluctantly agreeing that some form of value pricing appears to be the safe and sane way to provide consumer value without endangering the critical margins of manufacturers and trade. Importantly, the lower pricing has also helped the grocery chains regain the business they lost to membership outlets.

The effect of EDLP on the identity of the company's brands is not as clear. In theory, reducing the price of a premium packaged goods brand could make that brand appear to be less special. After all, most Americans have been raised to believe that the best products and services cost more. However, as pointed out earlier, higher prices no longer equate automatically to superior performance. In fact, the resurgence of the P&G brands implies that they are often succeeding, *because of* their perceived better value.

What Can We Learn from Procter & Gamble?

John Lipsky, chief economist at Salomon Brothers, has concluded: "In broad terms, it looks as if Procter & Gamble ran up against a clash of preexisting strategies of creating brand identities and the cyclical developments of the economy at large."[12] Translation: In order to save and build its key brand lines, Procter & Gamble had to be flexible enough to send out new positioning prompts to consumers, altering their brands' identities from premium quality/premium priced, to premium quality/ value priced, much the same way that McDonald's and other fast-food chains had done a year or two earlier.

P&G in changing positioning prompts also demonstrated the power of positioning. It's no easy task to lower prices and maintain brand identities that are based on strong product performance. P&G had been among the leading companies that helped the American consumer accept higher pricing for high-quality national brands. Now, P&G had found a better way to lower price—by reallocating funds and bolstering its "new" identities as excellent products at reasonable prices.

There are also some caveats that should be added to this value repositioning story. First, EDLP is not necessarily the answer for many categories, distribution and sales organizations, or brands. Nor is it always right for companies that don't have the resources of a P&G. As a group, Procter & Gamble brands have some of the greatest clout in the supermarket. P&G's total company leverage permitted it to take chances that most companies might have lived to regret. It took the largest packaged brand company, the largest sales force, the largest array of leading brands, and the largest consumer advertising budget to survive standoffs with the retail chains, some of which are still going on. What Procter did is not necessarily right for every company, or even for most companies, but it was apparently right for P&G.

In addition, the company has admitted that they were slow in seeing the writing on the wall about where consumers wanted to head, and how difficult the road would be given the intransigence of the trade. Procter, like most of its competitors, was not crazy about lowering prices on brands that had been delivering strong profits. Unfortunately, consumers have little interest in delivering profits, only in receiving good values.

It wasn't that many years ago that Procter & Gamble was considered more or less invincible in virtually any category in which it competed. More recently, the company has encountered a series of unexpected challenges that have tested its ability to cope with change. No challenge has been greater than the redefining of value in the marketplace that prompted identity shifts across more brands than at any other time in marketing history. Only time will tell how successful those moves will be.

8

Cases II
One Old, One New, One Blue

Mature brands are not guaranteed a future; new brands can reach maturity in a matter of months. In today's hostile marketplace, the difference between success and subpar depends more on the sturdiness of an identity than on the age of the brand. This chapter looks first at an older brand with fundamental strengths that needed reigniting, a brand called the Southwestern Bell Yellow Pages. Then, we'll explore the creation of a relatively new brand, Saturn, which was developed separate from its corporate parent, a waif by design. Burger King, the last brand in this chapter, is decades old, and only just now beginning to tap its full potential.

THE SWBYP'S STORY: REENERGIZING THE YELLOW PAGES

The "yellow pages." It's the household reference book that's used all the time, but forgotten within seconds after it has served its purpose. The yellow pages is the tome that some people would rather drive 10 miles to avoid opening. It's the doorstop, the paperweight, that big heavy thing that dares you to crack it open. Not exactly the stuff that make brand fantasies.

And yet, yellow pages directories are indispensable tools in virtually every household in America. They are also the products that have provided much of the profit that fueled the expansion of AT&T before the 1984 divestiture, and the seven "Baby Bells" afterwards.

"What Do They Mean, *Baby* Bell?"

In 1982, Federal Judge Harold Greene ordered AT&T to be vivisected and redistributed within two years. In so doing, he changed forever the brand identities of eight of America's largest telecommunications companies, including seven "Baby Bells," or regional Bell operating companies (RBOCs). One of those prodigious babies, Southwestern Bell, was given a five-state region in the south-central part of the country as its marketing area (Missouri, Kansas, Arkansas, Oklahoma, and Texas). As with the other Bell companies, Southwestern Bell was permitted to keep a prized possession, its yellow pages business, a highly profitable family of hundreds of community directories that carry ads for mostly local and regional companies.

Over the years, the yellow pages industry has grown into an enigma. One of the largest and most profitable advertising media in the country, directories now generate more than $9 billion nationally in revenues. They're also one of the most frequently used media; typical households will page through directories several times a week. And when they do, they're ready and willing to purchase, not just shop, giving them a distinct advantage over most other advertising media.

At the same time, directories are one of the least talked about media, always in danger of being taken for granted, considered old-fashioned compared to other media. Although several yellow pages companies are well along in developing computer-based, interactive consumer services, the directories themselves are considered by the advertising industry to be one of the most conservative vehicles for commercial messages.

Business as Usual

Let's say you're the owner of a three-store chain of local jewelry stores. Your father and your father's father founded the business. They gave you two pieces of advice when they retired: "Give the people what they want. Not what you want, what *they* want . . ." And, "No matter how tough times get, don't drop your yellow pages ads."

Many small to mid-sized companies, not just in Southwestern Bell territory but all over the industrialized world, will advertise in the yellow pages as long as they are in business because a huge percentage of their traffic traces to that medium. Plumbers, locksmiths, carpet cleaners, furniture movers, restaurants, travel agents—and, nowadays, some very wealthy lawyers and physicians—depend heavily on the yellow pages to keep the customers coming.

In many consumer households, however, directories sit quietly by the phone in the hallway or buried in some magazine rack. They're portable, but usually too big to carry around the house. They are often more difficult to use than any other reference books the consumer encounters, though most companies have introduced indexes and other aids to help in sorting through the categories of ads. Typically, a directory is 400 to 500 pages in length and carries more than 2,000 ads and listings, a cornucopia of information, but also clutter in the extreme.

Yellow pages are constantly in danger of being outflanked by more contemporary ways to advertise, such as local radio, direct mail, and cable television. The yellow pages industry must continuously contemporize itself to remain relevant as a medium. If it does not, the consumer will no longer bother to wade through its ads, and the retailer will no longer bother to advertise in a medium ignored by prospective customers.

Rethinking the Yellow Pages

Southwestern Bell was rightly concerned that the faster-paced world of the 1990s might bring with it a rapid migration of consumers from the yellow pages toward more top-of-mind media. The company was also feeling increasing pressure from new yellow pages directories in various states that claimed to be more modern alternatives to traditional directories.

Until 1984, the vast majority of communities in this country had only one yellow pages directory, usually published by AT&T. It was common knowledge that the AT&T books were exceptionally profitable, so when deregulation arrived, dozens of independent companies showed up to reap some profit of their own.

In an unexpected turn of fate, the competitive books were also free to use one of the best-known brand icons in the country—the "walking fingers" logo. Remarkably, the symbol had never been copyrighted. AT&T management had left it unprotected because, in their consolidated days as Ma Bell, they wanted as many small business advertisers as possible to use the logo in their local signage. Consequently, what was a key brand identity strength for the AT&T Bell yellow pages, became public domain a few years later when the new independent directories felt free to let *their* fingers do the walking, usually right across the front covers of their own books.

Most yellow pages companies try to position their books as encyclopedias of goods and services. The same "it's all in here" strategy was standard boilerplate in the industry. Because they had depended so long on the halo effect from the AT&T brand, few directory companies had yet figured out since the divestiture how to successfully brand their books. In fact, most books were really making category pitches, without proprietary appeals that they could call their own.

Here, then, was the problem for Southwestern Bell: Their yellow pages directories had been thrown into highly competitive, unregulated environments, with a heritage of sameness, and with little to differentiate them. If ever there was a need for a new brand identity, this marketing situation was certainly a prime candidate.

The Branding of Swbyp's

Southwestern Bell Yellow Pages called upon their communications agency, Ketchum, to help them rethink what their books should stand for in the marketplace. Their business objective was simple: increase consumer usage, and enable the sales force to use updated usage numbers to generate more advertising revenue from local and regional business customers.

After reviewing existing research and talking to customers and company employees, the Ketchum/Southwestern Bell team realized that the company would be falling into the same old trap if it continued to think of its end product as just a book. The directory, Ketchum strategists argued, was really more of a "place," a central information station that people "visited" in search of what they needed in their lives. The Southwestern Bell Yellow Pages was a place where consumers would find services and products that would help them meet challenges, capitalize on opportunities, and solve problems they couldn't handle on their own. That thinking ultimately became the brand's new positioning proposition: " Southwestern Bell Yellow Pages will be positioned as the place where people get what they want out of life."

With that change, the book of thousands of ads on yellow paper bound into heavy books became, instead, a repository of ways to improve people's lives. Consumers were not just looking up company names when they opened the yellow pages, they were in search of things to make their lives better, to help accomplish goals, to solve problems, even to realize their full potential as human beings. The tome that was so often thought of as a dusty reference book was, in reality, a ticket to a better life. What had been advertising messages could be restaged as a catalyst to make a person's life easier and more rewarding.

As the brand team worked, they began to piece together the Swbyp's' personality. Using adjective lists, "what if?" scenarios, anthropomorphic comparisons, and other techniques, the team began to see the new brand personality as "human, trustworthy, accessible, helpful, with a good sense of humor." The brand's inner strategic composition and outer face were forming into a cohesive whole—the beginnings of a reshaped brand identity. Assuming, of course, that consumers and advertisers accepted it as such.

But how could Southwestern Bell convince their advertisers and readers that they should look at those same old books in entirely new ways? The marketing team held sales rep focus groups to get a better fix on their needs, and to learn how a new campaign might help them do their job better. They found that the reps had not particularly liked the previous campaigns, which tended to sell the category and not the brand. What the sales force was looking for was a proprietary "conversation starter," marketing communications that would help them open the door to sales with new and existing small business customers.

In the end, the key was to take the positioning literally. A Ketchum creative group head named Steve Merson came up with a concept that brought the positioning to life in an unlikely, somewhat difficult to pronounce acronym: "Swbyp's" (pronounced Swa' bips) from Southwestern Bell Yellow Pages.

Swbyp's was not a book, it was almost literally—as the positioning called for—a place where people could get what they wanted for their lives. This particular "place" was an imaginary shopping mall where you could find virtually anything you needed, from legal advice (Attorneys, page 64) to accordions (Music Stores, page 475) to house toppers (Roofers, page 736). Ketchum crafted a department store–like logo, to underscore the shopping mall imagery, and the logo was placed on yellow shopping bags that became central to the company's new graphic system. "Where people get what they want" was used as the theme line, and a campy musical theme was composed that was reminiscent of the days when department stores were symbols of stylish shopping.

The Swbyp's television campaign used converted consumers who proclaimed to the world that they had found "this great place" where they could get just about anything they wanted. The campaign was rough-produced and pitted against another, more traditional approach in a battery of communications tests.

The results indicated that both campaigns were strong, but the Swbyp's idea loomed as the high-risk/high-yield option.

After evaluating the options, the marketing/agency team, led by Vice President for Marketing Virginia Vann, finally decided that a "no guts, no glory" tack was the only way to go. In a meeting in November of 1991, the team presented CEO Mac Geschwind with the test results and recommended the Swbyp's campaign. Geschwind recognized that what was being recommended would not only change his company's ad campaign, it would change his company's brand (a particularly sobering thought when your company is part of a 100-year-old corporation). When it was time to make the final decision, Geschwind didn't hesitate. "Let's go with Swbyp's," he said. "It may be tough to pronounce, but it's a big idea."

The Selling In and Rolling Out of Swbyp's

Before the campaign could be launched publicly, the Southwestern Bell Yellow Pages organization—soon to be called "Team Swbyp's"—had to sign up for the idea. As it happened, they were the toughest audience to convert. Fortunately, Virginia Vann had had the foresight to involve an employee representative team as a task force to help evaluate the new campaigns that were being considered, and to help employees understand the potential of the repositioning and the new communications program.

Beyond the task force, though, there were thousands of employees who had sold and supported yellow pages programs for decades in their own way. These people had serious doubts about re-branding their book into something that was unlike anything that had ever been attempted in the industry. More to the point, the corporate Southwestern Bell brand parentage was very strong and the sales force was not sure they wanted to add any more elements to their mother brand. The marketing team spent many weeks working with the sales and support staffs, explaining how the Swbyp's program would enhance their own best efforts, without diminishing the Southwestern Bell heritage.

After getting the nod from key managers throughout the organization, the Swbyp's program began rolling out the Swbyp's campaign in the five-state Southwestern Bell marketing area during the course of 1992 and 1993. The Swbyp's campaign was to be a convergent communications approach, with advertising, direct marketing, public relations, and community relations all focusing on the strategic concept of Swbyp's as the shopping place where people got what they wanted out of life.

Before the full campaign hit, a series of teaser outdoor boards piqued the interest of the local population wherever they appeared. Television commercials used funny, interesting, everyday people who had "shopped" at Swbyp's. Direct mail pieces were sent to customers and prospects in retention and lead generation programs, all carrying the Swbyp's graphics and the "Where people get what they want" theme.

Gradually, as the Swbyp's concept began to take hold, Geschwind and Vann decided to make the first major graphic branding change in years on the directories themselves. The Swbyp's logo would adorn each cover from that point forward, not a small decision since the company spends more than $100 million every year on directory production alone.

The logo was also put on anything and everything that employees and customers might wear, hold, and tote: coffee mugs, umbrellas, T-shirts, golf bags—whatever carried the Southwestern Bell name, now also carried the Swbyp's logo. The company store that distributed logo'ed items to employees sold more Swbyp's paraphernalia in the first six months of the campaign than had been sold in the previous three years using the old graphics. Eventually, the Swbyp's logo became more dominant on directories than the Southwestern Bell corporate logo.

The people of Southwestern Bell Yellow Pages still work for Southwestern Bell, but they also work for Swbyp's. It's the name, the personality, the brand identity of their company. Today, if you visit any Southwestern Bell Yellow Pages facility, you will find the Swbyp's logo on the signage throughout their offices, the stationery on their desks, the business cards in their wallets. The full Swbyp's graphic treatment is even a major part of the

EXHIBIT 8-1

OPENED 24 HOURS A DAY

Location.
Location.
Location.

| Every year people in Odessa use us 5 million times. | An impressive 50% of calls result in a purchase. | 20% of those calls result in new customers. |

Call 684-4051 and put your business right where the customers are. "Where People Get What They Want."

Southwestern Bell Yellow Pages

The unique Swbyp's advertising gave Southwestern Bell Yellow Pages a whole new identity that created new momentum for the brand.

yellow pages company section of the Southwestern Bell Corporation annual report.

An important aspect of the Swbyp's makeover was also the updating of the books themselves. Directories were "re-scoped" to cover expanded geographical areas so local residents wouldn't have to look in several books to check out various retail outlets. Four-color capability was added to all Swbyp's books to make them more readable and contemporary looking. Indexes were made more streamlined and helpful, and sections featuring maps, stadium/auditorium seating schematics, and other community information were strengthened. The product, in short, was made to be as fresh as the new Swbyp's identity itself.

How Swbyp's Got What *It* Wanted Out of Life

The Swbyp's repositioning has been a study in how to breathe new life into an aging product. Even more than that, it's a lesson about how to brand the difficult to brand.

According to tracking studies, after only a few months in the marketplace, the Swbyp's name was recognized by an astounding 75 percent of consumers. That figure rose to more than 80 percent the following year, and to more than 90 percent in some markets, after only a year or two of exposure. The research company involved reported that they had not seen those kinds of levels registered so quickly since the AT&T "Reach Out and Touch Someone" campaign. Just as important, consumer usage of the Swbyp's books has begun to rise for the first time in recent memory.

Similar results were seen among the company's business customers. Among advertisers, about 75 percent generally preferred the Swbyp's directories before they saw the advertising. After they saw the advertising, that preference rose to over 90 percent.

Clearly, the population of the Swbyp's states have felt the new vitality in the Southwestern Bell brand and are turning toward their books in increasing numbers. In 1993, the Swbyp's campaign was awarded an EFFIE, a prestigious award given by

THE SWBYP'S STORIES—
A BRAND IDENTITY AT WORK

When you change a corporate culture, you change the way people think and act about their company. When a new brand identity changes a corporate culture, it demonstrates the power of brand identity.

The Swbyp's phenomenon has so gripped the Southwestern Bell Yellow Pages company that the halls are filled with stories about how the name and personality makeover has swept through their five-state marketing area and well beyond. Some of the more popular Swbyp's stories:

- Each year, San Antonio holds a festival, complete with floats that literally float down the town's central river, with colorful displays by the local groups and companies. Southwestern Bell Corporation employees enter a float each year. The first year of the Swbyp's campaign, the Southwestern Bell float was laden with Swbyp's signage. As the float passed by the main group of spectators, hundreds of school children spontaneously began to sing the Swbyp's jingle.
- Swbyp's marketing director Laurie Vincent was climbing a Mayan pyramid in Chichén Itzá on the Yucatan peninsula, when she squinted into the sun and looked up to see how much farther she had to ascend. There, near the summit of the pyramid was a solitary man, a tourist from Kansas City bedecked in Bermuda shorts and camera, walking carefully across the narrow ledges. As Vincent watched, the man turned and strolled across the 2,000-year-old ruins, gently swinging a bright yellow Swbyp's bag filled with tourista booty. As Vincent tells the story, "It was like seeing a postcard from home."
- Another employee was returning from a trip abroad. When she arrived back in St. Louis and proceeded through the TWA terminal to U.S. Customs, the agent

welcomed her back and asked her where she worked. "Southwestern Bell," she replied. "Really?" the agent inquired. "Then maybe you can tell me what 'Swbyp's' stands for?"

- One manager, who happened to be wearing a Swbyp's T-shirt, was traveling across Missouri and stopped at a toll booth to pay her due. A line of less-than-enthusiastic motorists had to wait behind her car when the toll booth personnel decided to serenade her with the Swbyp's theme song before letting her go on her way.

- The Swbyp's customer service center is used to getting all kinds of calls, but this one touched even the veteran rep who received it. An 8-year-old boy called in to say that he knew Swbyp's was "where people get what they want." He was going on a trip with his family and was worried about whether his grandparents would be able to find them when they arrived. "Do you think Swbyp's," he asked, "can tell me where my grandparents are?"

- A sales rep from St. Louis reported that spontaneous singing of the Swbyp's jingle would take place in shopping malls whenever he wore his company shirt. He gave up wearing his Swbyp's golf shirt because the repeated singing by passing duffers disturbed the concentration of his golfing buddies.[1]

the New York chapter of the American Marketing Association, for one of the best in-market performances in the country.

A far-reaching change in the Southwestern Bell Yellow Pages organization has been in the way its sales force and support personnel throughout the five-state area have merchandised the Swbyp's concept. Employees wear the Swbyp's T-shirts and drink out of Swbyp's coffee mugs because they want to, not because they are told they must. They are proud to be associated with the fun and excitement of a fresh new way of thinking about their business. Now, when the sales reps walk into customers' doors, they often hear, "Hey there, it's the Swbyp's guy (or lady)!" Customers make out their checks to "Swbyp's," and customer service and telemarketing reps answer the phone "Swbyp's" as well. All of this is a revolutionary change in a company that had succeeded in the past by sticking with what traditionally worked in the past.

The Swbyp's brand team is now in the process of evolving the brand's identity from a place of information to an information resource. Swbyp's is stepping beyond its yellow page directories and looking toward the time when consumers will come to them for where to find goods and services, but also how to shop for certain items, how to entertain out-of-town guests, or where to take a family on a Sunday afternoon.

What Can We Learn from Swbyp's?

There's nothing more gratifying in marketing than to update a brand in need of new energy. The Southwestern Bell Yellow Pages would have continued to deliver profits to its parent even if Swbyp's had not been created. But, it's also likely that its venerable directories would have suffered from the hardening of the arteries that has overtaken many of its counterparts at other regional Bell companies, leaving them wide open to attack from competitive directories and alternative advertising media.

The Swbyp's story is also a story of commitment, but of a sort closer to that found at Disney than at Nike. The Swbyp's people were already committed to their organization; what was new was a recommitment to both a company and a newly fashioned brand. At Swbyp's, as at Disney, the time had come to reconsider what the brand stood for and what it had to offer that needed magnification. Unlike Disney, the heritage of the Swbyp's directories was not always as laden with fond memories and warm feelings. To consumers especially, directories had been more or less functional reference books, so their reconstitution into exciting places to shop was all the more imperative.

There's also something to be learned about how to sell in a risky new concept within an organization, a task that is sometimes more daunting than the sale to the outside world. Employees, particularly in service organizations, are often as important an audience as the customer, and often as skeptical of change as customers. But if the marketing team can involve them as collaborators, as partners in the change, they can become the catalyst that makes the new concept a winner. Some of the best brand contacts are made by employees, as demonstrated everyday at Swbyp's, Disney, Saturn, Nike, and other companies where employees are treated as living extensions of the brand.

Finally, the Swbyp's experience reminds us how the power of the positioning is that much more compelling if it can be translated into a personality that seamlessly flows from it. The personality of Swbyp's is a logical and emotional extension of what the brand stands for in the marketplace. The melding of the "Where people get what they want" strategy with the Swbyp's personality is a convincing testament to the power of a well-constructed brand identity.

THE SATURN MIRACLE: A NEW KIND OF IDENTITY

Until 1989, Americans thought of Saturn, when they thought of it at all, as the sixth planet from the sun. After 1989, Saturn the planet was preempted by Saturn the brand, a new shape of matter that signaled the comeback of a renovated universe called Detroit.

Mr. Smith Goes to Spring Hill

Roger Smith struggled through more than his share of problems during his tenure as the CEO of General Motors, but he godfathered at least one extraordinary idea, a concept that he believed could revolutionize the way GM made cars. It was conceived as a laboratory for learning how to compete better, particularly against offshore carmakers who had flat out whipped GM and most of Detroit when it came to delivering value to the American buyer. (At the time, the average American car cost $1,500–2,000 more to make than its Japanese counterpart, and that didn't include the additional differences in dealer markups.) The corporation would eventually invest heavily in the project, holding it up as a model for the revamping of a then outmoded GM.

After three years in planning, the project went public at the General Motors Technical Center in Warren, Michigan. In the first week of 1985, Roger Smith announced the creation of a largely independent subsidiary division called Saturn Corporation. It was the first new car line for GM since 1918, when the first Chevrolet rolled off the assembly line. GM said they would spend $5 billion to develop and jump-start Saturn. Industry analysts were split on the Saturn's prospects, but they agreed that it was good to see conservative-minded GM try to create a daring new brand, even if it failed.

The Saturn Concept Becomes the Saturn Identity

The Saturn team knew that the key to their brand's success would not depend on adding a few extra accessories or on keeping the suggested retail price a few hundred dollars below competition. Technologically speaking, Saturn was to be a good, but not advanced automobile, meaning that it was designed to offer the styling and amenities of a more expensive car at a lower price to the buyer.

The value that was to be built into Saturns would be the value *perceived by its buyers*. Saturn hit the road at a time when Americans considered value to be the eleventh commandment, and when they were feeling a bit guilty about buying foreign makes. Timing, as they say, is everything.

The Saturn team instantly set themselves apart from most other U.S. carmakers when management invited the heavy involvement of employees and dealers in the brand they had to sell. That overriding principle gave birth to some company characteristics that made Saturn unique at the time among U.S. automakers:

■ First, the Saturn concept hinged on the idea of partner-ships—between management and labor, company and supplier, dealer and customer. Before Saturn, Detroit automakers had talked the partnership talk, but had not often walked the walk.

■ The Saturn workers were all given stakes in the new com-pany. Their profit sharing would be tied directly to the perform-ance of the Saturn Corporation only, not General Motors overall.

■ As part of their partnership approach, the company estab-lished a collegial working environment, involving management, worker, dealer, company, and union. This not only made it a better place to work, it also created an ideal workshop in which to build a brand identity because all the key players became co-builders of the brand. That gave them an added feeling of brand ownership, which translated to an entrepreneurial fervor that could be felt by every customer who walked in the manufactur-ing plant or a dealership.

The partnership agreement also gave a GM company the op-portunity to reset union guidelines so the new car would not be burdened by excessive labor costs before it ever hit the show-room. (That arrangement with the unions later became a major stumbling block that complicated the union/management rela-tionship).

■ Among the many innovations that were to contribute to the Saturn identity was "reverse designing," the developing of the car to take maximum advantage of the new technology that was to be used in building Saturns, rather than the more com-mon method of building or refitting the plant to meet the specs of the car.

■ The Saturn dealers were also treated differently than those with other car companies. In previous years, the relations be-tween the "factory" and the dealer groups had sometimes soured for the Big Three companies, and Saturn was determined not to let that happen. Dealers were always referred to as "re-tailers" because, as Saturn executives put it, they wanted their dealers to be in the retailing business, not in the "deal" business. Retailers were also considered partners with the corporation, not just sales brokers, and company management worked hard to keep those relationships strong. However, it was the brand that was preeminent; the retail stores were uniformly called "Saturn of (location)" to ensure that the Saturn brand identity was paramount, rather than the retailer's name.

- A "no dicker sticker" policy was put in place. The Saturn retail buying experience was to be as smooth and hassle-free as possible. Honesty and directness were to be the watchwords among a class of retail salespersons who were not always known for those traits.

- The entire Saturn team focused their efforts on the customer as an individual. They took the time to think through how an individual might feel when accosted by a dealer's overly aggressive sales teams, and they encouraged their retailers to let shoppers spend time alone with the car. They thought about how individuals can grow attached to their cars, how they talk about them to their friends and family, and how the Saturn team might recreate and incorporate that positive feeling as part of their brand. They thought about how an individual feels when he or she is inconvenienced by a mechanical problem, and then they went out of their way to ensure that the post-sale service experience was as convenient and pleasant as possible.

- Saturn created more than a group of users; a feeling of "family" developed between owners, dealers, and the company. That was vividly demonstrated in June 1994 when an estimated 44,000 Saturn owners converged on Spring Hill for the Saturn Homecoming. Simultaneously, another 100,000 more owners participated in dealer picnics and parties across the country. Combined, those events involved approximately 20 percent of all Saturn owners. How many brands could count on one-fifth of their current users joining in on a celebration of the franchise's success?

Behind many of these innovations was the Saturn team's understanding of, and appreciation for, the lifetime value of the customer. Years before, Americans had been "Ford people" or part of the "Chrysler family," or would tend to restrict their choices to within the GM line. Sons and daughters often bought what their parents had bought because their parents had put their trust in a particular make, and that was good enough for the next generation. These Americans counted on the family brand to deliver what was expected of it, model year in and model year out.

Saturn is attempting to bring back to U.S. automobile making that reliance on a single brand that potentially can grow into a family tradition.

A Different Kind of Company, a Different Kind of Advertising

One of the most important decisions made by Saturn management was to involve its ad agency as early as possible in the marketing planning process. Hal Riney & Partners was hired a full 29 months before the first Saturn was available for sale. The agency teams talked with the people of Spring Hill, Tennessee, where the car was to be born, researched the origins of the young company, studied the philosophy that was bringing the brand to life, and generally immersed itself in this unique selling experience.

The Riney organization had produced the famous "It's Morning Again in America" long-form commercial for the Ronald Reagan election committee in 1980. In April of 1989, they released "Spring in Spring Hill," a film with a feel similar to "Morning," that told the story about the people and ethos of the Saturn environment. Hal Riney and creative director Bruce Campbell were nominated for an Academy Award for their creation of "Spring" as a short documentary. "Spring" never showed a single car, and only mentioned the word "Saturn" once, at the very end. The film was used for recruiting, internal training, and for talking with suppliers. Some Saturn retailers even used it to help secure loans from banks. Eventually, it aired as an infomercial during the Saturn introduction.

The Riney crew also had a hand in virtually all major brand communications, including retail brochures and signage, letters to prospective owners apologizing for delays in delivery, even the want ads seeking help for short-handed retailers.

Saturn advertising was unique within the automobile industry, maintaining that Saturn represented a whole new way to do things in the car business, and using the positioning line: "A different kind of company. A different kind of car." The initial advertising spent very little time showing the new car itself because the Saturn team believed that the car was only one of several reasons why people would buy a Saturn, the other critical one being an interest in doing business—from factory to retailer—with a company that cared as much about its product, its company and its customers as it did about making money.

The campaign was, and is, a long, beautifully rendered explanation of why what's American-made is good enough to buy again. The television work is a love story about the people and customers of a company that happens to make cars. The music and cinematography capture a world of simple honesty, an America that Americans had almost forgotten. In the print ads, the reader comes face-to-face with serious-minded people who are intent on making the best car they can humanly craft.

As in the case of Nike, the importance of the individual crystallizes as you scan the advertising, which slowly persuades you that this is not a company of workers, but a peer group of singular team members drawn together by a common cause. Their cheerful determination to do their job right is injected into their cars as you watch, and that alone seems remarkable enough in the assembly-line world of carmaking.

Reality Bites Back

A good many pundits were proven wrong about GM's ability to sustain such a grand experiment, and to resist the temptation to interfere until the fate of the Saturn brand could be solidified. The public response and positive awareness of the brand speaks for itself, as did the fact that Saturn was named in its introductory years as one of the top three new brands in customer satisfaction in the J.D. Power & Associates annual studies. The company's own research reports claimed in 1994 that 80 percent of its current owners plan to buy another Saturn.[2]

Saturn's financial and fiscal outlook is not as clear. The orig-

HOW A RECALL *STRENGTHENED* THE SATURN IDENTITY

In August of 1993, less than three years into its life, Saturn announced a voluntary recall of 353,000 cars, or 80 percent of the vehicles it had made to date. Rather than permitting the recall—which had been triggered by isolated engine fires—to turn into a public relations disaster, the Saturn team skillfully turned the problem into an opportunity to demonstrate that they meant what they said about customer service.

The company marketing and sales teams instinctively took a one-on-one approach to their crisis. They contacted each customer with a direct, simple-to-understand one-page letter. Many of the Saturn retailers also called customers individually to inform them of the recall.

While the repairs normally took less than half an hour, the extra workload the recall put on the retailers could have caused major inconveniences for their customers. Instead, retailers extended their hours and used these unexpected customer contacts as opportunities to hold barbecues, parties, and customer service feedback discussions. Some retailers even gave customers the admission price for movies or other distractions down the street if the corrective work took longer than anticipated. In other words, the factory and retailers stuck to their mission: Be the friendliest, best-liked car company in the United States.

Saturn management decided not to refer to the recall in their advertising, but to let the goodwill created by the advertising speak for itself. (However, a previous recall of 1,480 cars because of faulty seat-back recliners was the subject of a spot about a Saturn employee traveling all the way to Alaska to install a new one.) One of the team's strong beliefs had been that every brand contact during the good times was to be a positive communication about the brand and the car, with no comparisons to competition. That policy helped soften the blow when problems arose because people were less likely to find fault with a company that would not find fault with competition.

Unlikely as it might seem, the recall was ultimately seen as a *positive* event for Saturn because it reinforced the brand as being made up of people who were willing to admit to a mistake without losing confidence in their products or their brand.

---

inal business objective for the Saturn Corporation was to make 400,000 to 500,000 vehicles annually, but to date the company has sold well below that level (see Exhibit 8-2 for Saturn sales).

Saturn is in a continuous struggle to remain viable and independent as a profitable division of GM. The company was expected to post its first operating profit in 1994, with sales rising rapidly near the end of the year. That's encouraging, but perhaps not all that satisfying to GM management, given the fact that the division is five years old and has cost the corporation an estimated $5 billion to date.

Part of the original concept was for Saturn to have been an introduction for new customers to the GM company, customers who could have been cross-sold into other GM lines. Apparently, there is little evidence that this is happening, and even some indication that the line is cannibalizing some of GM's other brands.

In the fall of 1994, GM made a good news/bad news series of announcements: Saturn would be folded into a small car division that would share parts and transportation systems (and likely reduce company autonomy); but its president, Richard LeFauve, was to head the group that would use Saturn's operating philosophy to build business.

A key problem is that Saturn is operating with designs that are getting to be ancient by auto industry standards, and now is facing serious competition from Chrysler's Neon and other new subcompacts. The brand is not scheduled to get new designs off the assembly line until the 1996 and 1997 model years. That means that the original designs will have been on the road for

EXHIBIT 8-2

Model Year	1991	1992	1993	1994
Units	72,000	170,000	229,000	286,000

Saturn unit sales.
Source: Published company reports.

the better part of a decade, definitely having a negative effect on the brand's identity.

The Saturn experiment was a great success by many standards during its early years, but it will not be able to sustain its success without a continuing commitment from General Motors, and those in charge in Detroit are not the same team who signed off on the Saturn project in the 1980s.

What Can We Learn from Saturn?

The Saturn experience has been a demonstration in what can be achieved when an identity is meticulously planned and integrated from the very beginnings of a brand's existence. Despite considerable doubt and criticism, Saturn's creators stayed true to their original positioning as the caring car company.

The Saturn builders visualized from the outset how the car would be designed, manufactured, sold, and serviced; and they indi*visual*ized how customers wanted to be treated from the showroom to the repair shop. They had in mind that they could create that most unusual of enterprises in the automobile industry—a company that really did care about each of its customers, and could prove it on demand.

Like Disney and Swbyp's, everything counted in the building of the brand—every design element, every consumer letter, every car bolt, every brochure, every phone call to the service department. Everything that emerged from Saturn and the Saturn people became an important brand contact that could potentially contribute to the brand's value to the customer. If Saturn truly cared about its customers, then every part of the Saturn experience must reflect it.

Saturn's marketing communications proved that the product alone did not have to be the focus of attention, even when it was going to be a purchase greater than $12,000. In a unique fashion, the Saturn communications programs also showcased the people behind, in front, and inside the product (an intriguing contrast to Infiniti, which also tried to introduce its brand without showing the product, but its humanless pastoral scenes failed to be as engaging as Saturn's work). And, as does Nike, Saturn celebrates the optimism and spirit of the individual. What you see in the advertising, in the collateral material, in the cars themselves, is about what individuals can do when commitment to a team is what motivates them to strive.

The Saturn brand is the successful coming together of individuals, their building of relationships with one another, and with their vehicles. Saturn reminds us that we all buy *things* for utilitarian purposes, but we buy *brands*—and buy into brand identities—because of human connections that reaffirm our individuality.

In 1992, it was with justifiable pride and satisfaction that Donald Hudler, Saturn's vice president for sales, service, and marketing, told the press: "If we have any legacy at Saturn, it will be that we built an outstanding brand."[3]

THE BURGER KING ADVENTURE: AN IDENTITY THAT HAS BEEN LONG IN COMING

Burger King has been struggling for many years to realize its full potential as a leading fast-food brand. BK maintains a large group of company-owned and franchise operations around the world. They market a strong line of quality fast-food menus. Their advertising and promotional budgets, while not as large as McDonald's, certainly are substantial enough to make a major impact on the category.

But the brand is still not all that it could be, not by a long shot. Burger King has every right to be challenging for the category lead, even considering the potent marketing machine beneath the golden arches. To get where they want to go, however, their erractic marketing programs of the past, and the internal disagreements that created them, must be put behind them forever. It's become clear to many, including those on the Burger King marketing team, that BK must create a powerful, consistent brand identity, or be content to be a number two brand.

The Miami Whopper

The Burger King chain began humbly enough, founded by Miami businessmen James W. McLamore and David Edgerton as an "Insta Burger King" store in Miami on March 1, 1954. After eating a huge hamburger at a rival store, Edgerton came up with the Whopper and the partners were off and running. They started advertising a year later with their first campaign, "Burger King, the home of the Whopper." Variations on that campaign ran until 1968, the first and last time the chain stayed with a single positioning for anywhere near that length of time.

The Pillsbury Company bought the independent Burger King in 1968, and that became the first turning point for the young brand. It's been speculated that, had Burger King gone public instead of selling out, their competition with McDonald's might have been a much closer race because BK would have had sufficient investment capital without the interference of a corporate management.

The company grew dynamically during the mid-1970s, but eventually fell victim to inconsistent product and service delivery, and a parade of rotating positioning efforts that prevented the creation of a stable brand identity. Pillsbury ultimately lost control of the chain when it was absorbed in a semi-hostile takeover in January 1989 by Burger King's current owner, the English conglomerate, Grand Metropolitan PLC.

Inconsistency Reigns

Strategically and executionally, Burger King's advertising has been a moving target. A brief timeline: In 1968, the chain was focusing on the Whopper and its advantage over McDonald's with a campaign called "The Bigger the Burger the Better the Burger." In 1970, the company continued that tack with "It Takes Two Hands to Handle a Whopper." In 1974, they shifted the emphasis to a customized approach called "Have It Your Way." In 1977, they switched to "America loves burgers and we're America's burger." A year later, they went with the more competitive "Who's got the best darn burger?" Within 18 months, they were advertising "Make it special. Make it Burger King." Less than two years after that, it was "Aren't you hungry for Burger King now?" Also during that period, they again got competitive with "Battle of the Burgers," followed immediately with the "Broiling vs. Frying" campaign. We're now up to 1983 when the infamous "Search for Herb" program was launched. That lasted 7 months, and was followed by "This is a Burger King town." Seven months after that, it was "The best food for fast times." That campaign lasted nearly a year, replaced by "We do it like you'd do it." Then there was the enigmatic "Gotta break the rules," which survived for 18 months. "Your way. Right away" had a similar half-life and died in its sleep as the leaves changed in 1992. Reinforcements came in the form of the young and restless "BK Tee Vee: I love this place!" which loved this world until its fall from grace about a year later. To make matters worse, BK tied in with the summer of 1993 movie, Arnold Schwarzenegger's *The Last Action Hero,* one of the all-time Hollywood bombs. As of this writing, the brand is now in its first year of its current campaign, "Get your burger's worth."

Why such incredible lack of continuity? There appear to be several reasons, but the most important is that, since 1967, the company has changed owners twice, CEOs 10 times, and replaced 7 marketing chiefs and 6 advertising agencies, resulting in somewhere around 20 advertising campaigns.

These rapid changes in a brand's primary communications

vehicle (in this case, advertising) can do incalculable harm to a brand's identity or, as in the case of Burger King, prevent it from fully forming. It's impossible for the franchisees, employees, and management of any company to craft and support a long-term positioning and personality for a brand in that kind of fluid marketing environment.

Burger King may sell a lot of Whoppers, but it lacks the coherent identity that could help it sell the *store*. That is, if BK (like McDonald's) can persuade more fast-food families that they can trust the brand, then customers will walk through their doors even when both chains have similar products, promotions, or friendly employees. Of course, many people are relatively loyal to BK; but there won't be enough of them to close the gap with McDonald's until the maximum number of brand switchers are sure of, and like, what BK stands for, year in and year out.

Common Beginnings, Separate Lives

The chain's past problems are particularly ironic when you consider the similarities between BK and McDonald's. Burger King was founded in 1954 by entrepreneurs who turned it into a successful chain of stores nationwide. McDonald's was founded in 1955 by an entrepreneur who turned it into a successful chain of stores nationwide. McDonald's sells a strong set of good tasting, value-priced food items that families love. So does Burger King. When you drive the interstates from sea to shining sea, you frequently see both brands' stores sitting side by side.

So, what happened? Why did one become a model for identity building with sales exceeding $14 billion, and the other a textbook case of identity crisis at less than half that size?

The answer, in a nutshell, is that McDonald's has had better control over its brand. McDonald's has always been a centrally run organization in which the franchisees follow strict instructions from headquarters. Corporate management has kept a steady bead on its brand identity, and forced its franchises to do the same.

Burger King, on the other hand, has endured a long line of

managers and franchisees, each of whom has had his own idea of how the brand should be marketed. As *Adweek* put it back in 1991: "McDonald's won the burger wars of the 1980s because it had a uniform brand image, from its advertising right down to its restaurants. Burger King, meanwhile, appeared to be a loose confederation of disgruntled fiefdoms."[4]

According to one former marketing head, Gary Langstaff (he lasted 18 months), at least some of the brand's problems originated with a vocal minority of franchisees that had veto power over the entire system. After leaving the company, Langstaff explained, "We wanted to do, 'Have it your way.' I had no pride of ownership in that, and it's a very preemptive position. But about 15 percent of the system said, 'We won't do that.' It was unbelievable. It was not, 'We *can't* do that.' It was: 'We *won't* do that.' . . . So we were precluded from going down that path."[5]

Put another way, McDonald's stuck to an all-family, broad-target positioning for decades, and only recently has added its value story. The company has consistently stood for "food, folks, and fun," even when it changed executional campaigns from time to time. The result has been a permanent strategic reassurance from McDonald's, replenished with fresh ways of expressing their positioning. That has not been the case in the Burger King kingdom.

BK's Unrealized Strengths

The Burger King business may be an also-ran in terms of share of market, but it's still the number two fast-food chain in the country, generating revenue of more than $7 billion a year. The BK chain consists of more than 7,400 restaurants, about 85 percent of which are in the United States. Their overseas expansion has delivered handsome profits for their parent Grand Met.

BK's Whopper, and its line extensions, are still some of the most dominant products in fast food today (they sell more than 700 million a year). Their problems, although significant in size and scope, are not incapacitating. Yet the situation must surely be disturbing to a corporate and franchisee corps who know what might be accomplished with a marketing program that presents a consistent identity over time.

Burger King's past marketing efforts have sometimes been very effective, and have provided a guide for what may work in the near future. During the late 1970s when former McDonald's executive Don Smith took the reins, Burger King trailed not only McDonald's, but the old Burger Chef chain as well. Smith pulled together a team of former McDonald's players and built the brand into a force in the category, largely by pushing the advantages of the Whopper. More recently, even the much-maligned BKTV campaign reportedly delivered some of the best awareness and recall numbers in a generation, although sales momentum couldn't be sustained.

Later, when CEO Jim Adamson began pushing the dinner option, Jerome Ruenheck, president of the franchisee association, reported in March 1993 that dinner sales had increased as much as 20 percent in certain markets. At that time, share was on the rise and McDonald's was sliding by 3 percentage points. Unfortunately, the price wars started by Taco Bell continued to take their toll, as did the McDonald's Super Value meals, launched in 1991, which ultimately came to represent almost half of that company's sales. Burger King was late getting to the value game and paid the price at the cash register.

Nevertheless, the chain has some potent ammunition to use in the fast-food wars, for example, its ability to customize meals to individual tastes ("Have It Your Way"). Without changing one thing in their current restaurants, BK's customers can right now order a Whopper sandwich 1,024 ways. We are living in the age of the individual and BK could be perfectly positioned to take advantage of that trend.

In fact, the chain's newest efforts appear to be bringing the focus back onto Burger King's strengths. The new "Get Your Burger's Worth" campaign combines BK's traditional forte of making great burgers with their need to be a lead player in the value game. The advertising demonstrates BK's size and price advantages vs. McDonald's burgers, and it capitalizes on BK's broiling feature and their ability to customize to individual tastes. BK's new, more aggressive pricing strategy seems to have the category leader looking over their McShoulders.

Plus, the company took full advantage of its *Lion King* promotion in the summer of 1994, that allowed it to partner with one of the highest-grossing movies ever. That move put it in good stead with its franchisees, possibly setting the scene for a real resurgence in the minds of fast-food families.

No one is hungrier for a win than the management, franchisees, and owners of Burger King. While they have not exactly starved to death, they are reportedly weary of the continuous changes in personnel, and advertising and promotional strategies, even though their predecessors must take responsibility for that heritage of discontinuity. The BK team longs for a clear, focused direction that will help them challenge for the lead of the category. Fortunately for BK, this may be one of the best categories for such an upset to happen: Fast-food experts say that there is less brand loyalty within this particular business than in most. That's particularly the case now that value pricing has become the byword of the industry, encouraging more consumers to switch for the right deal.

What Can We Learn from Burger King?

The Burger King history has been a lesson in the need for identity continuity. Until recently, BK has not seriously challenged its beatable rival because of the company's failure to build a sustainable brand identity. How can there be commitment to a brand identity when there is no agreement on positioning and personality? The brand has suffered from an incessant tug of war between franchisees—who own nearly 90 percent of the chain's restaurants—and the corporate staff, and an unwillingness to do whatever's necessary to settle on a clear vision of the brand's place in the category.

It can be argued that BK's problems are at least partially caused by listening more to what management calls their "customers" (the franchisees) rather than their real customers (those folks who actually buy the Whoppers). Is it possible to listen too much to franchisees even though they run the retail operations? Should franchisees permit *themselves* to hold such sway over the company's marketing options, or should they resign themselves to being only knowledgeable consultants?

The Burger King story demonstrates that a hostile marketplace can exist *within* an organization, as well as threaten it from the outside. Internal strife can be more painful than anything the outside world can inject because the "opponents" know so much about one another. It's like the members of a squabbling family who are far too proficient at hurting one another.

It's not fun for anyone but McDonald's to see such a potentially outstanding brand fail to reach its goal. Without question, Burger King can close the gap between itself and the leader, but not without building a focused brand identity, and not without having the courage to stick with one that works.

This is a brand that's on the cusp of achieving the kind of share growth it has sought for so long. Perhaps the best indication of their promising future can be found in a quote from September 1994 by Burger King's CEO: "Whatever the competition does," Jim Adamson said, "that's up to them. We're staying our course."[6] As long as that "course" is toward a formidable, unswerving brand identity, BK is definitely heading in the right direction.

Common Goals, Uncommon Determination

The most obvious and important lesson to be learned from the group of strong brands in this chapter is their strategists' commitment to what has been called, "the long view," the business version of patience: patience to plan carefully, patience to execute meticulously, patience to find a strong position and personality in the marketplace and stay with it.

Those brands that have succeeded at identity building are, for the most part, run by individuals who treat their identities as rare wine, not to be hurried, shaken, or exposed to too many changes in temperature. Effective brand identities are too important and too complex to risk fiddling. The people who created and cared for the Disney, Nike, P&G brands', Swbyp's, and Saturn identities understood that, and their successors understand it today. The loyalty and devotion of their best customers to each brand pales in comparison to their own dedication. The same could not always be said of Burger King, although that may be changing at this moment.

Implicit in this philosophy is the acknowledgment of the lifetime value of a customer. As we will discuss in more detail in the next chapter, direct marketers have long understood the importance of considering the customer as someone in the act of a succession of purchases and referrals, not simply as an individual who is buying on a one-time basis.

Successful brand stewards also have a high degree of control over an above-average number of brand contact points. The Saturn company and their retailers attempt to control how their brand is seen before it's sold, while it's being purchased, and for the lifetime of their vehicles. Nike's brand contacts reach far beyond sports and well into all parts of our lives. It's about as likely to find an unmanaged Disney brand exposure as it is to find a rude employee in Disneyland.

From today's view, they seem almost predestined to succeed, with a great heritage like Disney, great products like those at Nike, a great positioning like Swbyp's, a great focus like that of the Saturn team. But hundreds, if not thousands, of other companies, including Burger King, have had those and many more advantages. Yet their brands are not where they should be because their brand identities were never nourished in the same way.

By creating durable brand identities, companies create the closest thing in business to immortality. Brands are going to need all the immortality they can muster in the next few years, particularly in light of the potentially disruptive changes we're about to experience in communications and marketing, as we will discuss in our next chapter.

9

Creating the Interactive Identity

For a while there, we thought we had caught up with the future. The economy slowed and staggered, values headed backward in an attempt to recapture the imagined goodnesses of the past, people started talking about pausing to smell the roses instead of racing headlong into career leaps that might end in unhappy success. We seemed willing, after the speed trips of the 1980s, to wonder about "now" as if it really mattered.

Somehow, though, the chip wizards never got the message. They had learned to drive in California where a stop sign means you seriously consider taking your foot off the accelerator. Speed was never a relative term in their world, only an immutable goal. How fast can we process a billion bits? If we can split protons into quarks, how can we split intervals into multiple nothings? Is there an infinite number of times data can be compressed?

They got us right back onto the road again, and an interested politician named Al Gore dubbed it a "superhighway."[1] Before we knew it, the telephone poles were flying by, stretching into fiber-optic strands. The limits of communications bulged and bent. We began to talk about "real time" as if it were a rare commodity. Meanwhile, most Americans lingered on the roadside, still hoping to watch it all unfold from the rest stop.

Living I.T.R.W.

You may remember reading about David Alsberg. He was the 42-year-old computer programmer, cyberspace traveler, and innocent bystander who was tragically killed by a stray bullet during a robbery in New York City. Only days before, he had advocated gun control in a heated debate over the Internet, the global network of computer users. When word of Alsberg's death got around "the Net," Alsberg was mourned by hundreds who knew him only by his computer address. Using the Net as a rostrum, they shared eulogies and meditations about the man and the sad event.

One legacy Alsberg left was a renewed debate about what cyberspace is, who populates it, and how cyberspace dwellers relate to one another despite the physical distance that separates them. As Peter H. Lewis of the *New York Times* wrote after David Alsberg's death:

> One cannot travel very far on the data networks without coming across new communities, new friendships and spontaneous acts of kindness among strangers, phenomena that sometimes seem to be all too rare "in the real world"—or I.T.R.W., as it is known in the shorthand of cyberspace.[2]

They are modern pen pals, these fellow travelers, bringing back the all but lost art of relationships through correspondence, a stronger binding than we tend to find I.T.R.W. To them, and gradually to the rest of us, cyberspace is becoming more real by the minute.

Interactive communications are here, not in their ultimate form and only a fraction of their ultimate size, but their existence is undeniable, and their future is assured. The reason is that interactive communications answer the most basic of human needs—the need to express our individuality. Here are the facts about interactive communications as we see them:

■ In its broadest sense, interactive will become a major, although not necessarily dominant, form of communcations within the next 10 to 15 years. A 1994 *Advertising Age* survey of 1,000 U.S. adults revealed that awareness of interactive media had increased 64 percent to nearly a third of the population in only one year. Nearly 40 percent said they would pay for interactive media services.[3] That's no guarantee of interactive's success, but it's a start.

■ The most common forms of interactive media will be the least flashy types, for example, kiosks (interactive stand-alones such as bank ATMs), online services (computer networks such as Internet and the subscriber nets), and CD-ROMs (high-capacity compact disks—as direct mail pieces, as sold separately in CD stores, and as the engine "drivers" of kiosks). Interactive television will continue to be the darling of the press, but it will not be widely available in the United States for at least ten years. It's highly unlikely that there will be a single type of interactive television approach but, instead, a patchwork quilt of solutions that will vary by locale or by distributor.

■ Interactive communications will be primarily commercial-driven, however, not in the same way that commercial media are today. Subscriber-funded media will be less important than commercial. Many systems are likely to offer both options.

Although nearly half of total respondents to the 1994 *Advertising Age* survey said that advertising was "not at all acceptable" in interactive media, 50 to 60 percent said they would find it more acceptable if it lowered fees, and if it gave the viewer more choices. Importantly, the younger respondents were much more likely to accept advertising than their elders, boding well for the future of commercially supported interactive media.

■ "Convergence" (not to be confused with "convergent communications" in chapter 6) is more than a buzzword of our time, it is the destiny of the interactive industry. It refers to the converging of formerly divergent hardware into a single form, or set of forms, which will be the primary way that audiences and consumers interface with content. All of this will bring much more overlap between media and message, media and media, customer and seller, and distributor and content supplier, than we have seen up to this point.

Will it all work? Of course it will, because everyone involved will want it to work. Will it work exactly the way communications futurists think? Not likely, since the power brokers of interactive media are changing strategy weekly. No one company can predict with certainty where it will be on the superhighway, but as a group they are determined to be players. Those that plan to be standing when the battles are over are also expecting to lose major money before they make a single dollar. As a popular cyber age saying goes, there will be many multimillionaires made in the interactive TV industry; unfortunately, most of them will start out as multi*billion*aires.

Interactive Branding in the New Media

For brand stewards, interactive media offer an advanced form of direct (or "relationship") marketing. As dramatic as its effects might be, this pending revolution will more likely be an evolution, moving us from our current method of one-way lecturing to a more natural, less formal exchange of information between buyer and seller.

Generally speaking, we don't like people who talk at us; we are more inclined toward those who talk *with* us. We feel an affinity with individuals who pull us into a conversation by letting us talk, too. The interactive communications evolution is, more than anything else, a recognition of what we are all most comfortable with, that is, information exchange instead of information dump.

Branding and marketing communications are heading toward a place of exciting opportunity and risky new ventures. The fragile bond called brand loyalty will be more precious than ever in this newly fractionated world, and more supportable in a marketplace where each individual's needs can be clearly identified and fulfilled. Still, there is a real question about how many of today's successful marketers will be able to make the turn into a contemporized selling environment.

Since we got serious about marketing to masses of consumers starting in the 1950s, we have basically been constructing more and more sophisticated loudspeakers. Newspapers, magazines, and some out-of-home media were our first microphones, followed by radio, television, and eventually a flock of "alternative" media that used increasingly creative ways to talk at audiences. Each of these mass communicators was designed to get the word out to as many people as possible, so that the content could attract as many people as possible. Later, as consumers' individual tastes were identified, the wonders of demographic and attitudinal analysis enabled the orange to be sliced in new ways. Still, the communications dynamics did not change: We talk, you listen.

In the future, regardless of what specific kind of marketing communications are involved, the act of creating a healthy brand will be more the result of give and take. When Hewlett-Packard ran television commercials or print ads peppered with Dalmatians strolling around printers, they were hoping that cute dogs would make the message more memorable and likable. They used dogs because they were concerned about the many distractions that might intefere with their message getting across. Someday soon, however, HP will be able to engage its prime prospects in an interactive game called, say, "Firefighter" that will encase their message in a story mixing Dalmatian heroism with printer specs. Hewlett-Packard will not be talking at its target, they will be dialoguing with its new friend. A dog's life, indeed.

Who's Targeting Whom?

Before we get too carried away with our visions of the future, we need to keep in mind that nothing is likely to happen uniformly in the interactive world. Households, and individuals within households, will adapt to the coming interactive environment in a thousand different ways according to their income, their age, their comfort level with technology, their vocation, their television viewing habits, their childhood experiences, their interest in national politics, their sleeping habits . . . in short, according to their unique characteristics as individuals. The fundamental allure of interactivity is the opportunity it offers to express our individuality. It stands to reason that this new communications form will be practiced according to individual biases.

As we move closer to the personalizing of media and message, the term "targeting" will take on a new meaning. Marketers will not be searching for targets, targets will search for marketers, meaning that the seller becomes the one who is sought if, that is, what is offered for sale appears to be worth the effort. Once contacted, we will no longer need to accept wastage as a given, it will be the exception to the rule. Buyers will come with a willingness, if not an eagerness, to buy. Most will also begrudgingly accept commercial messaging, especially if it's niftily enrobed in the content, or if they've been given an incentive to be exposed to a seller's message.

One of the most exciting consequences of this future scenario is that marketers will be able to finally focus their attention on the core of their franchises, the super-heavy users whose demographic territories have become known in some new media circles as the "cream zones." This is the kind of information that direct marketers have been seeking for years through their testing matrices. As always, heavy users of a brand will likely be more interested in the commercial message than the average person, and more inclined to act upon it.

Thus, marketers' messages will be more efficient, dollar for dollar invested. This should go a long way toward enriching the quality of a brand's franchise because more concentrated efforts can be focused on those customers with the greatest lifetime value, and far fewer resources will be diverted to users and prospects who are of lesser value to the brand down the road. The result will be a gradual distilling of the user group through planned or circumstantial attrition until the maximum return on investment is achieved. Consequently, marketers will make most of their money in the future by concentrating on retaining their best customers rather than fishing for new ones.

Our Debt to Direct Marketing

With our penchant for what's new, we sometimes forget what we owe to the pioneers who first understood the potential of relationship marketing. Direct marketers have been preaching the interactive sermon for many years. Direct marketing (DM) offers the marketer an opportunity to exchange, rather than only transmit, communications with a prospect. Those of us who are looking forward to the opportunities of the interactive marketplace owe a large debt of gratitude to the direct marketing industry for pointing the way toward what will be a permanent reconfiguring of the way brands are sold.

Since the advent of direct marketing, consumers and brands enjoy literally interactive relationships, even though the interactive era has only recently been officially anointed as a legitimate media phenom. No longer are many marketers satisfied with one-time sales or even traditional brand loyalty. As databases multiply, relationship marketing enables sellers to achieve strong returns on investment over the course of years with a given brand user. The interactivity between consumer and brand is the prelude to the knitting together of the two into a brand relationship that potentially is much stronger than whatever loyalty consumers feel toward their favorite broadly advertised brands.

As long as there are printed and broadcast media that can carry response devices, 800 numbers that can accept and deliver voice messages, and other means of encouraging dialogue, the conventional DM industry will flourish. In fact, direct-marketing industry leaders Stan Rapp and Tom Collins believe that traditional marketing communications, such as broadscale advertising, will soon give way to relationship marketing as the primary way of planning all communications. Several years ago, they wrote:

> To win in the 90's, we believe, a basic turnaround in thinking is needed. You will no longer start by concentrating on the cleverness of your advertising message in selling your product. You will start with the end—the kind of individual relationship you want with prospects and customers—and then turn back and plan your re-

search, media, awareness advertising, sales promotion, and dealer merchandising strategies accordingly.[4]

Unquestionably, the relationship model is gaining ground at an accelerating rate among American marketers, particularly service companies and those selling high-ticket items such as automobiles. Packaged goods brands, on the other hand, have not climbed on board as fast, mostly due to slimmer profit margins that make it more difficult to achieve satisfactory costs-per-lead/sale.

While Messrs. Rapp and Collins are right when they predict that the individual relationship will be the focal point of future marketing efforts, the more probable outcome is that "direct" and "interactive" marketing will become more closely related, perhaps merged, disciplines as they become one of many elements to travel onto the so-called superhighway. In fact, a strong case can be made that interactive is simply an advanced form of direct marketing.

Conventional direct marketing, like conventional mass marketing, will likely be enhanced, but not totally preempted, by the advent of interactive communications. The fact that Buick has mailed out more than one million interactive disks and CD-ROMs since 1986 has not obviated the need for the brand to advertise its attributes over broadcast television. The seven Baby Bells have all engaged in significant direct mail efforts for a decade or more, yet they continue to invest heavily in various broadscale media to spread their messages to customer and prospect alike.

The day may come when only direct and interactive marketing efforts will dominate marketing plans. But that day is a long way off for logistical and financial reasons, and because more narrow communications still do not carry the kind of broadscale impact necessary to sustain most widely marketed brands.

Brand Identity–Building through Relationship Marketing

This migration toward relationship marketing will perhaps have its most profound effect on branding. It's generally believed (not necessarily rightly) that relationships between brands and customers cannot be forged using "mass" communications. Developing a relationship with nationally advertised brands has been considered very difficult to pull off because, historically, mass communications are designed to build awareness or to inform, but rarely to create bonds with the customer. (In chapter 6, we pointed out that relationships between brand and customer *can* be forged using broadscale communications, but it's definitely more of a challenge than when direct marketing is employed.)

In contrast, direct marketing efforts regularly create some sort of relationship, however short-lived, because the interaction on the part of the buyer usually requires some personal involvement such as calling an 800 number or returning a postcard. Once established, the connection between buyer and brand has the potential to strengthen and intensify.

For instance, if you read an ad about a certain mutual fund and then purchase some shares, you may follow that brand of funds in the newspaper stock quotes, but that may be the extent of your involvement. On the other hand, if you express an interest in the services of Charles Schwab's mutual fund program, the company tries to establish a dialogue by sending you a series of carefully designed mailings and phone calls that begin to pull you toward a brand relationship.

After receiving this information and talking with a Schwab representative, you may begin to think of it as more than just a company, and more like *your* company, or at least a group of people working on your behalf. In the case of Schwab, the direct marketing efforts of the firm are also reinforced with pointed, high-profile direct-response television efforts starring the founder himself.

Of course, the greatest long-term contribution of direct marketing is that it helps create a database of leads and existing customers who can be a source for new brand growth. Database collection and management could well become the discipline with the greatest impact on how brands are marketed in the twenty-first century. Perhaps the most important benefits of database collection to new media marketers will be its capability to capture relevant information about who has the inclination to interact with brands.

In those instances where consumers are willing to provide information about themselves and their families, interactive marketers will no longer have to solicit an endless stream of new customers, and instead can spend their time harvesting pre-qualified leads, that is, people who have already expressed some interest in the brand.

As the interactive marketing industry ramps up, it will depend heavily on direct marketers' expertise to help them understand the advantages of relationship data management. When an interactive brand becomes that familiar with its clientele, it will be like salespeople who are no longer dealing with "cold leads," but who have new confidence because of knowledge that can make them more valuable to their customers. That kind of confidence is almost palpable, and of tremendous value to the brand team as they market in an increasingly diffused marketing environment.

The more involved consumers become with the brand, the more they respond to direct-marketing efforts by the marketer, and the clearer they are about what the brand's positioning and personality are all about. In fact, a relationship that, prior to direct marketing, might have been built on habit can be now firmly grounded in knowledge and familiarity about the brand. Ultimately, the stronger the relationship established by direct marketing, the stronger the brand identity in the eyes of the customer, because that customer has chosen to be involved with the brand.

Vapor-Wired: The Unanswered Questions of the Interactive Age

The term "vaporware" refers to software that a company has announced, but failed to distribute to the marketplace. In the interactive industry, many of us have been exposed to its country cousin, "vapor-wired," meaning, all the hype about our interactive future, much of which is yet to be demonstrated, let alone implemented.

Things are not working out as quickly in the interactive world as many thought would be the case, primarily because of those old stumbling blocks, time and money. For example, though rapid changes are being made in the U.S. telecommunications infrastructure, we are still largely an analog bunch. What our homes must aspire to be, of course, is digitized, renewed by the same surgings of "ones" and "ohs" that power computer microprocessors.

More than that, our digital inputting also must be compressed, which is made more difficult by the fact that we are largely tethered to our world by the old "twisted pair" telephone wires so assiduously laid by Ma Bell many years ago, as well as to the slightly less mundane coaxial cable. In order for all those video bytes to squeeze into our homes, we will ultimately require fiber-optic cabling at least most of the way up to the house, plus a gaggle of off-site or at-home video servers and digital compressors. To fully participate in the interactive dream, homes must be wired and plugged into a network of infotainment services fed by these "broadband" carriers.

Sadly, it *is* as complicated as it sounds.

Technological issues aside, at the core of our interactive future is this question: Do people really *want* to interact regularly with communications appliances for entertainment, information, or educational purposes, or would they prefer to be more or less passive onlookers? Are we fundamentally participants or couch potatoes? After all, passivity has its benefits. When someone else makes the choices for you, life can be easier and less disruptive. No one—not the distributors, the content providers, the telephone company executives, or the cable company moguls—is certain how many Americans are willing to be blessed by the benefits of the interactive age.

One fact that is certain is that the younger the audience, the more comfortable they are with interactive. Boomers, who now head the plurality of households, are more open to interactive communications than their parents because many have learned to cope with high-speed information technology at their workplaces. As the number of information and service businesses surpassed those in manufacturing, computer literacy became a virtual necessity for many jobs.

The children of these workers, in turn, will not have any

qualms whatsoever about interactive environments since most will have been exposed to computers in some form during their school hours. They have also been weaned on video games, a pastime so effective at teaching interactive skills that NASA and the commercial airlines use them to train their pilots. In fact, video *anything* is likely to be accepted readily by Generation X and younger, as long as the price is right.

One of the more intriguing questions currently being posed is whether the interactive revolution will lead to less real human contact, and more "virtual" contact through the growing communities of computer networks. Futurists wonder whether all this interacting with a monitor-cum-smartbox will turn us into a nation of high-tech/low-touch netnoids. Will socialization be changed at its roots, reverting to feudalism where we all hunker down in our "castles" (called "cocooning" by futurist Faith Popcorn)? Will we "create" our friends or sort through social contacts based on how we rate and rank them? Will there be any point in meeting with other human beings face to face? Will those who cannot learn the ways of the techno-savvy be thrust to the lower rungs of society, creating a less employable, more dependent underclass? Will increasing crime, onerous urban frustrations, and the AIDS pandemic feed our need to nestle closer to the remote (an aptly named appliance, as it's turning out)?

Beyond sociological issues, there are important brand-related questions that marketers need to explore:

- First and foremost, will commercial interests play a major role in the interactive drama, or be just one of the spear carriers?
- What form will brand messages take and how will they differ from today's current forms?
- Will broadscale branding become a thing of the past, replaced entirely by "personal" brands, that is, brands that are customized to the needs and wants of individual customers?
- How much will consumers be willing to pay for the opportunity to bring the interactive good life into their own

home? Or to access it away from home? Will interactive services be price elastic?

■ What kind of services will be the most likely to entice the interactive voyeur? The existing fare that they or their children were "trained on," such as video games and TV game shows? Or, newer conveniences like virtual shopping and telecommuting?

■ How soon will a majority of Americans routinely rely on interactive communications to go about their daily lives?

Many of these questions and theories are expected to be resolved by in-market testing and eventual rolling out of the interactive experiments. Yet, the studies themselves are raising still more questions among researchers about whether the test sites and respondents are representative of those who ultimately will be offered the services when the tests expand. It may not tell us a lot if upscale, computer-literate families lap up interactive goodies in ways that the majority of Americans will not.

Eventually, however, the answers will come in increments, paving the way for this new, experimental media stage to become a mainstream player in the communications of the next century.

The New Media Options Along the Superhighway

The "information superhighway," "I-bahn," or whatever metaphor works for you, is the coming together of human communications on a single, interglobal network of sights, sounds, and data. For the individual cybertraveler, the vision promises to be a treasure of communications choices. For the brand marketer, the highway offers new and better ways to find out what individuals want and deliver it to them within more efficient brand packaging.

The vehicles that will traverse the highway as carriers of brand messages are in various states of development and speculation:

■ *On-line*—One of the most advanced of the highway's options, on-line services are accessed through computer networks. The mother of all networks is the Internet (or "the Net"), a complex web of thousands of private and public on-line subnets that began as an informal link established in the late 1960s by the Department of Defense, and that soon spread to educational and research institutions. The Internet is now monitored by the National Science Foundation, but it would be an exaggeration to say that it's "managed" by anyone or anything, other than the forces of a free-access communications marketplace. By various accounts, there will be anywhere from 15 to 35 million Net users worldwide by the end of '95 (don't bet the ranch on those numbers, by the way; no one knows for sure how many are on the Net right now, let alone in the future).

While the total Internet is the dominant on-line player, it has a constantly shifting, unwieldy structure with a restricted commercial platform because of its legacy as a free forum for the exchange of information and ideas. A subsection called Commercenet has been created to bring some order to the Net as a whole. Financed by the federal government and industry, Commercenet is designed specifically for business-to-business commercial messages.

A subnet that exploded overnight in 1995 into a major advertising medium is the World Wide Web, boasting 3000-plus "sites," including Planet Reebok and the MGD (Miller Beer) Tap Room.

Other major networks are subscriber-funded, including CompuServe, which reportedly has a user base of about 2.5 million, with data-driven commercial and noncommercial fare; Prodigy, with a reported 2.0 million subscribers, offering broad commercial messaging with improving, but somewhat limited graphics due in part to its PC-based heritage; the fast-rising America Online, claiming over 1 1/2 million subscribers, and sporting a very receptive graphic platform for commercial use, springing from its Macintosh-driven origins; plus several other nets including Delphi and Apple's E-World.

What's particularly fascinating about on-line from a marketer's perspective, is that it encourages a computer game behavior among its users, that is, the opportunity to "get on a net" and stay there for hours at a time, navigating through its seemingly unlimited twists and turns. That kind of involvement can be an ideal setting for the presentation of a brand's story, because it allows for lengthy, in-depth contact with prospects. The information exchange format can also make interactive brand messages more habit forming than any form previously used.

■ *Interactive Place-Based*—The oldest, commonly used form of place-based interactive media is the kiosk known as the bank automated teller machine (ATM). Without realizing it, Americans have been training for the interactive age each time they've punched the "cash" button or manipulated funds at their local ATM. About half of all Americans use ATMs, and that figure is expected to rise dramatically as younger people, who are more comfortable with interactive formats, become regular bank customers. Bankers are also learning how to use the ATM screens to cross-sell products and services, thereby reinforcing their brand identities to customers who are candidates for relationship banking because they have checking accounts. For example, the Bank of America, boasting the largest ATM network in the world, sells its "Quick Look" mini-statement feature and advertises its quarterly promotions via ATM screens.

Interactive place-based platforms offer marketers excellent opportunities to associate a brand with contemporary technology, to involve the user with the brand, and even to collect personal data that can be used later to reinforce the brand identity and potential relationship with the prospect. Kiosks and other interactive out-of-home stand-alone structures provide passersby the opportunity to learn about something new (for instance, Acura's car preview kiosks in auto shows), play a video game (Sega's game samplers in electronics stores), sample compact disks before they buy (Muze kiosks in retail outlets), or order something (the Ticket Machine, a California-based kiosk system that orders and prints your tickets to sporting and cultural events while you wait).

■ *In-Home Shopping*—QVC, the Home Shopping Network, and others have cultivated a growing following who love to shop while they view, using their telephone to order and their credit cards to pay. It's entertaining (sort of), and delivers the same kind of armchair voyeurism that's stimulated catalog sales in recent years.

More to the point, in-home shopping is transaction-based, which means that it is proving with every sale that consumers are willing to buy by remote control. It's only a small leap from QVC to interactive TV shopping sprees that could provide the stimulus for a series of interactive brand building opportunities.

The "home" part of home shopping is becoming more appealing as crime in the streets and crazies in the malls are encouraging more people to try their luck with couch browsing. There are also shopping networks being tested or planned by major retail companies, such as Macy's and Nordstrom. While these early versions are literally interactive, they will be made even more involving by the introduction of interactive formats that will permit viewers to shop within a "virtual store" (as described at the beginning of chapter 1).

Right now, in-home shopping formats are not seeking major new advertiser support, so the opportunities for brand content are limited. However, plans are in the works for a number of in-home shopping outlets featuring upscale goods and services that will be more compatible for brand identity building.

■ *CD-ROM (Compact Disk/Read-Only Memory) and Floppy Disk*—There is a broad category of interactive software on floppy disks and CD-ROMs that can be mailed or distributed in a variety of ways to target audiences. The increased capacity of CD-ROMs has permitted interactive audiences to see motion video and sophisticated color reproduction, hear quality music tracks, and access much more data than on a standard floppy disk. They are, or can be, superior carriers of brand messages.

There were an estimated 1,700 consumer CD-ROM titles worldwide by the end of 1994, triple what was available three years earlier. Worldwide revenues from CD-ROM titles were close to $4 billion, with an installed base of multimedia PCs at 12 million, growing at double-digit rates. In addition to their stand-alone uses, CD-ROMs also serve as the drivers of kiosk

INFOMERCIALS FINALLY MAKE THE BIG TIME

Direct response television (DRTV) has been around for more than three decades and is a breed of direct marketing that began picking up steam as more book publishers (Time-Life Books), collectibles (Franklin Mint), and fitness equipment manufacturers (Nautilus) have discovered the profitability of selling in low-cost TV slots with 800-number response devices.

The "informercial" is an offshoot of DRTV that has recently become a strong contender for advertising dollars. These long-form (usually 30-minute) sales pitches were originally used by kitchen utensil companies and other low-end products, luring insomniacs and graveyard shifters with low-budget monologues shot on cheap sets.

Today, the format is being used by some of the largest marketers seeking more efficient ways to generate sales and sales leads. Infomercials offer advertisers the advantages of TV and the measurability of direct response. There were 500 to 600 infomercials produced in 1994, compared to only half that many three years earlier. An estimated 100-plus big-name brands are now using infomercials, including: GTE, Bank of America, Apple Computer, American Airlines, Coca-Cola, Eastman Kodak, Ford, Hyatt Resorts, McDonald's, Sears, Visa, and Volkswagen. Infomercials now account for as much as 25 percent of the programming time for many cable systems, raking in approximately $200 million in revenue. Sales from infomercials were estimated to be $900 million in 1993, and are expected to top $1.8 billion by the end of 1995.

Infomercials can be used to acquire leads (as used by Bell Atlantic and Volvo), to build awareness for a product or a category (appliances such as juicers), or simply to sell products (GTE, Kodak, diet and fitness products).

The increased demand for infomercials is driving spot TV and cable rates higher by an average of 10 to 15 percent compared to the same quarters the previous year. Plus, the cost of producing infomercials has risen dramatically, from less than $100,000 on average only a few years ago, to today's range, which starts at about $150,000 and can approach $1 million for the most elaborate productions. The dilemma: infomercials do not rely on audience accumulation, but on a relatively high response and conversion rate. Thus, the higher the costs, the tougher it is to create advertising that pays out.

Surprisingly, infomercials are attracting a relatively affluent group of consumers, not the lower income folk that advertisers assumed scanned the late-night TV fare for excitement. Based on industry research, the typical buyer is married, college-educated, and with an annual income exceeding $30,000. Just the kind of buyer that makes up major brand franchises.

Infomercials have a bright future in direct marketing, both in their present form and however they might evolve as they incorporate more interactive techniques. Their long-form format and repetitive structure makes them ideal for providing involving, brand identity messages. And their transactional successes offer a template for interactive marketing plans of the future.

interactive programs (although their limited capacity may lead to their replacement by laser disks and hard drives on kiosks).

Some of the most prominent interactive applications include magazines, such as interactive subscription versions of *Newsweek* and *BusinessWeek*; as encyclopedias and other multimedia reference sources such as *Compton's*; as games like those marketed by *Sega CD* and *3DO*; and as catalogs such as seen in *En Passant*, an interactive catalog of catalogs developed by Apple Computer carrying merchandise from the likes of Williams-Sonoma, L.L. Bean, Neiman-Marcus, and Lands' End.

CD-ROMs are being used by a wide variety of marketers to reinforce brand messages, and currently represent the most widespread brand identity–building channel within the interactive world. Cadillac, Chrysler, and many other upscale advertisers use CD-ROMs to reinforce their brand messages with mailings to key prospects.

■ *ITV*—Interactive television (ITV) is the most talked about and least developed of the new interactive media. ITV is seeking to be the fully realized "superhighway" that will allow virtually anyone to obtain a wide range of interactive services without leaving the home, as well as communicate and share those services with other households. The brand identity and general selling opportunities are enormous for interactive television, although there are many obstacles standing between ITV and its full implementation.

Interactive Television: The Gold Rush of the 1990s

This is what California must have been like 150 years ago. Rumors over drinks at the 1990s sushi bars, just like in the saloons of the 1840s. There's fame and fortune in those interactive television "hills," and it could be lying around like a 2-ounce nugget in a shallow stream, with that nugget representing untold sales revenue. Or, it could take years of research and billions in investments to uncover the real vein, treasures that only those with the most resources will be able to mine. The right idea and the right backer might be all you need to hit it big and never work again. The wrong idea and you might wipe out your corporate nest egg.

Even among the more experienced groupies, there is some confusion about what is meant by interactive television. One of the better definitions was nestled in a speech by Joseph Segel, founder of QVC and the Franklin Mint, at the 1993 Direct Marketing Association convention in Toronto. Segel explained the ITV stretch of the superhighway this way:

> What we're talking about is a high-capacity two-way electronic pipeline to the home—capable of simultaneously transmitting a huge number of different TV programs and other electronic services—with phone-like connectability between users and services and between users and other users.[5]

Thanks to several years of publicity, the key players in the ITV game-to-come are well known:

- Bell Atlantic, one of the most adventurous of the Baby Bells, with several ITV and kiosk tests underway throughout the United States and an approval from Uncle Sam to create interactive television systems, the first Bell operating company to get that kind of go-ahead.
- Tele-Communications, Inc. (T.C.I.), the largest cable company in the country and former partner with Bell Atlantic in a joint ITV venture; currently planning significant testing within its extensive cable markets.
- Time-Warner, a leading entertainment company and potential ITV content provider; partner with U.S. West in the Full Service Network test in Orlando.
- U.S. West, another pioneering Baby Bell and a strong financial and switching technology partner in Orlando; also with other ventures of its own, including hotel room ITV and cable sytems.
- AT&T, a player and investor in numerous interactive projects, including a planned test with Viacom in Castro Valley, California, scheduled to begin in 1995.
- Viacom, owner of Paramount, MTV, Nickelodeon, and numerous content packagers, plus significant cable operations.
- Several other potentially major players, including Pacific Bell, which plans to build its own ITV network in California; Southwestern Bell, former partner with Cox Cable, which plans an ITV test in Richardson, Texas, in 1995–96; plus numerous important content producers such as Microsoft, Apple Computer, IBM, Intel, Sega, 3DO, Blockbuster Video (teamed with Paramount), and several major Hollywood studios.

Before ITV can become a common reality, some critical issues must be settled, most notably, what kind of formatting and access (that is, "user interface") will be offered to the viewer? For example, will it be hundreds of channels that micro-focus on subjects of interest to only a sliver of the homes using television at the time? Will it be one self-programmable channel that the consumer creates on each viewing occasion? Or a series of 10 or more favorites, with an option to rotate in a new one from time to time, including a "shuffle play," similar to audio CD players, that builds in spontaneity to the channel choices?

Some observers have even suggested that the terms "channels" and "viewers" will become obsolete, replaced by the concepts of "interactive communications experiences." Each experience would be different than the previous one, each completely personalized, each less of a viewing occasion and more of a "sharing" between the individual, the medium, and its message.

There are currently more than 100 interactive television tests going on in North America. However, the most anticipated test, coproduced by Time-Warner and U.S. West in Orlando, Florida, was postponed several times due to technical setbacks, and finally began with 12 households in late 1994. Outside the United States, testing has been underway for a number of years in Canada and elsewhere. Quebec, for example, has been running their Videoway interactive programming since 1989 with a base of 220,000 subscribers. The same system ran interactive telecasting of the Lillehammer Olympics in February 1994 with Ford as a major sponsor, using interactive advertising that involved the viewer in questions about that company's products.

A version of ITV has been introduced in the United States in a big way in the form of the RCA DSS, or "direct TV." With an 18-inch satellite disk and a monthly charge roughly comparable to cable, households can get 150 channels, including near-video-on-demand via a staggered movie rotation schedule. The disks are priced at $700, and sold out fast during the 1994 holiday season.

ITV isn't just for home consumption. In 1993, U.S. West established their City Key interactive tourist services through in-room television in a number of San Francisco hotels. That was followed the next year by Bell Atlantic's Info Travel test in Santa Clara, California. In the Bell Atlantic test, guests can obtain information from 200 advertisers, including maps, cultural event updates, places to eat, and places for family entertainment in the area. Advertisers, whose messages are folded into the programming, are mostly local at this point. The U.S. West and Bell Atlantic programs are efforts to explore how best to convert their traditional yellow pages businesses into ITV forums for advertisers.

Marketers are interested in ITV as an interactive conduit for building identity by involving viewers in a brand's story. If it pans out as that, ITV has the potential to be the best tool ever offered to a brand steward.

Shotgun Weddings Falter at the Altar

The idea of telephone companies striking strategic alliances with cable companies made good sense, given that they were on a collision course that might cause havoc in lieu of cooperation in the burgeoning interactive industry. The Baby Bells brought money, switching capabilities, and billing systems to the table. Cable companies could provide digital compression, cable for phone use, broadband (high-capacity) networks capable of carrying a vast variety of content, their relationships with the entertainment content producers, and fiber-optic wiring into homes.

These marriages may have looked good in the boardroom, but they began to unravel in the light of day. Cultures and ledgers clashed as the two types of organizations got to know one another better. Despite more than a decade since the breakup of AT&T, the telephone companies are still much more fiscally conservative, vertically organized, and price-regulated than the cable industry. Proposed deal pricing was pegged at from 10 to 11 times cash flow, which is considered to be acceptable among nonregulated, fast-growing industries, but not so in the increasingly government-controlled environment that the cable industry was about to face.

When the FCC ordered a two-tier cable pricing format, resulting in an average 17 percent drop in cable bills in early 1994, the financial attractiveness of the cable interests was called into question, further souring the Bell Atlantic-T.C.I. deal in February 1994 (see inset), and the $4.6 billion joint venture between South-

LOVE ON THE ROCKS:
THE BELL ATLANTIC/T.C.I. BREAKUP

John C. Malone, the histrionic CEO of cable giant TeleCommunications, Inc. (T.C.I.), didn't get where he is today by beating around the bush. In February of 1994, four months and ten days after the announcement to merge T.C.I. and Bell Atlantic, Malone turned to Bell Atlantic CEO Raymond W. Smith and said, "This deal isn't going to make it, so let's shoot it."[6]

The plan, unveiled in October 1993, had called for Bell Atlantic's $33 billion purchase of T.C.I. in order for the two firms to gain communications control over a large number of cabled households. Bell Atlantic would supply the money, and switching and networking know-how; T.C.I. would kick in the message carriers and the inside track to much of the software and content needed to fill up all those channels-to-be.

The deal was scuttled because of several issues. First, the Clinton administration and Congress began showing an eagerness to more closely control the cable companies which, after a long maturation process, had suddenly become big and profitable; critics claimed, they got that way by charging the consumer far more than normal profit goals required. There were also serious questions about how little the industry pays to maintain its systems. The cables' investments in maintenance were estimated to be slightly greater than $1 billion a year compared to twenty times that rate for the Baby Bells, a frugality that could lead to disastrous problems when the complex ITV networks are switched on.

The two companies had an intense desire to be major players in the interactive game, but that's about all they could agree on. Malone's T.C.I. was hell-bent on growth and he didn't care much for the "what will the analysts think?" approach to management that is a strategic given for companies like Bell Atlantic. As Malone told the *New York Times*,

"Ray (Smith) was always dealing with a financial mind-set within his company that focused on near-term reported earnings instead of creating wealth in the long term—the old phone company mentality."[7] T.C.I. has been characterized as many things, but an "old phone company" was not one of them. The two companies simply operated their books in entirely different ways—Bell Atlantic as the conservative blue chip, T.C.I. as a highly leveraged corporation with net income and dividends frequently plowed back into growth-driving ventures.

Bell Atlantic was also not happy to hear that the cable companies had been hit with significant revenue declines from government-mandated rate rollbacks. This damper, in tandem with more government regulation in general, gave Ray Smith real pause. He questioned how much of his shareholders' money should be backing the ITV dream that had a long way to go before fully materializing.

Beyond the effect on the two companies, the falling-out mercifully put the brakes on the superhighway hype that was beginning to resemble the speculating on Wall Street just before the crash of 1989. Since early 1994 when this mega-deal was scotched, there has been considerably less bravado about how quickly and how broadly the highway will be constructed.

The 1994 on-again/off-again media marriages also sent out early warnings to marketers that they need to be careful where they place their brand messages and their hard-earned investments in new media. It's more important than ever that brand stewards test their way into reliable media vehicles that will be around for years to come as strong brand identity builders.

---

western Bell and Cox Communications six weeks later. At about the same time, U.S. District Judge Harold H. Greene (the same Judge Greene who orchestrated the AT&T breakup in 1984) postponed the proposed AT&T $12.6 billion purchase of McCaw Cellular Communications, although that was eventually OK'd to proceed as planned. As if to confirm the doubts of the cable companies' proposed partners, stock values for a number of the cables plummeted 30 to 40 percent after the proposed deals were sacked.

The Big Blur

A few years from now, your neighbor may pound on your front door in the dead of night and scream to the house, "Run for your lives! They're converging! THEY'RE CONVERGING!" Go back to bed; it will just be your digitized hardware mating in the family room.

Unbeknownst to most of us, we've been living our lives without the most scientifically elegant solutions in hand. Call us crazy, but we've managed to get along with unintegrated hardware, naively assuming that it's acceptable for the phone to be in one corner of the house and the television in another. Silly us.

It's time to grow up and get our digitized act together. That goes double for messages that the convergees will carry. They, too, must merge so that words and pictures and ideas all blur into a bigger and better concept called "content." The Three Musketeers had the right idea—"All for one and one for all!" Our mantra, it seems, for the new millennium.

The Merging of Appliances

Copiers have been merged with faxes, faxes with computers, televisions into computers, computers into telephones, and vice versa. Entertainment appliances have all have been folded into audio/video consoles. The prevailing school of thought is that the ultimate access point for home or office will be some sort of technological mongrel of our three favorite tools: the telephone, the TV, and the computer.

The telephone was first in the house, but it is woefully inadequate in its present form to do the necessary video pyrotechnics, although telephone wires may play a key role as carriers of "video dial tones," interactivity via phone line. The computer is currently best able to handle the load (digital, of course, is its middle name), but only a minority of Americans are comfortable in front of a computer keyboard. Thus, the television—or, "video monitor" as it's called now that it has reached technological maturity—is considered by many to be the leading candidate for the role of host body for the merger of household technologies.

The opposing camp is still expecting the computer to prevail because of its superior digitality and the inroads the PC industry is making in improving its user friendliness. The computer contingent points to past failures of CD-based technology in the set-top, as well as delays in even agreeing on the standards for High-definition TV, as reasons to put your money on the computer. Their case was made stronger by the announcement that in 1994, for the first time ever, more personal computers were sold in the United States than television sets.

As long as we're wagering, why not put some money on the games hardware? Thirty-two-bit video-game players by Sony will soon be the fastest guns in town, capable of performing up to 500 million instructions per second, compared to a paltry 66 million by the advanced Pentium PC chip, and the Sony players will sell for one-fifth the price. This means that gamesters could be sitting on the potential hub of the convergence wheel particularly as the "game computers" run sophisticated action video and realistic audio.

There is also a splinter group who expect very little appliance mating to go on, but instead see appliances as remaining separate, much as they do in the modern home. The grafting together of the refrigerator, stove, television, and kitchen sink is technologically possible, but not even General Electric has tried to force it on us, probably because they make more money in the long run by selling five appliances instead of one. It's not necessary, this group argues, for all that is digitized to be unitized.

The Merging of Media and Message

You may not be familiar with the advernewstainmentshopping-promo platform, so brace yourself. Until recently, the media options available to the marketer were relatively discrete. There were the broadcast, print, and out-of-home options for advertising; those in public relations could use publicity, event marketing, community affairs, and government relations to make their cases; and direct marketing usually took the form of direct mail and direct response print and broadcast. It was a relatively straightforward palate from which marketers chose one or more colors, then dabbled at will.

Things have gotten a bit more complicated on the way to becoming a bit more simple. The media are overlapping more than ever before, both in format and message. So-called embedded advertising—ads that are integrated into the content of programming—is becoming more popular by the month. Messages in the evolving media are moving from divergence to proximity to convergence to immergence. The ads look like news, the news looks like ads, the shows like commercials and vice versa.

In a blending of news and commercial messages, companies like Frito-Lay have released information to local TV stations in the form of "advernewscasts." Segments about the filming of a Frito-Lay commercial starring Chevy Chase, for instance, were used 1,734 times by local stations in 1993, racking up an estimated 729.5 million impressions (1,000 impressions = 1,000 people seeing an ad once, or one person seeing an ad 1,000 times). That was roughly four times what their $1.6 million investment yielded in Super Bowl advertising using the commercial itself. These program clips are variations on a PR format called "video news releases," packaged video material on subjects of general interest that can be picked up by TV stations with lots of news time to fill and not enough material to fill it.

Another form, InfoVision, is getting broad exposure with its half-hour programs highlighting businesses or brands that pay to be included in this quasi "news" program that resembles a news magazine. Then there's the commercial-based syndicated program, "Main Floor," which began airing on as many as 110 stations in September 1994, and appears to be a "program" that takes viewers into department stores to see what's hot and what's not. The video browsing is, in reality, a vehicle for selling sponsors' goods that are highlighted on the tour, including Chanel, Lee jeans, and Estee Lauder.

A more subtle form of embedded advertising is called "seamless programming," and is being seen on most of the major TV networks. Advertising has traditionally been placed between programs or at the end of each segment of a show, but the trend now is to embed the ads within the show only, and run one program right into the next with no commercial break. The networks' research reportedly indicates that "channel surfing" is common among about 3 to 5 percent of viewers during in-program commercials (a low, suspiciously self-serving level), but that number triples between shows. Seamless programming is expected to reduce surfing, particularly when two popular programs are run together without break.

The Ownership of Media Vehicles

There's also been a renaissance of the totally sponsored media vehicle that allows advertisers even more options to weave in their messages. As mentioned earlier, more than a dozen magazines are being produced as quasi-editorial vehicles that are actually platforms for their sole sponsors. Some examples: *Sun* magazine (from Ray-Ban), *Beauty* (from Mary Kay Cosmetics), *Know How* (from General Motors), and *Profit* (from IBM). In one of the most ambitious ventures to date, *Sony Style* became a semi-annual publication (actually, it's a catalog) selling for $4.95 on the newsstand and claiming a circulation of 500,000.

This trend has important ramifications for interactive branding because embedding options might be the only way for marketers to sell their brands if noncommercial interactive environments become more common. The potential for identity building is enormous with these advertiser-owned vehicles. Among the advantages: more opportunity to meld the brand positioning into the vehicle's story line; more time to develop the brand's personality; and the availability of more techniques to involve the viewer in the brand's claims.

However, media pundits worry about the ethics of publishing ventures that are owned by the sponsor, versus an independent venture that is supported only by commercial messaging. They point out that both the editorial integrity and the credibility of the sponsor's own messages could be undermined by the approach. That's sound advice; advertisers need to keep a sharp eye on this medium in case skeptical readers question the objectivity of the content, and then the integrity of the advertised brands.

The same issue holds for the broadcast field where an extravagant version of this new form appeared as an entire "TV special" aired on NBC in 1994. Called "Treasure Island: The Adventure Begins . . .", the special was actually one very elaborate commercial for the Las Vegas resort of the same name, dramatized as legitimate entertainment.

Branding the Vehicle

One of the more interesting developments on the evolving media landscape has been the evolution of vehicles from mere conduits for programming and brand messages into brands themselves. This idea hit the print ranks more than 60 years ago when Henry Luce established *Time* and *Life* as branded news and entertainment sources.

In broadcast, the three major networks had differentiated themselves based mostly on their news divisions and newscaster personalities. Ted Turner then created a new kind of global information source that he branded as CNN, as well as his unique Headline News and WTBS "super station," all out of his Atlanta home base. Time-Warner's ESPN and Viacom's MTV also created highly focused specialty networks.

The broadcast networks finally began to brand their properties when they included their logos during parts or all of their programming. For example, NBC keeps its peacock logo in the corner of the screen continuously during *The Today Show* and the evening news. The peacock even hovered in the corner of commercials used in their NBC Viewer Service, which offers more information about advertised brands through an 800 service. However, the broadcast networks' branding attempts have not yet created full-fledged brands because their programming is so diverse that it's extremely difficult for them to establish an identity as clear and distinct as their more specialized cable competitors.

Also part of this trend are "promercials," the merging of a commercial message with a promotion for the media vehicle. Introduced during a September 1993 edition of *60 Minutes*, the promercial format was a 20-second CBS promotion plug integrated into a 30-second paid commercial for K-Mart, ostensibly providing that advertiser with a 50-second message for the cost of a 30 seconds. In exchange for the value, K-Mart gave heavy exposure for CBS in 2,300 K-mart stores, whose name and logo were also featured in 76 million dropped coupons.

The Benefits of Merge/Purge

Given the option, most viewers would probably pass on the opportunity to see the latest Right Guard underarm deodorant commercial or Spray 'n' Wash stain removal demonstration. It's always been a real challenge for advertisers to make their messages as alluring as the programming or editorial. With seemingly unlimited choices and options to control what they see in the future interactive world, some consumers may opt to never see stand alone commercials again. When and if that occurs, the merging of commercial content with programming may be one of the few alternatives left for advertisers.

To capitalize on these trends, marketers need to hearken back to the advantages of convergent communications. By focusing messages from several different media on prospects' needs and brand benefits, a marketer can use combinations of these new media options to better persuade potential buyers to buy. The new media/message overlapping can be a strategic advantage for the marketer who learns how to deftly use the technique, eventually folding messages into a single, multilayered stream of what may be called "persuasive commercial communications."

A Two-Headed Monster Called Choice and Control

Until recently, most conventional media have sent their messages along crudely targeted channels, with the message attract-

LAZARUS REDUX:
THE RUMORED DEATH OF ADVERTISING

The advertising industry had seen better days. During the first half of this decade, advertising agencies watched margins dwindle as the traditional commission system was methodically preempted by less lucrative fees. Advertisers diverted much of their diminishing communications budgets away from traditional advertising. Mass media (network television, national magazines) began to lose their grip on the advertisers' purse strings, and were gradually whittled away at by more fragmented media that often translated to more work and less profitability for advertising practitioners.

Then came the insult to cap the injury. Advertising itself—that is, the basic business of buying time and space for the purposes of telling a commercial message—began to be called into question by those who see interactive as the opportunity to turn a new leaf and limit, rechannel, or even delete commercial messaging. As this particular vision goes, most interactive media vehicles will be affordable without dependence on advertising content, thus eliminating the need to sell off some of the vehicle's time/space to provide supplemental revenue. Instead, consumers would simply pay higher fees and enjoy a commercial-free environment, à la public television.

In May of 1994, Ed Artzt, chairman and CEO of the world's largest advertiser, Procter & Gamble, told the American Association of Advertising Agencies that the future television medium may not be driven by advertising at all. "From where we stand today, we can't be sure that ad-supported TV programming will have a future in the world being created—a world of video on-demand, pay-per-view and subscription TV."[8]

What seems most likely is that commercial message forms will have to change with their environment, exactly as they have had to do in the past. In future years, there will be a much greater need to demonstrate the inherent value of commercial content to the vehicle's audiences in order to convince the vehicle's producers that sponsored messages have a place in their productions.

An interactive medium's owners will have three roads to reach profitability: 1) maintain higher usage or subscription rates to pay content, maintenance, and R&D costs; 2) suffer lower margins or losses in the beginning of the medium's life until a critical mass of customers can be achieved and rates can be increased; or 3) enlist the financial support of advertisers to help defray costs. Consequently, the real task ahead for marketers and their communications consultants will be to design viable new relationship models involving advertiser, medium, and consumer that provide all parties with what they want out of the media.

However, just because producers accept the advertiser's money does not necessarily mean that advertising will be accepted by consumers. Advertisers will have to completely rethink how they go about creating commercial messages in order to entice viewers who will have the choice to edit them out of their lives. In this kind of environment, either marketers will have to live from hand to mouth with an endless series of one-time sales, or virtually irresistible brand identities will have to be created in order to hold audiences who have stronger control over their viewing fare.

---

ing broad classes of audiences, depending on their types of appeal. Even the most narrow of segmented vehicles (for example, "buff" magazines, classical radio, micro-niched cable channels), are no better than refined versions of mass media.

In contrast, interactive vehicles will be capable of "learning" and reacting to participant responses, allowing program producers to adjust messages to individual tastes. This will provide viewers with both a choice of what to watch and of what to "program" for themselves—they can either choose from a selection of predetermined options or create selections of their own choosing. They will also have the choice to manipulate what they have chosen, or to choose not to choose, that is, to let a computer decide for them what they see and hear. Finally, they will be able to choose between commercial-interrupted, commercial-embedded, or commercial-free viewing. The consumer benefit of choice will thus translate to the consumer advantage of control.

In the interactive setting, consumers will also have the hardware and software features to screen out many, if not most, of the commercial messages that do not meet their selection criteria. A famous World War I song asked the musical question, "How do you keep them down on the farm after they've seen Paree?" Our era's slightly less poetic equivalent will be, "How do you interest them in maintaining a brand relationship once they've experienced noncommercial interactivity?"

The option to eliminate commercial messages may cost viewers money, or those who choose not to listen to sponsor content may lose out on incentives. Unfortunately, those who can afford to do either happen to be the very same households whose larger disposable incomes make them the prime targets of many brands. One more reason why commercial content will have to be more enticing than intrusive. In fact, intrusive brands may not even be given an opportunity to intrude. The advertiser will involuntarily move from the role of omnipotent sponsor to plaintive petitioner, from the money source who can pretty much dictate how often a message appears, to a comparatively helpless supplicant.

Another complicating issue is that some of the art directors and copywriters who are currently responsible for advertising content at advertising agencies do not necessarily want their work "interacted with." This is a real conundrum for traditional communications agencies that must be resolved if they hope to be major players in the interactive content-producing arena.

In the long run, marketers will simply have to get better at what they do, making their messages more entertaining and informative in order to win the favor of the significantly more powerful consumer. Whether they deal in humor or hard sell, product demonstrations or soft-focus "image," advertisers will have to be more persuasive than ever before. With the interactive platform, commercial messages must be nothing short of riveting, or viewers will exercise their sacred right to zap.

Clutter, Privacy, and the Politicians

During the 1993 Super Bowl, football fans were expecting to see the usual 9 minutes or so of commercials during a typical hour of football. Instead, what they endured during one 45-minute period was 20 minutes of commercial pods, a full 44 percent of total airtime. Viewers who stuck it out for the entire 3-hour, 25-minute telecast survived 24 breaks showing 68 commercials. It was no surprise when a study by Performance Research indicated that viewer commercial recall suffered terribly compared to that during normal programming. One brand that was recalled well by viewers was Lee Jeans, which had established their effective "The Brand That Fits" positioning via a likable campaign that broke through the clutter and helped to establish a positive brand identity for Lee.

Viewers in the interactive age will demand more information-rich content, and they will be less tolerant of information that they have not asked for. The Super Bowl experience will not be acceptable in most new viewing environments, (although the Super Bowl format itself may remain as an anachronistic vehicle to show off new ads).

Today, the word "clutter" refers to an excessive number of commercial messages in a given time period or physical space. In the future, it's more likely to be called "information overload," and it will refer as much to intruding on an individual's space as it will to the cramming of too many messages in too little media time. In the interactive environment there may be fewer brand exposure opportunities and each brand exposure will generate fewer impressions due to the narrowness of the vehicles.

Users are worried that the interactive networks and other cyberlinks are virtually free opportunities for all comers to advertise whatever they want, under the guise of providing "content." The growing alarm about the commercialization of the nets could lead regulatory bodies to lay down rules that might severely hamper the efforts of marketers. While policing is rarely welcomed by the marketing industry, there may be a need for at least some moderate self-regulation about how products and services can be presented on the nets to prevent more stringent legislation. One way to accomplish that is to place advertising into specific areas of the nets so they can be perused whenever a user is looking for a product. As mentioned earlier, the Internet's Commercenet is one such approach.

Closely related to the clutter issue is that of commercial intrusion. In 1994, real estate lawyer Laurence A. Canter of Phoenix advertised his services on worldwide Internet bulletin boards, and was promptly "flamed," that is, scorched by irate users who sent back angry responses to his commercialization of the Internet, and demanded that his Internet rights be rescinded. They claimed that Canter had ignored what's called "netiquette," the informal guidelines of the network that, among other things, discourage commercial messages in inappropriate places. In a similar case, a cruise line advertised via America Online's "Wine and Dine Online" feature, which was meant to be a sponsor-free service. The ads came in the form of what appeared to be spontaneous recommendations for cruises, and were roundly criticized for the way in which their commercialization had been cloaked.

In a related development, Prodigy announced in late 1994 that it would be revamping its format to eliminate the running billboard advertising that had attracted frequent complaints from subscribers. Instead, the ads are to be reduced in size and relegated to a small box in the corner of the screen, with clickable logos that lead to more brand information.

As strong as opposition is to clutter and intrusion, it's most fervent when it touches on the issue of privacy, the collection and release of individuals' names and personal information for commercial uses, with or without the permission of the consumer. The first to encounter privacy violation questions was the direct marketing industry because of its dependence on database management.

The abuse of mailing lists and area blanketing techniques has created a so-called "junk mail crisis" in the DM industry. (As the saying goes among DM practitioners: if the prospects are interested in the offer, it's "direct mail"; if they're not, it's "junk mail"). A large percentage of mail is derived from lists that may contain millions of names whose owners had no intention of being in contact with the companies involved. This has caused a chain reaction of public debate and legislation that is threatening to significantly limit the buying and selling of consumer names. The issue is now extending well beyond the mailbox as more Americans are receiving phone solicitations (usually at dinnertime) that can be even more annoying than the several pounds of unsolicited mail they receive every few days.

The privacy rights debate really picked up steam with the publicity surrounding what has come to be known as the "Clipper chip." The Clipper is an encryption (coding) chip that the National Security Agency and FBI sought to have placed on every phone and computer in America. The chip would scramble all messages to everyone but the user—everyone, that is, except the government, which would hold the "key" to your chip. The chip would be split in two, with the appropriate legal authority holding the half that matches your own.

It's been estimated by marketing research lobbyists that well over 500 pieces of legislation regarding privacy rights have been introduced in various legislative bodies throughout the United States during the last two years alone. The end result of the privacy controversy can only be detrimental to brands whose selling tools may be greatly curtailed by restrictive lawmakers.

From the consumer's perspective, a 1992 Harris-Equifax Consumer Privacy Survey found that 78 percent of those asked said they were concerned about threats to their personal privacy. About the same time, Lotus Development Corporation dropped plans to create "MarketPlace: Households" after it got 30,000 complaints against the concept of a database with personal information about 80 million households.

There are even more serious implications for the interactive industry whose greatest advantages from the seller's point of view may prove to be an Achilles heel. In order for interactive marketers to be successful in generating repeat purchases, data must be captured regarding those consumers who have chosen to participate in the games, video on demand, or whatever. In principle, marketers will have an opportunity to learn more about interested consumers than ever before. But that does not necessarily mean that extensive customer profile data will be released to advertisers, or even that it will be retained beyond what's needed for billing purposes. Still, interactive media operators will have an opportunity to make more money by selling user profile information, and they are not likely to pass up their chance for more revenue, nor are marketers going to turn down the opportunity to refine their target profiles.

Interactive media and their sponsors may be inclined to provide incentives to consumers in order to obtain otherwise confidential information about their demographic profiles, their purchase tendencies, and even their specific names and addresses. The marketer would then have all the information needed to maintain a long-term relationship with that individual, while also possibly knowing in-depth information about his or her purchase and lifestyle inclinations. Obviously, those consumers who don't care to give out such information would not be forced to do so.

Managing Brand Identities in the Interactive Environment

Brands that are succeeding despite the hostile marketplace in which they compete are living in a delicate balance with forces that may otherwise destroy them. Those hostile forces will likely be present, and perhaps be even more destructive, in the interactive era. As we have seen, some pioneering ITV alliances are not necessarily planning for commercial messages to be an important ingredient in their brew. There's no guarantee that marketers will be able to collect converts without intruding more than the viewer has in mind. The "sponsor" has always been considered a necessary evil, and the jumping off point for brands to establish long-term connections with customers. If audiences fall into the habit of noncommercial communications, why would they tolerate any sponsor whatsoever? Only if the brand is presenting messages that are gripping enough to persuade audiences to let them pass into their homes.

Another problem posed by interactive communications will

be the fractionalization offered by customized media vehicles. In Ed Artzt's speech to the advertising industry referred to earlier, the P&G chairman bared his fear that the narrowing of media will make it unaffordable for many of his brands to create a broad impact in the market because so many vehicles will be needed to reach enough households to sustain a large franchise.

Direct marketing futurists believe that all brands will be narrowly supported, but that would not be an easy transition for the companies that make up the lion's share of hundreds of product and service categories in this country. How long will it take, and how many resources will be required, before Kraft/General Foods or American Airlines or Hertz will rely primarily on one-on-one marketing support? Smaller firms may find it even more difficult. Marketers must find ways to capitalize on the advantages of interactive communications without having to completely scuttle their tried-and-true marketing approaches.

Most brand stewards probably haven't given much thought to the coming interactive selling environment, or how their particular brands will need to adjust in order to flourish. (In fact, it's been whispered in more than one executive floor hallway that senior managers would just as soon reach retirement age before interactive must be dealt with.) It may be that traditional methods will only need an adjustment or two to work in these new settings that are on the way. More likely, however, the relationship between buyer and seller will need to be stripped down and examined piece by piece before marketers will know for sure if what has been sold in the past has a chance of being bought in our interactive future.

Looking on the bright side, interactive media will offer marketers new opportunities to create stronger brand identities because interactive means relationships, and relationships often translate to brand loyalty. It won't be that simple, of course, because brands won't be just "presented" within the interactive environment, they will be incorporated into the programming or software. Marketers will thus have to understand their brands even more than in the past in order to cast them into new roles as part of interactive content.

Marketers will also have the opportunity to create more convergent communications programs, using interactive platforms as the catalyst. For instance, if a viewer is enticed to participate in an interactive quiz, such as Pepsi has tested on the Interactive Network, there is an ideal chance to integrate the overall campaign message into a promotion that is thematically tied to the quiz. This, in turn, could be used in a public relations effort to publicize winners, and might also be incorporated into some local event marketing where the winners might attend an important baseball or football game.

Relationships behind the curtain are changing in preparation for the new ways in which people will be entertained and educated when the curtain is finally raised. These changing relationships may have a profound effect on the identities of participating brands.

Preparing Brands for Their Interactive Future

Brand stewards have a lot of work to do before they can capitalize on the advantages of interactive. To some, interactive marketing is a novelty, a phenomenon that is still a distant opportunity on the horizon. It would be a mistake to hold that view much longer. Interactive media and interactive branding are here in some forms right now, and will soon be available everywhere. It's vital that every brand marketer prepare now for the coming interactive age, or be prepared to be preempted by competitors. Here are some suggested ways to get started:

1. *Evaluate your brand's potential with an "interactive audit."* Brands, like the people who use them, adapt to new selling environments in different ways. Now is the time for marketing teams to determine how ready their brands are to deal with the realities of interactive marketing. For example, who would have thought that a commodity marketing board would have had an interest in interactive communications? Yet the National Potato Board is currently testing interactive kiosks in produce departments that offer reci-tips and buying suggestions for shoppers.

To find out where a brand stands, or should stand, in the

interactive arena, consider contacting an interactive branding consultant to conduct an "interactive audit" that evaluates the potential of interactive platforms to assist in the selling of a brand. One end product of such an audit can be an "interactive index," a comparative rating scale that ranks the usefulness of each interactive platform to a brand compared to other media, and relative to similar brands.

2. *Learn how to create interactive messages.* Whole new disciplines will need to be developed in order for brands to participate fully in the interactive media. Writing a 30-second television commercial, for instance, takes an entirely different set of skills than that required to construct a script for a CD-ROM, or to develop an effective message on the commercial segments of an on line service.

Right now, most of the scripting and art direction in interactive platforms is being done by the software developers themselves, who have not been trained to deal with the critical issues of branding. As more interactive opportunities arise, a brand's communications agency will need to train their people to marry: 1) direct marketing skills, with 2) appropriate content development disciplines, and 3) the identity crafting talents of traditional agency creative directors.

3. *Develop interactive media planning.* In the same way, media professionals will have to relearn how to plan, buy, and measure the effectiveness of a vehicle or a particular kind of communications format. Most interactive business propositions will probably look more like direct marketing deals than traditional arrangements, meaning that far more emphasis will be placed on costs and returns-per-lead/sale than on standard audience measurements, and advertisers may permit equity-sharing arrangements with media. At this moment, there are only a relatively few media professionals in the world who are qualified to do this type of buying and planning work.

4. *Practice convergent communications as interactive marketing takes hold.* The tenets of convergent communications explained in chapter 6 are even more crucial in interactive environments than in conventional settings. The brand messages communicated via various interactive platforms need to be coordinated

and focused on the customer's needs in a consistent stream of strategically compelling content. Just as conventional communications might concentrate PR, advertising, and sales promotion events on particular prospect needs, so interactive should ensure that all messages going out via on line, CD-ROM, ITV, and place-based media are similarly focused.

5. *Participate as soon as possible in testing.* Interactive marketing is no different than its traditional counterparts in at least one way: nothing can substitute for experience in the marketplace. The infotainment, CD-ROM mailers, and home shopping wings of interactive marketing are relatively far along in their development, so a brand can get involved in those areas as quickly as possible, wherever compatible with the brand's communications goals. CD-ROMs, as one example, offer many good selling opportunities for a wide range of brands such as Gillette (perhaps with sports highlights in support of their men's lines), Northwest Airlines (Asia travel package ideas), and Safeway Stores (long-form commercials about their line of private labels).

6. *Look for strategic alliances.* Huge telephone and cable companies are not the only firms that can benefit from partnerships to achieve more leverage in the interactive world. Brands might also consider whether they should navigate this new world in partnership with other brands inside or outside their brand family or corporate stable. For instance, a retail brand like Nordstrom might partner with another kind of retailer like Eddie Bauer in providing a CD-ROM on fashions of the day.

7. *Help in establishing industry clutter and privacy guidelines.* There's no denying that clutter concerns and privacy legislation will remain an ominous backdrop to interactive marketing. The smart brand teams are already considering these issues as part of their current planning. For those brands that are hoping to participate in the new media, it's time to come to grips with what clutter and privacy parameters would be appropriate, and to contribute to industry efforts to create sensible self-regulation.

The interactive age will enable brands to positively affect their identity if the stewards involved truly understand how to capitalize on the advantages of this new form of selling. Interactive is not a toy, or a fad, or a marginal player in the media game. Interactive media are the communications platforms of the future, and interactive marketing may turn out to be the most powerful tool ever for creating long-term relationships with brand customers.

10

Minding the Brand Identity

Clothe the Naked Product

It's a difficult time for brands. Premium product and service brands are under continuous attack from lower-priced competition. Lower-priced brands have had to raise their quality levels to maintain sales momentum. Value-conscious consumers are more discriminating than ever, more meticulous, more cautious, measurably more skeptical than just five years ago. The proliferation of line extensions, flankers, co-brands, and brand alliances is muddying an already murky pond. The exponential growth in commercial exposures, including selling message clutter and intrusive selling techniques, are tempting consumers to eliminate branded messages from their lives whenever they're given the opportunity.

As if in answer to that temptation, interactive media will soon provide consumers with the technology to electronically filter out all that offends. In the new media world, brands will have to earn their right to be included; they may be no more than passengers on the bus, if they're lucky enough to get a ride. Few founders of new media are insisting that commercial interests run the show, and many are openly dubious about how commercial they really want their vehicles to be.

In such an environment, the best that brands can do is to make themselves more distinctive and more attractive to both media owner and media audience. It's no wonder that some investment analysts are questioning more than ever whether brands are an asset or a liability. Even some battle-scarred veterans in the marketing industry itself are having second thoughts about the long term viability of brands.

Ironically, despite the perils of branding, there is a long waiting list of people, places, and events that are hoping to be branded. Jack Nicholson commands many millions per picture because Americans can't get enough of his brand. Our presidents must now become brands every four years in order to be elected. Even the Pope has been branded through a growing Vatican mini-industry of T-shirts, publishing, and memorabilia.

Every major media vehicle, from Fox Television to *People,* is working overtime to brand itself. Every significant sporting event seeks branded sponsors to help pay the bills, and most seek to become brands themselves. Gannett Outdoor New York has created a "brand train," an entire 10-car Lexington Avenue subway train that will carry only Donna Karan's DKNY advertising, and other advertisers are literally scrambling to jump on board trains of their own.

Logic leads us to our future: If PGA tournaments can be branded, why not the Westminster Kennel Club Dog Show? And if Westminster can, why can't the best-of-show winners—that prancing Welsh springer spaniel, or that pouty Pekinese—become brands? And if dogs can be branded, why not Humphrey the wayward California gray whale, who keeps swimming up the Sacramento River? For that matter, why can't a river be branded? Why hasn't some bright entrepreneur in the U.S. Department of the Interior figured out a way to brand the Mississippi ("The Mark Twain River™ Welcomes You to St. Louis") or the Suwannee ("Tours of the Stephen Foster Waterway® are available hourly").

While branding is a generally positive force in economic terms, individual brands are in danger of being swept away by their own desperate struggle to be heard above the clamor they helped create, dramatically devalued by the over-branding of all creatures great and small.

Through it all, brands, either as we know them today or in a new form into which they may evolve, will continue to be the common currency of consumer marketing. The reason can be found in the words of the eminently quotable Winston Churchill who said, in various ways, that democracy is a very bad form of government, but the others are so much worse. Brands can be difficult to manage, hypersensitive to change, vulnerable to a long list of communicable diseases, constantly in need of close supervision, continually a strain on the patience of their owners, and ludicrously expensive to maintain—the yachts of American business, holes in the water through which you throw money.

But the alternatives simply do not measure up because they fail to create an enduring trust between buyer and seller, still a firm prerequisite for long-term profitability. To sell a naked product or service, devoid of brand identity, is tantamount to starting over with each sale. It's difficult to imagine a more frustrating way to do business.

Managing the Brand Triad

Brands must fight the uncertainties of the future marketplace with a balance of consistency and flexibility. Consumers' concerns about value must be answered with reasonable pricing and commensurate quality. The proliferation of brand families and brand alliances should be approached with caution so that, in attempting to expand a brand's influence, marketers don't dilute the power of the very brand they are shepherding. Commercial clutter must be reduced by sane self-management of commercial media. Intrusion must be controlled by those brands that are most tempted to employ it.

As always, either brands make it in this environment or they will be replaced with a heartier breed. Ahead of us lies a *literally* customer-driven marketplace where consumers have the desire to act as individuals, the inclination to demonstrate their individuality in the brands they buy, and a growing army of companies that will be capable of mass customizing and personalizing, virtually on demand. That's a long way from the brand heaven of the 1950s, but heaven, like home, is where you make it.

We have left behind the days when most consumers bought what millions of others bought because millions of others bought it. We will never return to the separation between buyer and seller when marketing was not all that different from throwing sacks of food off of moving trucks into waiting throngs. We are dealing now and forevermore in various forms of intimate marketing where long-term relationships must be managed far more carefully than single sales.

As part of that relationship building, marketers will cross the line between buyer and seller and become more closely involved in the buyer's world. The benefits are obvious: the better marketers know their prospects, the better they can provide products and services to serve them, along with a reassurance that the customers can come back and get more of the same. The more closely customers work with marketers, the more likely that their needs will be filled to their satisfaction.

But, there is a key component missing in that formula—the brand itself. We've already established that successful brands have been positioned in a good place by customers within their mind-sets, and that the brands' personalities have been accepted as well. In those cases when a brand has been created to represent the product or service, it becomes a third partner in the relationship between customer and marketer. It is the coming together of *three* identities—the customer's, the marketer's, and the brand's—that forms a triad relationship, a long, enduring interdependence that yields benefits for all three parties.

In order for this partnership to be formed, the brand must be likable, accessible, credible, relevant, as loyal to its customers as we would have them be to the brand. The marketer, who is represented by the brand, must read the customer and manipulate the brand to deliver the desired benefits. The customer needs to be clear about what he or she needs, buy it when it's delivered, and ideally remain loyal to whatever brand finally gets it right. The marketer and customer and brand are three parts of the same whole: co-dependents, co-habitants, co-workers in the playing out of brand capitalism.

For all of that and more to happen, stewards must create and fortify the strongest possible brand identities because a sound brand identity provides the most viable link between the marketer and the customer.

So Who's Minding the Identity?

Cutbacks in marketing departments across this country have left brand managers wondering if they still like their jobs, and brands in dire danger of having no steward to keep the identity fires burning. Is it possible that all the changes in marketing organizations and the marketplace itself have overshadowed the importance of establishing a strong brand identity? Category managers have been created by a number of major packaged goods companies to concentrate on blocks of brands rather than the individuals. Elsewhere, the marketing function has been divided between business managers who mind the retail trade end of the enterprise and consumer managers who focus on that side of the house.

In many service companies, the marketing function is a staff group that merely provides the sales force with the selling materials they need. Still others experiment with a matrix management structure that distributes responsibilities for marketing across several groups in celebration of universal horizontalness.

The idea of a single person being charged with an entire brand is no longer considered to be ideal. That may make sense functionally as brands and markets become more complex and more duties must be shared for cost reasons, but it raises the question: who's the one person in charge of the care and feeding of the brand identity? If a company CEO cannot answer that question without hesitation, there may be serious brand trouble ahead.

The Brand Identity Strategy (Reprise)

No brand teams are defenseless against the hostilities in the marketplace or the disruptive reshuffling of their own organizations. The Brand Identity Strategy presented in chapter 1 and elaborated on throughout this book is our recommended way to fully capitalize on whatever strengths your brand may have. To recap, it calls for the brand team to:

- objectively analyze where their brand stands now;
- rediscover their customers and prospects as individuals, not just segments of a population;
- determine what kind of credible and relevant prompts can be communicated to customers and prospects, creating a power positioning in their minds, given the realities of their lives;
- construct a brand personality that seamlessly extends from the achieved positioning, and that humanizes the brand in a way that encourages close relationships with consumers;
- manage all possible brand contacts with customers and prospects, and to measure success according to how well the brand contacts perform "on the street," that is, in the everyday world of the consumer;
- regularly study those brands that have succeeded, and those that have not, in search of lessons that can be applied to their own brand identity experiences; and
- prepare for, and capitalize on, the coming opportunities and challenges offered by the interactive age.

The only device that the U.S. Patent Office will reject out of hand is a perpetual motion machine, yet that is exactly what brand stewards are asked to maintain. Now—before uncontrollable forces control your brand—control your brand's fate by establishing and maintaining a bulletproof brand identity that will withstand the test of time, and the travails of a hostile marketplace.

Listen to Dad

They call him "The Great One" because he is the greatest player ever to strap on hockey skates. He holds more than 60 major National Hockey League records, including the most goals scored (passing Gordie Howe's record in one-third fewer games). He has scored more often, and against more opponents, than anyone could have imagined possible 10 years ago, including once from behind the net by flipping the puck off a goalie's back. He has been named most valuable player of the league 9 times, scoring champion 9 times, and selected as a member of 12 NHL all-star teams. History might consider him selfish except that he also led the league in assists for 12 years.

Wayne Gretzky weighs 180 pounds after a big meal. He is not the strongest player in the league, nor is he the fastest skater, or the quickest, or the shooter with the hardest shot. He is not even close to being the toughest in a tough sport. In fact, he has won the Lady Byng Memorial Trophy three times for being "the most gentlemanly player" (a little-known honor in the macho NHL). To be blunt, Wayne Gretzky has always looked a little like a walk-on who hopes to play with the big boys, but who just doesn't have the strength and skills necessary to make the cut.

What is the secret to his remarkable success? His dad, Walter Gretzky, told him at an early age: "Wayne, never skate toward where the puck *is*. Skate toward where the puck *will be*."[1] The Great Gretzky, as it turns out, is one of our foremost futurists. He knows the ice, he knows his opponents, and he knows what's going to happen before it does.

Those of us with brands to tend might do well to study Wayne Gretzky's talent for anticipation. From this point forward, brands and their stewards must skate over slippery surfaces, not toward where the marketplace is, but toward where the marketplace will be. And, when we get there, we had best be carrying a hardwood stick called a brand identity.

It is shopping day in the year 2020. Thirty million Americans order goods and services via in-home interactive telecomputer programs, but you are one of the majority who still prefer to pick up what they need at mid-size shopping convenience centers. You are grateful that the trend toward hyper-stores was turned back by common sense a few years earlier; shopping was never meant to be a quest for survival.

There are 25,000 goods and services available, nearly 20 percent of which can be customized on the spot to fit your specific needs. You begin with a visit to the bank of virtual reality headsets near the center's entrance so you can plan your shopping before venturing out onto the moving trams that run down each aisle. A sensor at the center's front door alerts the computer to your presence. Once your headset is in place, it displays a list of your favorite brands and where they can be found, plus a list of items you have likely run short of based on usage information you voluntarily provided to the store.

As you visually "walk" down the aisle, you are presented with as many options as you historically have preferred to review in each category, no more, no less. In the hand control set at your fingertips, there is an "overload" button that permits you to eliminate from consideration any brand whose packaging or aisle advertising is making it too confusing for you to make a selection.

Also on your control set is an information access button that permits you to hear exactly how the brands that appear on shelf are chosen by the center's dry grocery, produce, meat, and services buyers. The selections available are based on a combination of your specified desires and new national and store (private label) brands, providing a wide spectrum of price and value choices. Private labels dominate in a minority of product and service categories where most of the center's shoppers believe that they offer the best value. In the majority of categories, regional and national brands still hold the largest share of shelf space and sales.

New products are rotated onto shelves, again, according to the desires of the shoppers who are exposed to a multimedia demonstration of the new items as they push the appropriate button on their control sets. Which brands are retained and which are discontinued is based entirely on consumer preference rather than retailer analysis. Retailers encourage brand manufacturers to limit the number of line extensions that represent only minor differences compared to the base brands. New product introductions have stabilized at about 17,000 per year (the level in 1995), and down from a high of 30,000 a few years ago. The grocery and drug chains share their scanning data with those manufacturers who are willing to pay part of the costs, and both groups work together to prevent the kind of industry warfare that led to the national grocery boycott of 2005.

You decide you will also need to stop at the center's service wing where shoppers are offered everything from insurance annuities to home decorating consultations, each of which can be "experienced" before committing to a purchase. Today, you will use the vacation services that are sold by an independent broker, one of two dozen whose credentials were presented to you a few months ago in an interactive video presentation transmitted to your home. The broker displays five options for you, also in a virtual reality booth, and each vacation alternative is presented by a group of brands that had been assembled according to your particular travel interests.

Forty-five minutes later, your shopping completed, you pull out of the center's holding area. As you accelerate your aircoupe, your driver's console flashes a signal that you are passing an environmentally embedded advertisement for your favorite brand of running shoe. Apparently, the brand is bringing out a new model that might be of interest to you. You press the "display" button and a commercial message is projected onto your console only, from a transmitter hidden among a grove of trees. You are reminded of your car trips as a child when commercial signs were everywhere, including on a baseball you snagged at a major league game. (Now, each ballpark has a specified limit to its commercial signage, and no sign can be placed behind home plate.)

You ask the computer for the "News of the Day" summary. Among the late-breaking items in the business report, the U.S. West/Microsoft/ Blockbuster research organization has issued its tenth annual "brand satisfaction" index. According to the report, many of the old standbys are still at the top, but consumers are keeping new brands alive and well as they seek those that offer the best value for the money based on their individual needs.

The news report ends and the console voice asks if you would like to review ways in which you can save money on your next shopping trip. But by then, you have put the aircoupe on autocruise and settled in to catch a few winks before touching down at home.

Chapter Notes

Chapter 1

1. Alvin Toffler, *The Third Wave* (New York: William Morrow, 1980), p. 248.

2. The term "mass customization" was coined by Stanley M. Davis in an article which was used as an introduction to his book, *Future Perfect* (Reading, Mass.: Addison-Wesley, 1987).

3. Willard Bishop Consulting brand study results as reported by Ira Teinowitz and Jennifer Lawrence, "Brand Proliferation Attacked," *Advertising Age*, May 10, 1993, p. 1.

4. Emily DeNitto, "Private Labels Mean Headaches for Brand Stocks," *Advertising Age*, July 29, 1993, p. 2.

5. Larry Light, "Advertising's Role in Building Brand Equity," speech to annual meeting of the Association of American Advertising Agencies, Laguna Niguel, California, April 22, 1993.

6. Jean-Noel Kapferer, *Strategic Brand Management—New Approaches to Creating and Evaluating Brand Equity* (New York: The Free Press, 1992), pp. 38–39.

7. David A. Aaker, *Managing Brand Equity: Capitalizing on the Value of a Brand Name* (New York: The Free Press, 1991), p. 15.

8. This list of brand terms is drawn from a variety of readings, including David Aaker and Jean-Noel Kapferer, plus *Brand Equity and Advertising* (Hillsdale, N.J.: Lawrence Erlbaum Associates, 1993), a compilation of papers presented at the 10th annual advertising and consumer psychology conference in May 1991, and edited by David Aaker and Alexander Biel; and *Mythmaking on Madison Avenue: How Advertisers Apply the Power of Myth and Symbolism to Create Leadership Brands* Sal Randazzo (Chicago: Probus Publishing, 1993).

9. The subject of brand equity is much more complex than the brief description in this chapter might imply. To obtain a considerably more in-depth (and broader) description of brand equity, see Aaker, *Managing Brand Equity*, and David A. Aaker, and Alexander L. Biel, eds., *Brand Equity and Advertising: Advertising's Role in Building Strong Brands* (Hillsdale, N.J.: Lawrence Erlbaum Associates, 1993).

10. Sal Randazzo, *Mythmaking on Madison Avenue: How Advertisers Apply the Power of Myth and Symbolism to Create Leadership Brands*. (Chicago: Probus, 1993), p. 17.

11. Frederick F. Reichheld, and Earl W. Sasser, Jr., "Zero Defections: Quality Comes to Services," *Harvard Business Review*, September–October 1990, pp. 93–95.

Chapter 2

1. From Alex Haley speaking tour, College of Marin, Kentfield, California; August 1980.

2. This is a reference made by Alexander Biel in his article "Converting Image into Equity" in *Brand Equity and Advertising,* Aaker and Biel, eds., *Brand Equity and Advertising,* p. 67, regarding a paper presented by John Sherry at the fourteenth annual Association for Consumer Research conference in Toronto, 1987.

Chapter 3

1. Robert B. Settle and Pamela L. Alreck, *Why They Buy—American Consumers Inside and Out* (New York: John Wiley, & Sons, 1986), p. 29.

2. John Boslough, *Stephen Hawking's Universe: An Introduction to the Most Remarkable Scientist of Our Time* (New York: Avon Books, 1985), p. 49.

3. From a speech by Judith Langer to the *American Demographics* 10th annual Conference on Consumer Markets, New York City, June 13, 1990.

4. This story about Jeanette MacDonald and Nelson Eddy was not confirmable, but the legend is as telling as whatever truth might lay behind it.

5. From Ketchum Communications focus groups held between 1992 and 1994 in northern and southern California.

6. Andrew Olds, "Planned and Delivered," *Advertising Age,* January 1, 1990, p. 9.

7. Cheryl Russel, *The Master Trend* (New York: Plenum, 1993).

8. Michael Treacy and Fred Wiersema, "Customer Intimacy and Other Value Disciplines," *Harvard Business Review,* January–February 1993, pp. 83–93.

9. All story excerpts from the July 12, 1994, edition of the *Wall Street Journal,* pp. A1 and C1.

10. Meredith F. Small, "Demogram—Chevy Chase, Maryland," *American Demographics,* (April 1994), p. 29; and Brad Edmondson, "Demogram—Taso, New Mexico," *American Demographics* (May 1994), p. 28.

11. Don Peppers and Martha Rogers, Ph.D., *The One to One Future—Building Relationships One Customer at a Time* (New York: Doubleday), pp. 56–58.

12. Paul D. Brown, *Lessons in the Art of Marketing* (New York: Harper & Row, 1988), p. 206.

Chapter 4

1. Alice Z. Cuneo, "Starbucks' Word-of-Mouth Wonder," *Advertising Age,* March 7, 1994, p. 12.

2. Al Ries, and Jack Trout. *Positioning: The Battle for Your Mind* (New York: Warner Books, 1981), p. 2.

3. Kevin J. Clancy and Robert S. Shulman, *Marketing Myths That Are Killing Business—The Cure for Death Wish Marketing* (New York: McGraw-Hill, 1994), pp. 122–24.

4. Derived from data in a variety of reports issued by Private Label Manufacturers Association, as reported in: "Private Label, Experts Predict, Will Reach 45% Market Share," *Brandweek,* February 8, 1993, p. 8; "Brands Besieged—They're Right to Worry," *Adweek,* October 25, 1993, p. 5; Jim Kirk, "The New Status Symbols," *Adweek,* October 5, 1992, pp. 38–39.

5. Greg Erickson, "Seeing Double," *Brandweek,* October 17, 1994, p. 31.

6. Telephone interview with Lynn Dornblaser, editor of *New Product News* magazine, August 19, 1994.

7. Molpus quote from Steve Winstein, "A Case for National Brands," *Progressive Grocer,* April 1994, p. 109.

8. Orville Redenbacher story as told by Orville to the author several times, and reconfirmed in August 1994.

Chapter 5

1. Alexander Biel, "Converting Image into Equity," in *Brand Equity & Advertising,* ed. David A. Aaker and Alexander L. Biel (Hillsdale, NJ: Lawrence Erlbaum Associates, 1993), pp. 71–74.

2. Max Blackston, "Beyond Brand Personality: Building Brand Relationships," in *Brand Equity & Advertising,* ed. David A. Aaker and Alexander L. Biel (Hillsdale, NJ: Lawrence Erlbaum Associates, 1993), p. 116.

3. Norman Smothers, "Can Products and Brands Have Charisma?" *Brand Equity and Advertising,* pp. 105–6.

4. David N. Martin, *Romancing the Brand* (New York: AMACOM, 1989), pp. 87–91.

5. Stuart Elliott, "A Study Shows That Celebrity Endorsements of Products Can Help a Company's Stock Price. A Little." *New York Times,* August 16, 1994, p. C6.

6. Greg Farrell, "Star Search," *Adweek* (Midwest Edition), December 6, 1993, p. 26.

7. Stuart Elliott, "Despite Mixed Reviews, Coke's Quirky Campaign Commands Encore," *New York Times,* February 8, 1994, p. C8.

8. Ibid.

9. Based on sales data referred to in: Stuart Elliott, "At Coke a Shift to Many Voices." *New York Times,* January 20, 1995, p. C6.

10. "Does Likeable TV Advertising Help Sell the Product?" study conducted January–April, 1985 by The Ogilvy Center For Research & Development; report issued September, 1985.

11. Data from 1989 ARF Copy Research Validity Study, as discussed at the 7th Annual ARF Copy Research Workshop, New York City, July 11–12, 1990.

12. Michael Ray and Rochelle Myers, *Creativity in Business* (New York: Doubleday, 1986), pp. 163–71.

13. David Aaker quote from "1993 Will Go Down as 'The Year of Efficiency,' " *Superbrands,* October 18, 1993, p. 35.

Chapter 6

1. Based on winter 1994 Nielsen data.

2. Don E. Schultz, Stanley I. Tannenbaum, and Robert F. Lauterborn, *Integrated Marketing Communications* (Lincolnwood, Ill.: NTC Publishing Group, 1993), pp. 132–40. To be clear on this point, Schultz, Tannenbaum, and Lauterborn were among the first to develop the concept of "contacts." The discussion in chapter 7 focuses that concept on the contacts the brand itself makes on current or potential customers, and how that relates to the brand identity.

3. John P. Cortez, "Put People behind the Wheel—Word-of-Mouth Advertising Works for Chrysler in Test-Drive Plan," *Advertising Age,* March 22, 1993, p. S28.

4. Alice Z. Cuneo, "Starbucks' Word-of-Mouth Wonder," *Advertising Age,* March 7, 1994, p. 12.

5. Ibid.

6. Jan Carlzon, *Moments of Truth* (New York: Harper Collins, 1987), p. 3.

7. Regis McKenna, "Marketing Is Everything," *Harvard Business Review* (January–February 1991), p. 69.

Chapter 7

1. Cyndee Miller, "Upscale Brands Regaining Popularity," *Marketing News,* May 23, 1984, p. 3.

2. Julie Mollne, "EPCOT Center: Orlando's Billion-Dollar Hit," *Meetings & Conventions,* April 1983, p. S40.

3. Patricia Leigh Brown, "In Fairy Dust, Disney Finds New Realism," *New York Times,* July 20, 1989, p. C1.

4. Mario Mota, "Disney-Bashing and the Disney Grooming Policy," *Los Angeles Times,* January 21, 1990, p. 11.

5. Nike 1993 annual report, inside cover.

6. David E. Thigpen, "Is Nike Getting Too Big for Its Shoes?" *Time,* April 26, 1993, p. 55.

7. Ibid.

8. Geraldine E. Willigan, "High-Performance Marketing: An Interview with Nike's Phil Knight," *Harvard Business Review* (July–August 1992), pp. 95–96.

9. Matthew Grimm, "Nike Vision," *Brandweek,* March 29, 1993, p. 18.

10. Warren Berger, "They Know Bo," *New York Times Magazine,* November 11, 1990, pp. 36, 48, 50, 52.

11. Grimm, "Nike Vision," *Brandweek,* p. 18.

12. Michael Janofsky, "Procter & Gamble in 12% Job Cut as Brand Names Lose Attraction," *New York Times,* July 16, 1993, p. C1.

Chapter 8

1. From verified employee/customer anecdotes reported to Swbyp's headquarters during the summer of 1994.

2. Saturn research, as reported by Doron P. Levin, "Car Buyers Turn Back to Detroit," *New York Times,* August 11, 1992, p. C1.

3. Raymond Serafin, "The Saturn Story," *Advertising Age,* November 16, 1992, p. 16.

4. Matthew Grimm, "The Biggest Battle at Burger King," *Adweek's Marketing Week,* April 8, 1991, p. 21.

5. Greg Farrell, "Something's Got to Give," *Brandweek,* May 17, 1993, p. 32.

6. Jeanne Whalen, and Gary Levin, "BK Puts Basics on Center Stage in Huge Ad Blitz," *Advertising Age,* September 5, 1994, p. 3.

Chapter 9

1. William Safire, "Footprints on the Infobahn," *New York Times,* April 17, 1994, p. 20. The term "information superhighway" has been attributed repeatedly to Vice-President Al Gore. According to *New York Times* columnist William Safire, "Vice-President Al Gore's staff claims, without citations, that he called for a national network of information superhighways in the early 1980s."

2. Peter H. Lewis, "Strangers, Not Their Computers, Build a Network in Time of Grief," *New York Times,* March 8, 1994, p. A1.

3. From *Advertising Age,* 1994 annual survey of 1,000 U.S. adults, conducted by Market Facts' Telenation research service.

4. Stan Rapp and Thomas L. Collins, *The Great Marketing Turnaround: The Age of the Individual and How to Profit from It* (Englewood Cliffs, N.J.: Prentice-Hall, 1990), p. 37.

5. Joseph Segel, excerpts from speech to a Direct Marketing Conference in Toronto, reprinted in *Direct Marketing* (February 1994), p. 18.

6. Steve Lohr, "How Bell Atlantic and T.C.I.'s Match Went Awry," *New York Times,* March 28, 1994, p. C1.

7. Ibid.

8. "P&G's Artzt: TV Advertising in Danger: Remedy Is to Embrace Technology and Return to Program Ownership," *Advertising Age,* May 23, 1994, p. 24.

Chapter 10

1. The story of Walter Gretzky's advice to his son was confirmed by Rick Minch of the Los Angeles Kings media relations staff in September 1994.

References

Aaker, David A. *Managing Brand Equity: Capitalizing on the Value of a Brand Name*. New York: The Free Press, 1991.

Aaker, David A., and Alexander L. Biel, eds. *Brand Equity and Advertising: Advertising's Role in Building Strong Brands*. Hillsdale, N.J.: Lawrence Erlbaum Associates, 1993.

Advertising Age. "The Best Awards." *Advertising Age*, May 3, 1993, pp. S1–S15.

"Adweek's Best of 1993." *Adweek*, January 31, 1994, pp. 32–37.

Agins, Teri. "Is It a TV Show? Or Is It Advertising?" *Wall Street Journal*, August 10, 1994, p. B1.

Bennet, James. "The Power of Cult Brands." *Adweek's Marketing Week*, February 24, 1992, p. 18.

———. "Culture of Complaint," *Brandweek*, July 26, 1993, p. 32.

———. "Chevrolet Is Seeking to Reclaim Old Glory." *New York Times*, March 16, 1994, pp. C1, C14.

———. "Saturn, G.M.'s Big Hope, Is Taking Its First Lumps." *New York Times*, March 29, 1994, pp. A1, A12.

———. "Saturn Invites the 'Family' to a Party." *New York Times*, June 21, 1994, p. C1.

Berger, Warren. "They Know Bo," *New York Times Magazine*, November 11, 1990, pp. 36, 48, 50, 52.

Berman, Phyllis, and Alger, Alexandra. "A One-Man Show." *Forbes*, February 14, 1994, p. 68.

Berry, Jonathan, Zachary Schiller, Richard A. Melcher, and Mark Maremont. "Attack of the Fighting Brands." *Business Week*, May 2, 1994, p. 125.

Bird, Laura. "First Advertorials; Now Advernewscasts." *Wall Street Journal*, September 24, 1993, p. B1.

———. "NBC Special Is One Long Prime-Time Ad." *Wall Street Journal*, January 21, 1994, p. B1.

———. "'Custom' Magazines Stir Credibility Issues." *Wall Street Journal*, February 14, 1994, p. B10.

330

_____. "Collagen Corp.'s Video Uses News Format." *Wall Street Journal,* March 29, 1994, p. B5.

"Brand Scorecard." *Advertising Age,* various issues, 1993–94.

"Brands on Trial: An *Adweek* Roundtable on the Turmoil Among Brands and the Challenge to Agencies to Protect Them." *Adweek,* May 24, 1993, p. 24.

"*Brandweek* Salutes the 1993 Effies." *Brandweek,* June 14, 1993, pp. 1–30.

Brown, Warren. "GM Making Last Stab at Small Cars: Saturn Represents Crucial Industry Test." *Washington Post,* January 13, 1985, p. E1.

Bryant, Adam. "New Logo Inspired by Public." *San Francisco Chronicle,* June 24, 1994, p. B3.

Bulkeley, William M. "Sponsoring Sports Gains in Popularity; John Hancock Learns How to Play to Win." *Wall Street Journal,* June 24, 1994, p. B1.

Butler, Charles. "Playing to Win." *Sales & Marketing Management,* August 1993, pp. 37–46.

Byrd, Veronica. "Consumers Wake Up to Increases in Cereal Prices." *New York Times,* August 10, 1993, pp. D1, D5.

Caminitti, Susan. "Her Own Best Customer" (segment of "Twenty Companies on a Roll"). *Fortune,* November 22, 1993, p. 22.

Campbell, Charlotte. "Likeability: Does It Deserve A Place at the Table?" Speech to Advertising Research Foundation. New York City, September 22, 1992, pp. 122–26.

Carlson, Tracy. "Brand Burnout." *Brandweek,* January 17, 1994, p. 23.

Carey, William R. with Rebecca Holdren Ball, and Sam Bowers. "The New You." *Inc.,* August 1991, p. 50.

Clancy, Kevin J., and Robert S. Shulman. *Marketing Myths That Are Killing Business—the Cure for Death-Wish Marketing.* New York: McGraw-Hill, 1994.

Collins, Glenn. "Xerox Attempts a New Beginning by Making Its Name the Last Word in a Corporate Rechristening." *New York Times,* August 4, 1994, p. C16.

Cortez, John P. "Put People behind the Wheel—Word of Mouth Advertising for Chrysler in Test-Drive Plan." *Advertising Age,* March 22, 1993, p. 528.

Costello, Richard. "Focus on the Brand." Speech to the Association of National Advertisers Issues Forum. San Francisco, September 14, 1992.

Crispell, Diane. "What's in a Brand?" *American Demographics,* May 1993, p. 26.

Cuneo, Alice Z. "Starbucks' Word-of-Mouth Wonder." *Advertising Age,* March 7, 1994, p. 12.

_____. "Nimble VF Strips Levi of Jeans Market Lead." *Advertising Age,* September 28, 1994, p. 30.

"December Trends: New Products Climb to 17,571 for 1993; Up Modest 4.6 Percent versus 1992." *New Product News,* January 8, 1994, pp. 3, 5, 10–11.

DeGeorge, Gail. "Sid Feltenstein Is Having It His Way." *Business Week,* November 23, 1992, pp. 64, 68.

DeNitto, Emily. "The Concept of EDLP Is Changing." Interview with Tim Hammonds. *Advertising Age,* August 16, 1993, pp. 33–34.

———. "They Aren't Private Labels Anymore—They're Brands." *Advertising Age,* September 13, 1993, p. 8.

Deveny, Kathleen. "Sale of Private Label Goods Keep Rising." *Wall Street Journal,* October 5, 1993, p. B1.

———. "How Country's Biggest Brands Are Faring at the Supermarket." *Wall Street Journal,* March 29, 1994, pp. B1, B8.

"Disney's Got Right Touch—and Top Spot." *Daily Variety* (special section), February 5, 1993, pp. 9–11.

Dougherty, Philip H. "Advertising: TV Spots Mark New G.E. Effort." *New York Times,* March 30, 1981, p. D9.

Edmondson, Brad. "Demogram: Taos, New Mexico." *American Demographics,* May 1994, p. 28.

Elliott, Stuart. "The Revolution in Television Technology Will Test the Industry's Ability to Rethink Brand Image Building" *New York Times,* April 26, 1993, p. C14.

———. "Once Again, Burger King Shops for an Agency." *New York Times,* October 21, 1993, pp. C1, C18.

———. "When a Stranger Offers to Buy a Drink at the Bar . . . ?" *New York Times,* January 14, 1994, p. C18.

Elmer-Dewitt, Philip. "Take a Trip into the Future on the Electronic Superhighway." *Time,* April 12, 1993, p. 50.

Erickson, Greg. "Seeing Double." *Brandweek,* October 17, 1994, pp. 31–34.

"The Equifax Report on Consumers in the Information Age," June 1990, conducted by Louis Harris & Associates.

Farrell, Greg. "Burger King: Whopper on the Rebound?" *Brandweek,* February 7, 1994, pp. 23–26.

———. "Something's Got to Give," *Brandweek,* May 17, 1993, p. 32.

Feder, Barnaby J. "Those with Things to Sell Love Word-of-Mouth Ads." *New York Times,* June 23, 1992, p. 18.

Fitzgerald, Kate. "Circle of 'Friends' Rounds Out MCI Base." *Advertising Age,* January 13, 1992, p. 2.

Fraser, Bruce W. "General Electric: They Know It's GE." *Marketing & Media Decisions,* March 22, 1983, p. 85.

Friedman, Martin. "The Day the Last National Brand Died (a Frightening Fable)." *New Product News,* January 8, 1994, pp. 12–13.

Gallagher, Patricia. "Value Pricing for Profits: Ed Artzt Has Pushed the Value Concept to the Front of P&G's Strategy." *Cincinnati Enquirer,* December 21, 1992, p. 1.

"General Motors: Planet Falls to Earth." *The Economist,* March 12, 1994, pp. 74–75.

Georges, Tuesday. "Guerrilla Marketer Makes Its Name with Bold Theatrics." *Wall Street Journal,* August 13, 1993, p. B1.

Gibson, Richard. "Cobranding Aims to Double the Appeal." *Wall Street Journal,* August 3, 1993, pp. B1, B7.

Goldman, Kevin. "Lee Aims at Bigger Targets: Pudgy People." *Wall Street Journal,* January 27, 1993, B7.

———. "As Ad Clutter Becomes Tradition at Super Bowl, Viewer Recall Slips." *Wall Street Journal,* February 3, 1993, p. B8.

———. "Volvo Features Accident Survivors in Ads." *Wall Street Journal,* October 8, 1993, p. B7.

———. "TV Promotional Clutter Irks Ad Industry." *Wall Street Journal,* February 11, 1994, p. B6.

———. "Year's Top Commercials Propelled by Star Power." *Wall Street Journal,* March 16, 1994, p. B1.

Green, Alan. "The Naked Consumer." *Best of Business Quarterly,* Summer 1991, pp. 30, 32–37.

Grimm, Matthew. "Nike Vision." *Brandweek,* March 29, 1993, p. 23.

Grover, Ronald. "The Shock Therapy Wall Street Gave Disney; Storming the Magic Kingdom: Wall Street, the Raiders, and the Battle for Disney." *Business Week,* May 18, 1987, pp. 26–27.

Gubernick, Lisa. "Mickey N'est Pas Fini." *Forbes,* February 14, 1994, pp. 42–43.

Heline, Holly. "Brand Loyalty Isn't Dead—But You're Not off the Hook." *Brandweek,* June 7, 1993, p. 14.

Helyar, John. "Signs Sprout at Sports Arenas as a Way to Get Cheap TV Ads." *Wall Street Journal,* March 8, 1994, p. B1.

Hoover's Handbook of American Business. "The Walt Disney Company, 1994," pp. 1106–7.

Huey, John. "The World's Best Brand." *Fortune,* May 31, 1993, pp. 44–54.

Hume, Scott. "Brand Loyalty Steady; NPD Sees No Correlation to Promotion Spending." *Advertising Age,* March 2, 1992, p. 19.

"InfoVision Straddles Line between Information and Advertising." *Marketing News,* February 14, 1994, p. 3.

"Integrated Marketing—Marketers Convinced: Its Time Has Arrived." *Advertising Age,* November 8, 1993, p. S1.

Jacob, Rahul. "Changing Demands: Beyond Quality and Value." *Fortune,* November 22, 1993, pp. 8–11.

Jaffe, Andrew. "Was Ayer to Blame for the Fate of the 'i Plan'?" *Adweek,* November 29, 1993, p. 46.

Janofsky, Michael. "Procter & Gamble in 12 Percent Job Cut as Brand Names Lose Attraction." *New York Times,* July 16, 1993, p. C1.

———. "A Former TV Celebrity Humanizes a Campaign for Weight Watchers." *New York Times,* March 9, 1994, p. C17.

———. "Heartstrings, Not Heartbeats, Drive Chevy's New Campaign." *New York Times,* March 17, 1994, p. C17.

Johnson, Bradley. "The Commercial, and the Product, That Changed Advertising." *Advertising Age,* January 10, 1994, pp. 1, 12–13.

———. "Intel Fends off PC Industry Critics." *Advertising Age,* October 10, 1994, p. 12.

Kanner, Bernice. "Mind Games." *Marketing Insights,* Spring 1991, pp. 50–58.

Kapferer, Jean-Noel. *Strategic Brand Management: New Approaches to Creating and Evaluating Brand Equity.* New York: Free Press, 1992.

Katz, Donald. *Just Do It: The Nike Spirit in the Corporate World.* New York: Random House, 1994.

Khermouch, Gerry. "Coke Goes Rough-and-Ready: Sealey Exits, Zyman Returns." *Brandweek,* July 26, 1993, p. 3.

Kim, Junu Bryan, ed. "*Advertising Age* Marketing 100." *Advertising Age,* July 5, 1993, pp. S1–S29.

Kirkpatrick, David. "Mac vs. Windows." *Fortune,* October 4, 1993, pp. 107–14.

Koepp, Stephen. "Do You Believe in Magic?" *Time,* April 25, 1988, pp. 66–69, 71–73.

Kotler, Philip. "From Mass Marketing to Mass Customization." *Planning Review,* September/October 1989, p. 10.

Krantz, Michael. "Marketing on the Super Highway." *Superbrands,* October 18, 1993, pp. 27–34.

Lane, Randall. "The Ultimate Sponsorship." *Forbes,* March 14, 1994, p. 106.

Langer, Judith. "How to Spot the Trends." Report presented at the American Demographics' Tenth Annual Conference on Consumer Markets, June 13, 1990.

Lautman, Martin R. "The ABCs of Positioning." *Marketing Research,* March 1993.

Lavin, Douglas. "Chrysler Directs Neon Campaign at Generation X." *Wall Street Journal,* August 29, 1994, pp. B1, B3.

Lawrence, Jennifer. "Steering P&G to Efficiency." *Advertising Age,* July 26, 1994, p. 17.

Lefton, Terry. "MasterCard Agenda: Build Momentum." *Brandweek,* September 6, 1993, pp. 26–27.

———. "Co-Branding Reshapes Credit Card Landscape." *Adweek,* October 4, 1993, p. 16.

Levin, Doron P. "Car Buyers Turn Back to Detroit." *New York Times,* August 11, 1992, p. C1.

Levin, Gary. "Package-Goods Puzzle—Interest in Mail Remains, but Marketers Slow to Jump In." *Advertising Age,* April 18, 1994, p. 29.

Liesse, Julie. "Kellogg's Prices Go Up, Up, Up." *Advertising Age,* August 9, 1993, pp. 1, 29.

———. "Private Label Losing Its 'Enemy' Status." *Advertising Age,* October 11, 1993, p. 27.

———. "Brands in Demand." *Advertising Age,* February 7, 1994, pp. S1, S10.

———. "Häagen-Dazs Spoons Up a Revival." *Advertising Age,* August 22, 1994, p. 38.

Liesse, Julie, and Gary Levin. "Here's the Genuine Article for Realin' in Consumer." *Advertising Age,* April 18, 1994, p. 3.

Light, Larry. "Trustmarketing: A Brand Relationship Approach to Marketing." *A.N.A./The Advertiser,* Summer 1993, p. 12.

Lindamood, Jean. "Honda Begets Acura." *Automobile Magazine,* April 1986, p. 105.

Lippert, Barbara. "Speed Freaks." *Adweek,* February 1, 1993, p. 22.

Lohr, Steve. "How Bell Atlantic and T.C.I.'s Match Went Awry," *New York Times,* March 28, 1994, p. C1.

Madison, Cathy. "Researchers Work Advertising into an Emotional State." *Adweek,* November 5, 1990, p. 30.

Magiera, Marcy. "Clearly Canadian in New Age Struggle." *Advertising Age,* January 31, 1994, p. 12.

Magiera, Marcy, and Jeff Jensen. "Dennis Hopper Ads Take Nike to Edge." *Advertising Age,* December 6, 1993, p. 44.

Mandel, Michael J., and Mark Landler. "The Entertainment Economy," *Business Week,* March 14, 1994, pp. 58–64.

Mandese, Joe. "Here Come the Newest Brands: NBC, CBS, ABC." *Advertising Age,* May 17, 1993, pp. 1, 44.

Markoff, John. "Internet Adding a Network for Wheeling and Dealing." *New York Times*, April 13, 1994, p. C3.

———. "Potent PC Surprises Those Betting on Interactive TV." *New York Times*, May 8, 1994, p. A1.

———. "Will Video Game Machines Turn into PC Killers?" *New York Times*, January 8, 1995, p. F7.

Martin, David N. *Romancing the Brand: The Power of Advertising and How to Use It*. New York: American Management Association, 1989.

McKenna, Regis. *Relationship Marketing: Successful Strategies for the Age of the Customer*. Reading, Mass.: Addison-Wesley, 1991.

———. "Marketing Is Everything." *Harvard Business Review*, January–February 1991: p. 69.

McManus, John. "Sayonara Time for Silos as Brand Groups Re-Align." *Brandweek*, January 17, 1994, p. 16.

———. "Don't Count Prosperity as Ally versus Store Brands." *Brandweek*, February 7, 1994, p. 14.

McMath, Robert. "A Clear Winner—or Clearly the Emperor's New Clothes?" *Superbrands*, October 18, 1993, pp. 46, 48.

Meyer, Michael, with Stryker McGuire, Charles Fleming, Mark Miller, Andrew Murr, and Daniel McGinn. "Of Mice and Men." *Newsweek*, September 5, 1994, pp. 41–47.

Meyers, Gerry. Excerpt from *Targeting the New Professional Woman*. *Brandweek*, January 31, 1994, pp. 18–24.

Miller, Cyndee. "Privacy vs. Direct Marketing: Industry Faces 'Something on the Order of a Survival Issue.'" *Marketing News*, March 1, 1993, p. 1.

———. "Focus Groups Go Where None Has Been Before." *Marketing News*, July 4, 1994, p. 4.

Morgan Brad. "'Everywhere' Will Remain Visa's Passport to Future Growth." *Brandweek*, September 6, 1993, p. 30.

Morgan, Richard. "Up in Smoke." *Adweek*, June 21, 1993, pp. 25–32.

Morgenson, Gretchen. "Barbie Does Budapest." *Forbes*, January 7, 1991, pp. 66, 68–69.

Motar, Mario. "Disney-Bashing and the Disney Grooming Policy." *Los Angeles Times*, January 21, 1990, p. 11.

Munk, Nina. "Disney's Magic Lamp." *Forbes*, November 22, 1993, pp. 42–43.

Naisbitt, John, and Patricia Aburdene. *Megatrends 2000: Ten New Directions for the 1990s*. New York: William Morrow, 1990.

Nayyar, Seema. "Private Label, Experts Predict, Will Reach 45 Percent Market Share." *Brandweek*, February 8, 1993, p. 8.

Nelson, Ted. "The Big Scare." *New Media,* April 1994, pp. 41–42.

"New Names Reflect Brand ID." *Marketing News,* August 2, 1993, p. 1.

"Nike Heads to the Street." *Marketing News,* March 14, 1994, p. 1.

Nike, Inc. *1993 Annual Report.*

O'Leary, Noreen. "Benetton's True Colors." *Adweek,* August 24, 1992, pp. 27–31.

Ono, Yumiko. "Campbell's New Ad Campaign Is Stirring Up Dormant Soup Sales." *Wall Street Journal,* March 17, 1994, p. B51.

Ourusoff, Alexandra. "Brands—What's Hot. What's Not." *Financial World,* August 2, 1994, pp. 40, 44–46, 48–50, 54, 56.

Ourusoff, Alexandra, and Meenakshi Panchapakesan. "Who Says Brands Are Dead?" *Financial World,* September 1, 1993, p. 40.

Papazian, Ed. "How Many Ads Do We See?" *TV Dimensions,* 1993, p. 403.

Pare, Terence P. "How to Find Out What They Want." *Fortune,* November 22, 1993, pp. 39–41.

Peppers, Don, and Martha Rogers, Ph.D. *The One-to-One Future: Building Relationships One Customer at a Time.* New York: Doubleday, 1993.

Pereira, Joseph. "Sports Sandals, Boots Step on Sneaker Sales." *Wall Street Journal,* April 14, 1994, pp. B1, B6.

Petersen, Lisa Marie. "A Studio at the Top of Its Form: Inside Disney." *Brandweek,* April 5, 1993, pp. 20, 22.

Phillips, Stephen, Amy Dunkin, James B. Treece, and Keith H. Hammonds. "King Customer: At Companies That Listen Hard and Respond Fast, Bottom Lines Thrive." *Business Week,* March 12, 1990, pp. 88–94.

Piirto, Rebecca. "Socks, Ties, and Videotape." *American Demographics,* September 1991, p. 6.

_____. "Beyond Mind Games." *American Demographics,* December 1991, pp. 52–57.

Portman, Jamie. "Nephew Gives a Fresh Face to Disney's Dream." *Vancouver Sun,* April 16, 1993, p. C1.

Powell, Bill, with Anne Underwood, Seema Nayyar, and Charles Fleming. "Eyes on the Future." *Newsweek,* May 31, 1993, p. 39.

Power, Christopher, with Walecia Konrad, Alice Z. Cuneo, and James B. Treece. "Value Marketing." *Business Week,* November 11, 1991, pp. 132–38.

Radding, Alan. "Consumer Worry Halts Data Bases." *Advertising Age,* February 11, 1991, p. 28.

"Radio's Personalities Help Find Snapple's Sales Targets." *Advertising Age,* October 18, 1993, p. R3.

Randazzo, Sal. *Mythmaking on Madison Avenue: How Advertisers Apply the Power of Myth and Symbolism to Create Leadership Brands.* Chicago: Probus, 1993.

Rapp, Stan, and Thomas L. Collins. *MaxiMarketing: The New Direction in Advertising, Promotion, and Marketing Strategy.* New York: McGraw-Hill, 1987.

——. *The Great Marketing Turnaround: The Age of the Individual—and How to Profit from It.* Englewood Cliffs, N.J.: Prentice Hall, 1990.

Ravo, Nick. "For the 90s, Lavish Amounts of Stinginess." *New York Times,* January 15, 1992, pp. B1, B5.

Ray, Michael, and Rochelle Myers. *Creativity in Business.* Garden City, N.Y.: Doubleday, 1986.

Ries, Al and Jack Trout. *Positioning: The Battle for Your Mind.* New York: Warner Books, 1981.

——. *Bottom-Up Marketing.* New York: McGraw-Hill, 1989.

——. *The Twenty-Two Immutable Laws of Marketing: Violate Them at Your Own Risk.* New York: Harper Collins, 1993.

Robichaux, Mark. "Highway of Hype: Despite Many Claims For 500-Channel TV, Long Road Lies Ahead." *Wall Street Journal,* November 29, 1993, p. A1.

Russell, Cheryl. "The Power of One." *Brandweek,* October 4, 1993, p. 27–32.

Ryan, Nancy. "Top Brands Struggle to Maintain Image in Sea of Labels." *Chicago Tribune,* April 12, 1992, pp. 1–5.

Rydholm, Joseph. "Right on the Mark," *Quirk's Research Review,* November, 1992, pp. 6–7, 40.

Saffo, Paul. "It's the Context, Stupid." *Wired,* March 1994, p. 74.

Samuelson, Robert J. "How Our American Dream Unraveled." *Newsweek,* March 2, 1992, p. 32.

Saporito, Bill. "Behind the Tumult at P&G." *Fortune,* March 7, 1994, pp. 74–76, 80–82.

Schiller, Zachary. "Stalking the New Consumer," *Business Week,* August 28, 1989, p. 54.

Schindler, Robert M. "The Real Lesson of New Coke." *Marketing Research,* December 1992, pp. 22–27.

Schrage, Michael. "Reinventing the Wheel—When Brand Advertising Becomes a Way to Justify Higher Prices . . ." *Adweek,* April 26, 1993, p. 23.

Schultz, Don E., Stanley I. Tannenbaum, and Robert F. Lauterborn. *Integrated Marketing Communications.* Lincolnwood, Ill.: NTC Publishing Group, 1994.

Sculley, John, with John A. Byrne. *Odyssey: Pepsi to Apple . . . A Journey of Adventure, Ideas, and the Future.* New York: Harper & Row, 1987.

Sellers, Patricia. "Winning Over the New Consumer." *Fortune,* July 29, 1991, p. 113.

_____. "Brands: It's Thrive or Die." *Fortune*, August 23, 1993, pp. 52–56.

_____. "The Best Way to Reach Your Buyers." *Fortune*, Nov. 22, 1993, pp. 14–17.

_____. "Keeping the Buyers You Already Have." *Fortune*, Nov. 22, 1993, p. 56.

Serafin, Raymond. "The Saturn Story." *Advertising Age*, November 16, 1992, p. 16.

_____. "BMW: From Yuppie-Mobile to Smart Car of the '90s." *Advertising Age*, October 3, 1994, p. S2.

_____. "Saturn Recall a Plus—for Saturn!" *Advertising Age*, August 16, 1994, p. 4.

Serafin, Raymond, "Chevy Claims 'Genuine' Icon Status: New Direction Aims to Recapture Position as 'America's Brand.' " *Advertising Age*, March 21, 1994, pp. 1, 44.

Serafin, Raymond, and Leah Rickard. "Lighting Up Neon." *Advertising Age*, February 7, 1994, pp. 16–17.

Settle, Robert B., and Pamela L. Alreck. *Why They Buy: American Consumers Inside and Out.* New York: John Wiley, 1986.

Sherman, Stratford. "How to Prosper in the Value Decade." *Fortune*, November 30, 1992, pp. 90–91.

Shuster, Gary. "Relationship Marketing." *Forbes*, April 3, 1989, p. 145.

Singer, Karen. "Ethnography: Research That's Up Close and Personal." *Adweek*, September 29, 1986, pp. 30, 32.

Small, Meredith F. "Demogram: Chevy Chase, Maryland." *American Demographics*, April 1994, p. 29.

Smyth, Jeff. "A '90s Taste for Private Label." *Advertising Age*, April 11, 1994, p. 29.

Snyder, Adam. "Coming Up for More Air: Channels Go Logo Crazy." *Brandweek*, December 6, 1993, p. 24.

Spethmann, Betsy. "Re-Engineering the Price-Value Equation." *Brandweek*, September 20, 1993, pp. 44–52.

Steenhuysen, Julie. "Adland's New Billion-Dollar Baby." *Advertising Age*, April 11, 1994, p. S8.

Stefanae, Suzanne. "Interactive Advertising." *New Media*, April 1994, pp. 43–52.

Stern, Gabriella. "As National Brands Chop Prices, Stores Scramble to Defend Private-Label Goods." *Wall Street Journal*, August 23, 1993, p. B1.

Sterngold, James. "Tokyo's Magic Kingdom Outshines Its Role Model." *New York Times*, March 7, 1994, pp. C1, C7.

Superbrands, supplement to *Adweek* magazines, May 18, 1993.

Tedlow, Richard S. *New and Improved: The Story of Mass Marketing in America.* New York: Basic Books, 1976.

Templin, Neal. "GM Unit Posts Operating Profit for First Time." *Wall Street Journal,* June 14, 1993, p. A5.

―――. "GM's Saturn Subsidiary Is Fighting for Its Future." *Wall Street Journal,* June 16, 1993, p. B3.

Therrien, Lois, Maria Mallory, and Zachary Schiller. "Brands on the Run." *Business Week,* April 19, 1993, p. 26.

Thigpen, David E. "Is Nike Getting Too Big for Its Shoes?" *Time,* April 26, 1993, p. 55.

Toffler, Alvin. *The Third Wave.* New York: William Morrow, 1980.

Triplett, Tim. "Generic Fear to Xerox Is Brand Equity to FedEx." *Marketing News,* August 15, 1994, p. 12.

"Two Brands are Better than One." *San Francisco Examiner,* July 24, 1994, p. C1.

Underwood, Elaine. "Marketers of the Year: Herbert Kelleher." *Brandweek,* November 8, 1993, p. 41.

―――. "Mall Busters, Like Crime, a Boon for Home Shopping." *Brandweek,* January 17, 1994, pp. 18, 20.

Vogel, Thomas T., Jr. "Disney Amazes Investors with Sale of 100-Year Bonds." *Wall Street Journal,* July 21, 1993, p. C1.

―――. "Walt Disney's Rating on Long-Term Debt Is Lowered by Moody's." *Wall Street Journal,* February 11, 1994, p. B2.

Walt Disney Company. *1993 Annual Report.*

Wandycz, Katarzyna. "Love Means Never Having to Say Anything." *Forbes,* April 1, 1991, pp. 88, 90.

Warner, Fara. "The New Formula: Brand Building for the '90s." *Superbrands,* October 18, 1993, pp. 17–22.

―――. "Inventive Events Marketers Cutting a Grassroots Edge." *Brandweek,* January 24, 1994, pp. 18–19.

―――. "DKNY Takes Upscale Ads Underground." *Wall Street Journal,* October 6, 1994, p. B5.

"Wayne Gretzky at a Glance." *Sacramento Bee,* March 23, 1994, p. E9.

Weisz, Pam. "Major Marketers Reorganize Teams." *Adweek,* January 17, 1994, p. 9.

Westcott, Michael, and Marc Braunstein. "Customer Conversations: The Benefits of Being a Good Listener." *Brandweek,* February 15, 1993, pp. 30–31.

Whalen, Jeanne, and Gary Levin. "BK Puts Basics on Center Stage in Huge Ad Blitz." *Advertising Age,* September 5, 1994, p. 3.

"What's In Store for EDLP?" *Sales & Marketing Management*, August 1993, pp. 56–59.

Whiteside, David, Richard Brandt, Zachary Schniller, and Andrea Gabor. "How GM's Saturn Could Run Rings around Old-Style Carmakers." *Business Week*, January 28, 1985, p. 126.

Whitworth, Brad. "Proof at Last; Effectiveness of Employee Communication Programs." *Communications World*, December 1990, pp. 28–31.

Willigan, Geraldine E. "High-Performance Marketing: An Interview with Nike's Phil Knight." *Harvard Business Review*, July–August 1992, pp. 90–101.

Yahn, Steve. "Advertising's Grave New World." *Advertising Age*, May 16, 1994, p. 1.

Yang, Dori James, Michael O'Neal, Charles Hoots, and Robert Neff. "Can Nike Just Do It?" *Business Week*, April 18, 1994, pp. 86–90.

"Yet Another Thing for Marketers to Worry About." *Adweek*, October 11, 1993, p. 23.

Young, Mary, and James E. Post. "Managing to Communicate, Communicating to Manage: How Leading Companies Communicate with Employees." *Organizational Dynamics*, Summer 1993, pp. 31–43.

Ziegler, Bart. "On-Ramps to the Info Superhighway." *Business Week*, February 7, 1994, p. 108.

_____. "Building the Highway: New Obstacles, New Solutions." *Wall Street Journal*, May 18, 1994, pp. B1, B6.

Ziegler, Bart and Robichaux, Mark. "Mutual Attraction of Phone and Cable Giants Fades Fast." *Wall Street Journal*, April 7, 1994, p. B1.

Index

Aaker, David, 13, 189
Absolut vodka, 84, 130, 168
Accountability, importance of, 195–96
Account planning, 91–92
Ace Hardware, 69
Acura
  brand identity of, 45
  customer profiling and, 100–101
  identity contacts and, 201
  loyalty to, 12
  positioning of, 119–20, 129
  preview kiosks of, 288
Adamson, Jim, 270, 272
Advil, 29
Aetna Life & Casualty, 130
Agrawal, Jagdish, 173
Airline industry
  brand names in, 103–4
  brand personalities in, 150–51, 181–82
  brand positioning in, 117–18, 147
  changing brand value in, 32
  frequent-flier liabilities in, 33, 35
  perceived attributes in, 65
  price wars in, 125
  selling environment and, 59, 63
  unsuccessful innovations in, 83
Alamo Rent a Car, 170
Alaska Airlines, 170
Alcoholic beverage industry, 52, 87
Aleve, 20, 31
Alleborn, Jim, 218
Alliances
  brand parity and, 7
  interactive marketing and, 314
  proliferation of, 316, 318
Allowances, 238
Allstate Insurance, 27, 152
Allyson, June, 176
Alreck, Pamela, 81
Alsberg, David, 275
Ambush marketing, 203
American Airlines
  frequent-flier liabilities of, 33
  image marketing strategies of, 198
  infomercials and, 290
  interactive communications and, 311

  marketing support for, 132
  personality of, 161
American Demographics, 95, 96–97
American Express
  co-branding and, 199
  personality of, 166, 173, 174
American Greeting Cards, 6
America Online
  advertising and, 308
  brand name acceptance of, 20
  features of, 287
  research conducted through, 87
Anheuser Busch, 22
Apple Computer
  brand parity and, 7
  co-branding and, 199
  E-world net of, 287
  image marketing strategies of, 197
  infomercials and, 290
  innovations by, 35
  interactive catalogs and, 291
  interactive television and, 293
  logo of, 64
  Newton campaign of, 122
  positioning of, 141–42, 145, 172
  PowerBook campaign of, 169–70
Arm & Hammer, 141
Armani, 164
Army, U.S., 67, 182–83
Arrow, 92
Artzt, Ed, 238–39, 304, 311
AT&T
  brand name power of, 19
  breakup of, 244, 295, 297
  co-branding and, 199
  corporate brands and, 61
  image of, 89
  innovations by, 35
  interactive television and, 293, 297
  marketing campaigns of, 197, 252
  marketing support for, 132
  personality of, 166–68, 177
  phone directory profits and, 244, 246
  positioning of, 131
Attends, 136
Attributes of brands, 44, 65

342